By the same author:

The Cuisine of the Sun

The Cuisine of the Rose

Classical French Cooking
from Burgundy and Lyonnais

Mireille Johnston

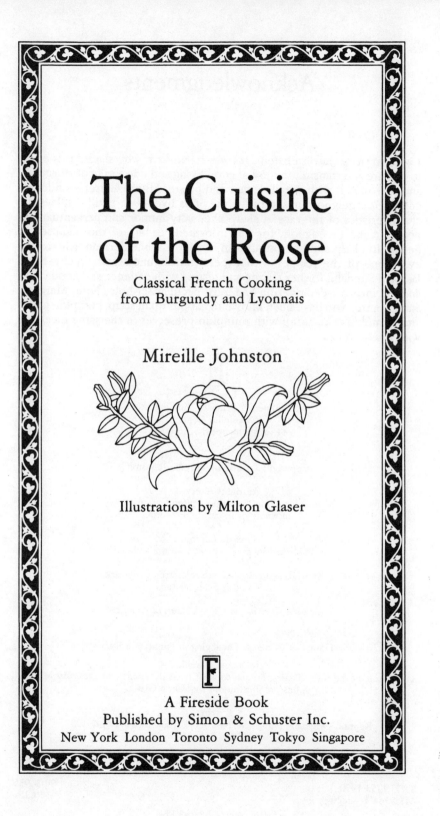

Illustrations by Milton Glaser

F

A Fireside Book
Published by Simon & Schuster Inc.
New York London Toronto Sydney Tokyo Singapore

Acknowledgments

I wish to thank Jason Epstein, *gourmet-en-residence,* who shared this effort to capture and transmit the joy of good living and fine eating of Burgundy and sustained it with unfailing flair and palate; Milton Glaser—undoubtedly a Bourguignon in one of his previous lives—who still displays the characteristics of the race: a sharp eye, salty humor and gargantuan appetite; Anne Freedgood, for her informed reading of the manuscript, her skillful help and her enthusiasm; Roberta Schneiderman, who tested every one of the recipes with expert thoroughness and precise taste; Barbara Sundahl, for her tasting and testing with patience and good cheer and the intricate deciphering of a most peculiar scribble; Tom, Margaret and Zabette, who have been known to eat pumpkin soup, pumpkin gratin and pumpkin cake along with pumpkin preserves in the same meal and with brave smiles.

Fireside
Simon & Schuster Building
Rockefeller Center
1230 Avenue of the Americas
New York, New York 10020

Copyright © 1982 by Mireille Johnston

First Fireside Edition, 1990
Published by arrangement with the author

FIRESIDE and colophon are registered trademarks
of Simon & Schuster Inc.

Manufactured in the United States of America

2   4   6   8   10   9   7   5   3   1   Pbk.

Library of Congress Cataloging in Publication Data
Johnston, Mireille.
The cuisine of the rose: classical French cooking from Burgundy and Lyonnais/ Mireille Johnston; illustrations by Milton Glaser.
—1st Fireside ed.
p. cm.
Reprint. Originally published: New York: Random House, © 1982.
"A Fireside book."
Includes index.
1. Cookery, French. 2. Burgundy (France)—Social life and customs. 3. Lyonnais (France)—Social life and customs. I. Title.
TX719.J53 1990   90-36935
641.5944'4—dc20   CIP

ISBN 0-671-70870-8 Pbk.

Contents

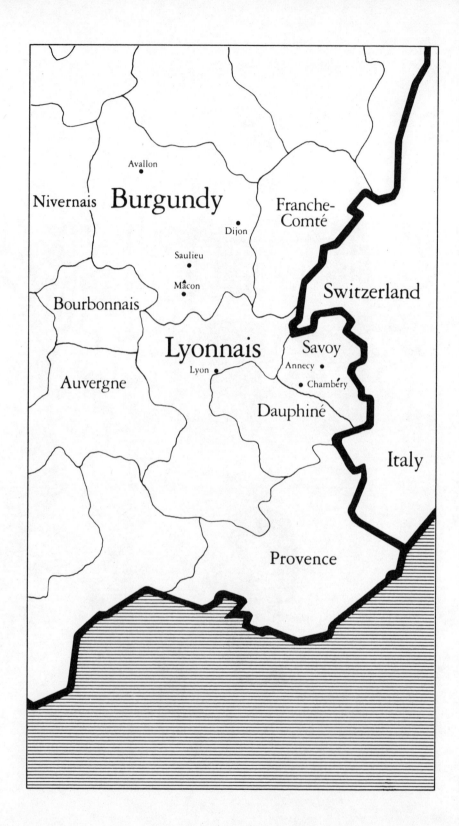

The Cuisine of the Rose

Introduction

As one enters Burgundy there should be a warning sign, "No one can come here if he is not ready to fall madly in love with life." Burgundy stands in the heart of France as both a celebration and a challenge, for life always seems more intense and sunnier here. The whole province blooms like a fluffy rose, the incarnation of the sheer joy of being alive. But just as a rose is a rose is a rose, Burgundy is difficult to introduce formally. She is larger than life, and a bundle of tastes, smells, and accents bursts forth whenever I think about her.

I remember the cattle fair in Digouin, the cream-colored Charolais cows and the huge blond bulls tied on the town green. Heavy bargaining between the breeders, red cheeks and sparkling eyes, rolling *r*'s, gray smocks over corduroy pants. Later would come the truce—a hearty snack in a café, energy and laughter, piles of fritters and sausages, everybody commenting on the quality of some bull, the flavor of a wine, fast sales, shared treats, who did what how. And above this turbulent exchange, softly drifting from the back rooms, the intoxicating smell of wild boar marinating in earthen bowls.

I remember long walks in the woods of Morvan, the thick mat of leaves silvery with frost on the ground, the elder trees and the oak trees bare, the air smelling of burnt wood, and nearby a flight of partridges, a glimpse of deer. Then back to the village with the caramel-colored roofs and, by the fire, a steaming glass of red wine simmered with clove and warm toast with hare pâté.

I remember the canal near Dijon with its long lines of symmetrical poplars, the lockhouses, the barges gliding slowly with flowerpots and drying linen on the deck, heavy with timber or sand—perhaps wine—the mellowest of sights.

Burgundy records only the rich hours. She seems to have a supplement of soul, an extra pinch of civilization given to her both by her past and by the rich nature she has been blessed with. She finds in her very old human identity and her

Introduction

diverse history—one of the oldest in Europe—the reason and the energy to believe in her future and to remain confident.

Rivers, canals and roads have crossed here for thousands of years carrying blood and energy through the whole country. All the strong moments of French history have left their traces. It is truly the mixed dreams and efforts of the Celts, the Romans, the Greeks and the Germans, and the spirit of the monks, merchants, pilgrims, sculptors, blacksmiths and wine-growers that have given Burgundy its vitality and its organic balance.

Civilization started here some twenty thousand years before Christianity spread over the country. One hundred thousand skeletons of wild horses have been found near Solutre dating to that period, and it is whispered that they have given Pouilly Fuissé wine its unique flavor. Reindeer and wild horses were hunted. The trade roads for tin, salt, amber and minerals crossed the region. Iron and timber were exploited; weaving, jewelry and sculpture flourished. There were rich markets and busy harbors long before the Romans arrived.

Then, when Caesar defeated the Gauls in Alesia, which is now Burgundy, a fruitful cooperation began. The Romans brought ceramics, olives, wines, and also law and order. They discovered a strong vine able to tolerate Burgundy's climate, and soon vineyards spread all along the rocky hillsides. Later, when the Burgundians—tall heavy drinkers from Scandinavia—invaded the region, they were welcomed by the Gallo Romans. They worked hard; forests were cleared and agriculture improved. A cohesive, busy community came into being.

In every branch of life, this constant outpouring of energy flooded through Burgundy, but during the Middle Ages the region knew a spirituality and an explosion of artistic and political activity that have not been matched since. The apogee of the dukedom came in the fifteenth century, when Burgundy encompassed Flanders, Luxembourg, Artois, Franche-Comté and the provinces along the Rhone Valley down to the Mediterranean Sea. It became the vibrant, tumultuous center of feudal Europe, and the great dukes of Burgundy were all lusty, earthy characters. Philip the Bold, John the Fearless and Philip the Good made the Burgundy court a model of fashion and manners all over Europe. Their appetite for life and irrepressible energy were felt in technology as well as in philosophy, sculpture, architecture and gas-

Introduction

tronomy. There was quality in every realm.

Today the pre-Roman crypts, Roman ruins, monasteries, fortified cities, castles, and Roman and Gothic cathedrals still seem to grow out of the land according to some natural law. The past lingers everywhere and enhances the present. A festive air blows over the province; mind and flesh mingle happily. There are as many Romanesque and Gothic works of art as wine and gastronomical meccas. A fortress built in the third century shows how the region was already fascinated by food and sculpture equally: fishmongers, butchers and fruit merchants appear in elaborate stone carvings. And perhaps the most durable work of the dukes of Burgundy, heralded as "lords of the best wines of Christendom," has been the standards they set for cuisine and wines. The splendor of their festivities, when guests spent nights and days at banquets, echoed throughout Europe. Each course contained ten dishes, and there were five to six courses, with acrobats and jugglers in between. Great attention was given to the production of wine. Farmers and monks created a unique vineyard under the vigilant eye of the dukes.

Even then, gastronomy reflected the formidable appetite and the respect for the past that prevail in Burgundy. Discoveries from other lands and other times were harmoniously mingled. The seasoning of garlic and parsley from Egypt became a favorite in Burgundy. The Romans brought olives and grapes. The Gauls favored sauces and pork. Sugar, cinnamon, pepper, ginger, saffron and shallots, discovered during the Crusades in the Orient, were added and led to a truly inventive cuisine. The changing of plain beef into a fragrant *boeuf bourguignon* and the slow development of great crus* that changed simple beverages into exquisite wines made every Bourguignon forever wish he "had a throat shaped like a screw, so food would go down more slowly and be enjoyed more."

The whole province has remained without a pause under the spell of food. High cuisine blossoms in Burgundy because it can rely on a rich countryside, a diversified and meticulous agriculture and a constant interest in taste. Here all the fruits of the land, rivers and woods are gathered in abundance. Throughout the province, open markets with crates of live

*Cru means a vineyard of high quality, worthy of recognition under the laws of classification.

snails, piles of vegetables and huge trays of cheese speak of a generous land.

Dijon, the capital of Burgundy, has been a true gastronomical center since the days of the Gauls. It has a splendid ducal palace whose kitchen walls are still lined with cooking devices of all sorts, ready to prepare sixty dishes a day. South is the Lyonnais region, and Lyon, now the second largest city of France and once the formal capital of Gaul, is where Rabelais wrote *Pantagruel* and *Gargantua,* where endless gourmets' clubs blossom, where legendary chefs and the famous Mothers, women chefs, offer true bourgeois regional cooking at its very best. It also claims the title of world capital of gastronomy.

But if Dijon and Lyon are the heart of the Burgundy rose, there are treats to be discovered under every petal. Beaune offers rich *oeufs en meurette;* Mâcon, *coq au vin* stewed in Chambertin wine and herbs, and *escargots* stuffed with butter, shallots and garlic; Morvan, a rich stew of wild boar and chestnuts and wild mushrooms; Charolles, its sumptuous beef with marrow; Auxerre, the famous pike-and-trout mousse and frog soufflé; Sens, its crispy *gougère,* its mushrooms stuffed with snails; and all along the Loire Valley, salmon and wild duck. In Franche-Comté there are corn dishes and carp stuffed with sorrel and simmered in cream and cheese. There are glorious gratins and walnut salads in Dauphiné; sausages with pistachios, raw ham, truffles and garlic in Lyon, and fritters and soups of all kinds. Permeating the whole region is the hearty fragrance of marinades, wild mushrooms and sumptuous sauces.

All the dishes here have developed slowly and carefully through the centuries. It has taken a constant taste for the good life to achieve this shared bliss in living. In medieval days the rich ate extravagantly; live birds under napkins and theatrical mixtures were part of endless banquets. In contrast, the poor always had more nose than money and used all their tricks to transform their basic potato, rye and milk into tasty dishes. Out of these two repertories of cooking, the bourgeois middle class created an interesting balance. In each family, experiences and observations on recipes were recorded, different versions of a regional dish were kept, simplified versions of elaborate haute cuisine recipes were developed, and one of the most inventive and satisfying cuisines was born.

Introduction

And so it is an artisan's heritage we have gathered here, a

medley of memories, experiences, secrets and records of splendid meals enjoyed through the years. I have added a few comments because a dish seems better when one speaks about it. Eating involves palate, eyes, memory and wit to enjoy it fully.

I have transcribed old recipes only in a form suitable to today's appetite. Most dishes cannot be as hearty and rich as they once were, since we cannot, as the early Burgundy gourmets did, digest both snails and their shells. The Nouvelle Cuisine came and went but did teach us a few things. Yet since raw fish and crisp vegetables lack diversity, I offer a few dangerously rich recipes, sumptuous sauces and medieval alliances of sweet and salty. But I always emphasize the pungent, the light, the sharper version of a recipe.

Cooking becomes refined among people long civilized, and today gourmandise is still taught early through daily practice in Burgundy. Each flower, each root, bark and leaf has value and is picked to become tea, sauce, syrup, marinade, condiment. The children are responsible for little odd jobs, which give them the very spirit of Burgundy gastronomy. The fresh cheese in the cellar must be washed with salty water, brandy and wine; the pears and quinces drying on the cupboard have to be inspected; the blue cheese in its earthenware pot, stirred with fresh butter; the snails have to be gathered and fed with flour; the frog, caught in the pond; the mushrooms, dandelions, elderberries, beechnuts, and hazelnuts, gathered regularly; the cream, skimmed off with a wooden spoon and kept until it becomes a rich ivory color and has a nutty taste.

Young palates are educated gently with an after-school snack of rye bread covered with yellow velvety fresh cream sprinkled with garlic, or with warm chestnuts, or a coarse paste of pear wrapped in crisp warm pastry and, when a child goes to share a shepherd's day, with snails in their shells, new potatoes in their skins, and goat cheese wrapped in leaves, all cooked gently under the ashes. And so, of course, it is no surprise that food becomes the criterion of all values. When asked whom he likes best, his mother or his father, the spirited child is likely to answer, "I like snails best, with plenty of butter and parsley." At all times, the kind and witty ghosts of Rabelais, Brillat-Savarin and Colette walk beside him. He is part of a strong race of peasants, artists and winegrowers who have transmitted to him the coherence of a heritage in which so many tendencies enrich each other.

Cooking acts as a catalyst; it awakens in the soul new potentialities. Whenever I think of the joy of living, the pleasure of a perfect dish served with a perfect wine and the deep joy that comes from perfect harmony, I see Burgundy: the light greens of the Charolais pastures with the cream-colored cattle, the dark green of the Morvan wood, the pink and gray stones of the castles and cathedrals, the silver of the ponds and creeks, the yellow gloss of the tiled roofs. I see the pink cheeks, the sparkling eyes crinkled as if they had faced the sun too much, the eloquent forceful faces.

The song of the world grabs me—I know I am in the right place to enjoy life. Burgundy is one of those perfect achievements in which nature and craft fulfill each other. It is reassuring to know there is an actual paradise in this world. Let the feast begin! *À table, que la fête commence!*

Ingredients

A serious meal depends largely on very serious shopping. You must learn how to smell, touch and select your ingredients and to demand freshness and quality. Although Burgundy and Lyonnais cooking uses a large variety of ingredients, most of them are easily available here.

A cooperative butcher is essential, but he can be found in most supermarkets. Spanish saffron, shallots, chestnuts, cheese, wine vinegar and canned snails are available in supermarket gourmet corners; and dried fish, olive oil, herbs and cured or smoked ham are worth a trip to Spanish, Hungarian and Greek shops.

Vegetables have become fresher and more varied in the past few years. Leeks, artichokes, shallots, green asparagus and fresh herbs are no longer luxury items.

The following is a descriptive list of all the basic Burgundy and Lyonnais ingredients used in this book.

Fonds de Cuisine

Staples to Have in Your Kitchen at All Times

Anchovies *(les Anchois)*
Anchovies are used in salads and with beef *(boeuf marinière),* and it is always best to buy them packed in salt or oil in Greek, Spanish or Italian markets. Before using the salt-packed variety, wash the fish thoroughly in cold running water. Cut along the back and pull out the bone, then remove the tail.

Bouquet Garni
This is a small bundle of herbs wrapped in a piece of cheesecloth and used to enhance the seasoning of soups, stews and the like. The basis is 2 or 3 sprigs of parsley, a bay leaf and

a sprig of thyme (or ¼ teaspoon of dried thyme); for a tastier bouquet garni, add a stalk of celery and a stalk of fennel. When the dish is ready, remove the bouquet garni.

Bread *(le Pain)*
Stale bread, once a standby for the frugal housewife, is now a traditional ingredient of many dishes in one of several forms: bread crumbs, croutons or *chapons.* Sometimes a slice is soaked in milk, which is squeezed out before the bread is used for a sauce or for stuffing. You can buy so-called French or Italian bread, but home-baked is best. I prefer baking my own firm white bread with unbleached flour.

Bread Crumbs *(la Panure, la Chapelure)*
The ready-made kind is uniformly bad, so bread crumbs simply have to be homemade.

To make a supply, either grate a few slices of stale bread or crumble them into a blender and blend at high speed for a few seconds. They will keep for at least two or three days in a jar and for three weeks in the freezer. When kept longer, they become moldy, but you can still use them if you remove the mold.

Cheese *(le Fromage)*
Goat cheese is used in some preparations and can be found in some supermarkets or in Greek or Italian groceries and specialty shops. Parmesan cheese keeps if it is enclosed in plastic wrap. Always have a large wedge of it on hand. Fresh cheese can be found under the name "farmer's cheese." Ricotta, although made with pasteurized cow's milk, can be used for *claqueret.*

Chestnuts *(les Marrons)*
You can buy canned chestnuts, already peeled and cooked, in most gourmet stores. Keep·a few cans for purée, stuffing and pastry. For other recipes, try to buy fresh ones, which are usually available in the fall and early winter.

Cream *(la Crème)*
You may use light or heavy cream, but to add taste and texture to a dish, try ½ heavy cream mixed with ½ sour cream.

Croutons *(les Croûtons)*
Ingredients These are used in many dishes in Burgundy and in Lyon. To make them, cut slices of good firm homemade bread in triangles and fry in butter or in vegetable oil.

You may, for a lighter touch, simply bake the croutons in a 350° oven for 4 minutes.

Dried Cod *(la Morue Sèche)*
Dried cod can be kept in a dry corner of your kitchen or in the freezer. It is sold in three forms. The dried whole fish (bone, skin and tail) requires about two days of soaking in cold water, with the water changed several times a day. Dried filleted cod, often sold in pound packages, requires an overnight soaking and four changes of water. Frozen fillets will require only about four hours' soaking with four changes of water.

Always ask your fish dealer how long his particular dried codfish should soak and follow his instructions. Most fish markets sell it, but for the tastier, drier kind you will probably have to go to Italian, Spanish or Greek markets. Buy a great amount since so many of Lyon's light, tasty, inexpensive dishes are made from it—*morue à la lyonnaise, beignets de morue,* and so on.

Flour *(la Farine)*
Always use unbleached flour, available in most supermarkets or by mail order.

Garlic *(l'Ail)*
Since I use great quantities of garlic, I buy it in a wreath and hang it in a dry place in the kitchen. Red garlic (usually from Mexico) is tastier and stronger than the white. All supermarkets carry some garlic in the vegetable department. Remember that a garlic clove cooked whole is much less strong than a minced or crushed one.

Gherkins *(les Cornichons)*
These little pickles originally came from India but have become an everyday staple in Burgundy cooking. They are called *cornichons* because they look like little horns *(corne).* They are eaten before they become mature. To make your own, choose very small (about 2-inch-long) cucumbers, all roughly the same size. Wash and dry them carefully and place them in a large bowl with rough salt or Kosher salt. Let them stand for 24 hours, tossing them from time to time.

Dry them with a piece of soft cloth. Place them in a jar with a few pearl onions, a few cloves, 4 garlic cloves, a sprig of tarragon and 10 peppercorns. Boil enough red-wine vinegar to cover them and pour over the vegetables. Let stand over-

Ingredients

night. In the morning, pour the vinegar into a pan and bring it to a boil. Pour over the cucumbers. Let them soak another night. Repeat the boiling and soaking. Add a sprig of thyme and 2 bay leaves. Close the jar tightly. The cornichons will be ready in 1 month. Use in hors d'oeuvres, with *boeuf mironton,* and in various sauces. If you cannot make them yourself, you can buy them in gourmet and specialty stores.

Lean Salt Pork *(le Petit Salé)*
Sautéing with salt pork is the essential first step in making stews and fish dishes. Always choose the leanest and keep a large piece in the refrigerator. Most supermarkets and all pork butchers sell good salt pork. Try to find some that is free of nitrate and nitrite.

Mustard *(la Moutarde)*
Always keep a large pot of Dijon-style mustard at hand (see p. 298).

Nuts *(les Noix; les Noisettes; les Amandes)*
Keep walnuts, hazelnuts and almonds frozen for freshness.

Oil *(l'Huile)*
For salad dressing I use either olive oil, or ½ peanut oil and ½ olive oil, or walnut oil. For cooking, I mostly use peanut oil. Many good brands of walnut oil and imported olive oil are sold in the United States. Experiment with them. Buy your favorite and keep it always in closed dark bottles. Refrigerate if you use it slowly.

Orange-Blossom Water *(l'Eau de Fleurs d'Oranger)*
This flavoring is used with fresh cheese or in desserts. It is available in dark blue bottles in specialty stores and some "apothecaries" (because it is supposed to calm nerves and put angry babies to sleep) and through mail order.

Pork Caul, or Lace Fat *(la Crépine)*
This thin, fatty membrane is sold by the pound in German, Italian, Chinese and Spanish butcher shops. If you cannot find it, substitute thin slices of bacon. It is used for *caillettes* and to cover terrines.

Salt *(le Sel)*
Kosher salt is coarse and tasty; I use it with *pot-au-feu* and also in cooking. *Sel gros* is excellent for cooking and available at some shops, but tends to be expensive. Since the amount of

Ingredients

salt used depends on individual preference, I recommend tasting each dish at least twice to check the seasoning adequately.

Shallots
Easily available in most supermarkets, they should always be kept on hand. They store well if they are kept in a dry part of your kitchen.

Swiss Cheese *(le Gruyère)*
The domestic brand sold in all supermarkets is very good. Grate it fresh and sprinkle on soups, pasta and stews. Always keep a large piece, tightly wrapped, in the refrigerator.

Vermouth
The dry white vermouth made in the United States is good in sauces. The sweet red vermouth is acceptable, too. Take a sip of your vermouth before using, since cooking intensifies its flavor—good or bad.

Vinegar *(le Vinaigre)*
Whether red or white, wine vinegar is available everywhere. Find a kind you like and keep a few bottles on hand.

Wine *(le Vin)*
I use California hearty red Burgundy to make stews and either a dry or sweet white wine or a dry or sweet white vermouth for fish, lamb or chicken sauces. Always taste before using and keep a few bottles of your favorite wines in your kitchen for cooking.

Les Épices et les Aromates

Spices and Flavorings

Aniseed *(les Graines d'Anis)*
Anise has a flavor somewhat like that of licorice. The seeds are used in confectionery and pastry or with fish.

Bay Leaf *(le Laurier)*
The California bay leaf is stronger than the French but very good. Use it in stews *(boeuf bourguignonne)* and sauces and with fish and rice *(riz aux herbes).*

Ingredients

Capers *(les Câpres)*
Capers are the buds of the caper bush. They are kept in vinegar or salt and used in hors d'oeuvre, with meat and in sauces.

Cayenne Pepper
Pungent and lively.

Chives *(la Ciboulette)*
Use the narrow big leaves, finely chopped, in omelets and with vegetables and fresh cheese *(claqueret)*.

Clove *(le Clou de Girofle)*
Stick one clove into a large onion, sauté the onion on all sides, and add it to soups and stews.

Coriander *(le Coriandre)*
The round seeds of coriander look like peppercorns. This spice must be used with discretion because it is powerful. It is used in marinades and with pork.

Ginger *(le Gingembre)*
Available in many supermarkets and in all Chinese vegetable shops. It was used often in old recipes, and Nouvelle Cuisine has fallen in love with it.

Mint *(la Menthe)*
This is used in salads, with fish and as a garnish with strawberries or custard. Brewed as tea, it is supposed to rekindle an honest man's passion and a pretty woman's vigor.

Nutmeg *(les Noix de Muscade)*
Buy whole nutmeg and grate it when needed at the last moment with a sharp knife. Use in sauces with fish and meat.

Parsley *(le Persil)*
This is the most commonly used of all herbs. Italian parsley, flat-leaved, is the most savory and will keep in a plastic bag in the refrigerator. Because parsley is rich in vitamins A and C, which heat destroys, add it, finely minced, at the last minute. Try to grow it (you might have a hanging basket in the kitchen), since there is constant use for it—sprinkled on black olives, in omelets, in sauces and with most meat and fish dishes. Always chop it as finely as possible with a chopper so that it is almost a paste.

Ingredients

Pepper *(le Poivre)*

White pepper made from the ripe berries of the pepper plant has a slightly stronger flavor than the black, which is made from the dried, underripe berries. But the major difference is color—add white pepper to dishes that should have a pale color and black to others. Peppercorns are sometimes added to a simmering liquid and then removed when the dish is done. For sprinkling, always use peppercorns to make freshly ground pepper.

Saffron *(le Safran)*

Use the stamens of Spanish saffron only. They are available in most gourmet counters in little metal cans. More expensive than the powdered kind, but well worth it.

Ingredients

Les Soupes

Soups

For centuries, soup was the core of a Burgundian meal. It was dinner as well as breakfast until World War I, when women decided that coffee and milk should replace it in the morning. *Faire la soupe* meant "to cook dinner," and *Venez souper* meant "Come for dinner." Every cook in Burgundy had a rich repertory of soups. Every woman learned how to create rich blends of flavors with ingredients as varied as plain sorrel, delicate crayfish and wild mushrooms.

Vegetable soups are prepared with leeks, turnips, asparagus, pumpkin, chestnuts and sorrel, often sautéed in butter and enriched with cream and egg yolks. *La porée à la ribelette* is the most famous. Vegetable purées—carrots, cauliflower, lentils, red beans and turnips—are often served with fried croutons.

Cereal soups are made with corn, barley, oatmeal or chestnut flour; *la soupe aux gaudes* is the classic among them.

The *mitonnées* are vegetable or meat soups in which pieces of bread are soaked to thicken the broth. The celebrated *gratinée lyonnaise* is the most sumptuous of them.

And then there are soups that are somewhere between stews and soups, such as *pochouse* and *potée,* and soups that are unique, such as the soup prepared with slices of thick custard of egg served with a hot broth, or the curious blend of frogs, leeks and turnips. Also somewhat strange are poached eggs sprinkled with truffles. There is a thick soup made with chicken and crayfish enriched with cream, and, finally, the beloved wine-cropper soup.

Most of the recipes included here will make delicious lunches as well as first-course dishes.

Les Soupes

Potage de Porée à la Ribelette de Lard

A Leek and Potato Soup Seasoned with Sautéed Onions and Pork and Served with Croutons

One of the oldest recipes in Burgundy, this is the kind of soup that evokes images of old copper dishes, a cat asleep by a high roaring fire and waxed oak furniture.

For 8 people:

3 *tablespoons sweet butter*
5 *leeks, only the white part, chopped*
1½ *quarts water*
6 *potatoes, peeled and diced*
Salt
Freshly ground black pepper
½ *cup lean salt pork, diced*
2 *onions, peeled and sliced*
8 *croutons, fried in peanut oil and butter*

Cook the leeks in the butter for a few minutes over low heat. When they are soft, add the water and potatoes, salt and pepper, and cook slowly.

After 30 minutes, sauté the salt pork and onions and add to the soup. Serve with croutons.

Soupe à L'Oeuf

Broth Served with an Egg Yolk and Broth Custard

This Lyon specialty can be prepared with a beef or chicken broth, highly seasoned. It is a perfect luncheon dish followed by a green salad and a light dessert.

Soups

For 8 people:

8 egg yolks
2 quarts strong beef broth (or chicken broth)

Beat the egg yolks until foamy and slowly add 2 cups of the broth while stirring. Pass through a sieve into a shallow dish. Place the dish over a pan of boiling water and cook until the mixture is thick. Remove the dish from the heat and let it cool.

Heat the remaining broth. Cut the custard into slices. Place a slice in each soup plate and pour the hot broth over it. Serve at once.

Soupe à la Bressane

A Tomato and Chicken Soup

Delicious and invigorating, this soup was traditionally prepared for weddings and brought to the bride's bedroom in the middle of her wedding night.

For 8 people:

1 chicken back, neck and gizzard
1 onion, peeled and chopped
1 whole clove
1 celery stalks, chopped
5 peppercorns
Thyme
2 onions, peeled and sliced
2 tablespoons lard
6 tomatoes, quartered
2 egg yolks
3 tablespoons heavy cream
3 tablespoons minced fresh herbs

Cover the chicken back, neck and gizzard with cold water. Bring to a boil, stirring from time to time. After 10 minutes, add the chopped onion, clove, celery, peppercorns and thyme. Cook, uncovered, for 1 hour. Strain through a sieve.

Sauté the sliced onions in the lard. Add the tomatoes and cook, covered, for 10 minutes. Pass the onions and tomatoes

Les Soupes

through a sieve into the hot chicken broth and cook for 20 minutes.

Meanwhile, whip the egg yolks and the cream. Remove the broth from the heat and stir in the egg mixture. Return to the stove over low heat, stirring vigorously for 5 minutes.

Sprinkle with fresh herbs and serve.

Soupe au Chou

A Cabbage, Carrot and Turnip Soup Enriched with Cream and Egg Yolks

A wonderful soup. Since all the vegetables are available all year round, you may enjoy it often with either of the two following garnishes.

Serves 8 people:

2 tablespoons sweet butter
1 tablespoon vegetable oil
1 cup lean salt pork, finely chopped
1 onion, peeled and minced
1 3-pound cabbage, trimmed and coarsely chopped
4 carrots, peeled and quartered
2 turnips, peeled and quartered
  Salt
5 peppercorns, crushed

Garnish I

½ cup cream
2 egg yolks

Garnish II

4 garlic cloves, peeled and crushed
½ cup pork fatback, finely chopped
2 tablespoons country ham, chopped

Heat the butter and oil and cook the salt pork over medium heat for about 3 minutes. Add the minced onion and sauté 3 minutes longer, then add the cabbage, carrots and turnips. Cook for 5 minutes, stirring from time to time, and sprinkle

Soups

with salt and the crushed peppercorns. Add 2 quarts of boiling water, then lower the heat. Simmer uncovered for 1½ hours. Just before serving, add Garnish I: beat the cream and egg yolks in a bowl and pour into the hot soup, stirring. Check the seasoning and serve.

For a heartier version, add Garnish II: Place the garlic and pork fatback in a food processor or a mortar and make a thick paste. Add to the hot soup just before serving along with the chopped country ham.

Soupe Arlequin

A Rich Vegetable Soup with Cream

A wonderful soup served cold, warm or hot.

For 8 people:

2 *cups shredded leeks (or ½ onion, ½ scallion)*
2 *tablespoons sweet butter*
1 *celery stalk, finely chopped*
1 *cup diced potatoes*
2 *cups diced peeled pumpkin*
  Salt
  Freshly ground black pepper
  Freshly grated nutmeg
6 *cups milk*
1 *egg yolk*
2 *cups heavy cream*
1 *tablespoon chopped chives*

Sauté the leeks in butter until soft. Add the celery and potatoes. Sauté for 5 minutes longer. Pour into a saucepan with the pumpkin, salt, pepper, nutmeg, and milk and cook for 20 minutes. Pass through a blender or a food processor. Add the egg yolk and the heavy cream. Return to the saucepan and reheat gently. Check the seasoning, since pumpkin is very bland. Sprinkle with chives and serve.

Les Soupes

Soupe au Riz et au Chou

A Rice and Cabbage Soup

A very hearty country soup I find easy to prepare ahead and reheat for chilly winter evenings.

For 8 people:

1 cup cooked rice
2 pounds cabbage, trimmed and quartered
2 onions, peeled and chopped
2 tablespoons sweet butter
2 quarts hot chicken or beef broth, well seasoned
Salt
Freshly ground black pepper
3 tablespoons grated Swiss cheese

Cook the rice and cabbage in salted water for 1 hour. Discard the water. Sauté the onions in hot butter for 5 minutes. Add to the rice and cabbage, then pour in the hot broth and bring to a boil. Season. Pass through a blender or a Moulinex mill. Sprinkle with grated cheese and serve.

La Soupe aux Gaudes

A Smooth Chicken Soup with Cream and Corn Meal

Although corn was first used by the American Indians, it has been made into soups in Europe in regions where poor harvests or poverty made wheat a luxury item.

In Burgundy, men who enjoyed their corn soups were traditionally called "yellow belts" and corn was called *gaudes*. This smooth soup should be served before a pungent dish such as *Travers de Porc aux Herbs* (p. 168).

Soups

23

For 8 people:

6 *yellow onions, peeled and thinly sliced*
2 *tablespoons sweet butter*
1 *tablespoon vegetable oil*
2 *cups fine corn meal*
4 *cups chicken broth (or milk)*
4 *cups cream (light or heavy)*
  Salt
  Freshly grated nutmeg
  Freshly ground white pepper
3 *tablespoons chives or scallions, minced*

Sauté the onions in butter and oil in a large skillet. Sprinkle them with a little salt and cook gently until soft and pale brown.

Pour the corn meal into a bowl filled with half of the broth (or milk). Stir, and add the rest of the broth. Beat carefully and add to the onions. Simmer for 30 minutes, then add the cream, salt, nutmeg, and pepper. Check the seasoning.

Sprinkle with the fresh herbs and serve at once.

Soupe Nevers

An Unusual Soup with Brussels Sprouts

Named for Nevers, the city it comes from, this soup is also a never-ending delight with its abundance of flavors.

For 8 people:

36 *Brussels sprouts, trimmed and quartered*
4 *carrots, peeled and diced*
3 *tablespoons sweet butter*
1 *tablespoon vegetable oil*
8 *cups chicken broth, hot*
  Salt
  Freshly ground black pepper
3 *tablespoons minced chives (or*
  parsley or chervil)

Les Soupes

Sauté the vegetables in the butter and oil, stirring for 5 minutes. Pour them into a large saucepan. Add the hot broth and bring to a boil. Cook for 35 minutes. Add salt and pepper, sprinkle with the fresh herbs and serve at once. The Brussels sprouts should not be overcooked.

Soupe au Vin

A Rich Wine and Vegetable Soup

This hearty soup does wonders on cold winter nights.

For 8 people:

> 2 big onions, peeled and sliced
> 3 carrots, peeled and diced
> 3 pink turnips (or 1 big waxy yellow one), peeled and diced
> 2 leeks (or 2 white onions), chopped
> 2 tablespoons sweet butter
> 1 tablespoon vegetable oil
> 2 cups hearty red wine
> 1½ quarts chicken broth
> Salt
> Freshly ground black pepper
> 1 tablespoon arrowroot
> 2 tablespoons minced chives

Sauté the vegetables in butter and oil over medium heat for 5 minutes, stirring from time to time. Add the wine and bring to a boil, uncovered. Simmer for 20 minutes. Add the broth. Simmer for 10 minutes more, stir, and add salt and pepper. Dissolve the arrowroot in 3 tablespoons of water, then stir it into the soup. Simmer for 3 minutes, sprinkle with chives and serve.

Soupe Savoyarde

A Hearty Vegetable, Swiss Cheese and Salami Soup

Made with fresh vegetables, simmered with bacon and served

with a crisp garnish, this soup is superb as a main dish for lunch on a cold winter day.

For 8 people:

2 tablespoons sweet butter
2 tablespoons vegetable oil
5 carrots, peeled and diced
4 pink turnips, peeled and diced
3 leeks (or 3 white onions), peeled and chopped
1 small green cabbage, minced
3 stalks celery, peeled and minced
3 potatoes, peeled and diced
½ cup bacon, chopped
1½ quarts boiling water
1 cup warm milk
Salt
Freshly ground black pepper
8 slices good bread, crusts removed
2 tablespoons sweet butter
1½ cups Swiss cheese, grated or shredded
10 slices good Italian or Danish salami
2 tablespoons chervil (or scallions), minced

Heat the butter and oil in a heavy skillet. Add the vegetables and cook over moderate heat for 15 minutes, stirring. Add the bacon and cover with the boiling water and milk. Bring to a boil. Add salt and pepper and simmer for 30 minutes.

Butter the slices of bread, sprinkle them with cheese, cover with salami and then a little more cheese and broil them for 3 minutes, until golden. Cut them diagonally in half.

Sprinkle the soup with chervil and float the cheese toast on top. Or place a slice of toast in the bottom of each individual soup bowl and pour the warm soup over it, then sprinkle with chervil and serve.

Soupe Dauphinoise

An Onion, Carrot, Turnip, Sorrel Soup Enriched with Cream

A fragrant velvety soup perfect for a light lunch or to start an elegant dinner.

For 8 people:

2 *veal bones*
Bouquet garni
6 *tablespoons sweet butter*
1 *tablespoon vegetable oil*
3 *onions, peeled and minced*
2 *leeks (or 2 white onions), chopped*
6 *carrots, peeled and diced*
2 *turnips, peeled and diced*
Salt
Freshly ground pepper
1 *cup sorrel (or watercress, in winter), finely shredded*
4 *tablespoons light cream*
5 *slices of bread (crusts removed), diced, and fried in*
4 tablespoons sweet butter and 1 tablespoon
vegetable oil (optional)

Bring 3 quarts of water, bones and bouquet garni to a boil and continue to boil, uncovered, for 1 hour.

Heat 3 tablespoons of butter and the oil in a large heavy-bottomed pan and sauté the onions, leeks, carrots and turnips for a few minutes, stirring. Add the hot broth and the seasonings and simmer for 30 minutes. Heat the remaining 3 tablespoons of butter and sauté the sorrel (or watercress) for 5 minutes. Add to the soup. Discard the bones and bouquet garni. Stir in the cream, and check the seasoning. Pour into a warmed soup tureen and serve at once. For a richer soup, add croutons to the soup.

Soupe au Fromage I

A Smooth Cheese Soup

7 *cups chicken broth*
5 *eggs*
8 *teaspoons Parmesan, Swiss or Romano cheese, grated*
or shredded
½ *cup bread crumbs*
Pinch of nutmeg
5 *teaspoons minced chives (or chervil)*

Soups

Bring the broth to a boil. Meanwhile, beat the eggs, cheese, bread crumbs and nutmeg together. Remove the pan from the burner and slowly beat some of the broth into the egg mixture; then slowly stir the egg mixture into the broth pan. Check the seasoning and correct. Sprinkle with the herbs and serve.

Soupe Verte

A Creamy Vegetable Soup

A fresh and rather fancy soup, delicious whether you make it with sorrel, spinach or watercress (my favorite is sorrel). It can be eaten cold or warm.

For 8 people:

> 6 *cups (about 2½ pounds) sorrel, spinach or water-cress, washed and dried (you may use ½ spinach and ½ sorrel)*
> 3 *tablespoons sweet butter*
> 1 *large onion, minced*
> 1½ *quarts chicken broth*
> *Salt*
> *Freshly ground black pepper*
> 3 *egg yolks*
> 1 *cup heavy cream*
> *Freshly grated nutmeg*
> 1 *tablespoon minced chervil*
> 8 *slices good bread, cubed and fried in butter (optional)*

Wash the sorrel (or spinach or watercress) under cold water and dry well.

Heat the butter in a heavy-bottomed pan, add the onion and cook for 3 minutes. Add the greens and cook for 5 minutes. Bring the broth to a boil, season with salt and pepper and then add the greens. Simmer for 10 minutes.

Drain the greens and put them through a food processor or a blender. Meanwhile, blend the egg yolks, cream and nutmeg in a large bowl and add the boiling stock, one cup at a time, stirring constantly. Next, stir in the purée. Pour the

Les Soupes

whole mixture into a saucepan and reheat very gently over low heat; do not boil. Check the seasoning and sprinkle with chervil. Add croutons if you want a richer soup.

Soupe au Fromage II

A Hearty Cheese Soup

For 8 people:

8 *potatoes, peeled and diced*
2 *large onions, peeled and chopped*
2 *quarts beef broth*
1 *pound Swiss cheese, grated or shredded*
2 *tablespoons grated Parmesan cheese*
2 *tablespoons chopped chives*
  Salt
  Freshly ground black pepper
1 *cup dry white wine*
2 *tablespoons minced parsley*
5 *slices of bread, diced*
3 *tablespoons sweet butter*

Prepare the vegetables while you bring the broth to a boil. Cook them in the broth for 20 minutes. Crush them with a fork; they should not be too smooth. Stir in the cheese and chives and reheat on a low flame until the mixture is thicker. Season carefully. Pour in the wine. Fry the bread dices in butter and serve the soup sprinkled with parsley and croutons.

La Soupe au Potiron

Pumpkin Soup

La soupe au potiron tout rond (made with the very round French cousin of the pumpkin) is a favorite in Burgundy. I have chosen two of the most interesting versions: one spectacular and rich, in the spirit of the Lyon Great Cook masters, and the other simpler, easier.

Soups

For 8 people:

I The rich version

- *1 cup peeled, minced shallots (or onions)*
- *5 tablespoons sweet butter*
- *3 cups diced bread, toasted*
- *Salt*
- *Freshly ground black pepper*
- *1½ cups grated cheese (Swiss, Parmesan or Romano)*
- *1 6-pound pumpkin (or orange butternut squash)*
- *5 cups light cream*
- *Freshly grated nutmeg*
- *2 bay leaves*

Cook the shallots in 3 tablespoons of butter over low heat for 10 minutes. Add the bread and cook for 2 minutes longer. Sprinkle with salt and pepper and add the cheese. Set aside.

Preheat the oven to 400°.

Cut the top off the pumpkin with a strong, sharp knife. Reserve the lid. Remove all the seeds with a long-handled spoon or a wide knife. Sprinkle salt over both the inside and the outside of the pumpkin. Fill with the mixture of shallot, bread and cheese. Stir in the cream, salt, pepper, nutmeg and bay leaves. Replace the lid on top of the pumpkin.

Bake the filled pumpkin on a large ovenproof dish for 2 hours. Twice, while it is cooking, lift the top and stir vigorously, reaching into the pumpkin with a long-handled spoon.

When you are ready to serve, place the pumpkin over a folded napkin on a shallow serving plate. Check the seasoning, stir carefully, add the remaining butter and serve.

II The simpler, lighter version

- *1 6-pound pumpkin (or acorn, hubbard or butternut squash)*
- *Salt*
- *Freshly ground black pepper*
- *2 bay leaves*
- *1 large onion, studded with 1 clove*
- *5 cups light cream*
- *4 tablespoons sweet butter*
- *2 cups diced bread, toasted*
- *½ cup grated cheese (Swiss, Parmesan or Romano)*
- *2 tablespoons minced chives*
- *Aniseed*
- *Grated nutmeg*

Les Soupes

Remove the seeds of the pumpkin. Scoop out all the flesh, dice it, and boil it in a large pot of salted water with pepper, bay leaves and the onion. Drain it carefully. Pass it through a blender or a food processor. Add the cream and pour into a saucepan. Simmer for 20 minutes, uncovered. Check the seasonings, and add the butter. It must be highly seasoned.

Serve, sprinkled with the diced bread, grated cheese, chives and aniseed and a little grated nutmeg.

Soups

Les Hors-d'Oeuvre

Appetizers

Meals are carefully planned in Burgundy, and as a rule, since the main course is indeed the most serious part of the meal, hors d'oeuvres are meant to be inviting, provocative, amusing, but always discreet so as not to compete with or overshadow what is to follow.

There are cold hors d'oeuvres, such as *cerneaux*—fresh green walnuts kept for a few days with salt, pepper and wine vinegar, and nibbled with a glass of good red wine. There are plump *cêpe* mushrooms marinated in oil, vinegar, garlic and herbs, and cold fritters of little wild mushrooms. There are all kinds of pork delicacies: piles of sausages, dried, cured, smoked; big tripe sausages, simmered in white wine; small broiled chitterlings; crispy *gratons* made with the residue of fried pork fat; pâtés made of veal and sweetbread, eel, chicken liver, hare. There is tender asparagus served with a mustard cream-and-herb sauce.

There are warm pies: a leek tart, a rich meat pie, a thick pancake stuffed with cheese, egg and rum. There are stews of snails, there is a *rigodon* pastry made with diced ham and *corniottes* (little pouches filled with egg and cream), and finally, the most famous of all, *la gougère,* the best friend of red Burgundy wines.

Crépinette aux Marrons

Fried Cakes of Pork, Chestnuts and Spices

Hors-d'Oeuvre

These crisp little patties are perfect as an hors d'oeuvre, warm or cold, in a buffet or to accompany a plain pork roast.

You will find chestnuts already peeled and blanched in the

gourmet department of most stores if you are reluctant to go to the trouble of boiling and peeling them.

For 8 people:

2 pounds lean salt pork (or bacon or country ham)
    with some fat, finely chopped
4 shallots, peeled and finely chopped
3 tablespoons finely chopped parsley
Salt
Freshly ground black pepper
1 teaspoon ground coriander
1 pound cooked, peeled chestnuts, chopped
16 slices of bacon (or one large pork caul cut in pieces)
8 tablespoons sweet butter
3 tablespoons vegetable oil
Freshly ground black pepper
3 tablespoons minced parsley

Mix the pork, shallots, parsley, salt, pepper and coriander together. Add the chestnuts. You must have a finely ground mixture. Use a blender if you cannot chop it fine enough.

Place one-sixteenth of this mixture on a piece of bacon (or caul) and make a tight little ball wrapped in bacon. Flatten it with the palm of your hand so it will cook more evenly.

Heat the butter and oil in a large skillet. Sauté the patties, five or six at a time, for 15 minutes over medium heat, turning with a spatula or a pair of tongs.

Sprinkle with pepper and parsley.

Bersaudes

A Highly Tasty Pork Spread

4 pounds lean salt pork, cut into very small dice
2 tablespoons lard
2 teaspoons thyme
2 bay leaves
1 garlic clove, peeled and chopped
1 onion, peeled and chopped
Salt
Freshly ground black pepper

Appetizers

Sauté the pork in the lard until crisp. Drain.

Place the pork in a saucepan with the thyme, bay leaves, garlic and onion, cover with cold water, and cook over medium heat for 3 hours, covered. Drain. Place the mixture in pots and cover with lard.

Delicious on hot toast as an appetizer with a glass of cool white or rosé wine.

Délices d'Endives

Endives and Ham, Chopped and Cooked with Cream in Individual
Dishes, Then Topped with a Poached Egg

Prepared in a few minutes, this is a lovely luncheon dish or an elegant first course for a more elaborate meal. This should be eaten with a spoon.

For 8 people:

*4 large endives or 8 small ones, trimmed and chopped
    or sliced
Juice of 1 lemon
4 tablespoons sweet butter
1 large onion, peeled and finely chopped
Salt
Pinch of sugar
Freshly ground black pepper
4 teaspoons cream
Pinch of nutmeg
4 large slices country ham or smoked ham, shredded
8 eggs
3 tablespoons sweet butter
Salt*

Trim and slice the endives. Bring a pot of salted water to a boil, add the lemon juice and the endives and cook for about 5 minutes. Drain carefully.

Preheat the oven to 400°.

Put the butter in a saucepan, add the onion and cover. Cook for about 5 minutes over low heat. Add the endives, salt, sugar, pepper, cream and nutmeg. Cover and simmer for 20 minutes. Remove the lid and cook for 5 minutes more, stirring. Add the shredded ham.

Pour the mixture into eight small ramekins or individual ovenproof dishes. Break an egg into the center of each dish. Dot with butter, sprinkle with salt and bake for 5 minutes or until just set. Serve at once.

L'Enchaud

Patties of Pork, Herb and Eggs

These can be served warm, but I find them tastier cold. A welcome addition to a picnic or a buffet meal.

For 8 people:

3 pounds pork tenderloin (use 2 pieces if it is small)
2 tablespoons sweet butter
1 clove garlic
¼ pound (about ¾ cup) chopped pork or chicken liver
½ pound (about 1⅓ cups) chopped lean salt pork (or country ham)
4 shallots (or small onions), peeled and chopped
2 garlic cloves, peeled and chopped
2 slices of bread, dipped in water, then squeezed
2 beaten eggs
3 tablespoons minced parsley
2 tablespoons brandy
2 teaspoons sage (or savory)
Salt
Freshly ground black pepper
1 halved lemon
Slices of bacon (enough to cover the meat)
3 bay leaves
Broth

Preheat the oven to 375°.

Split the pork tenderloin lengthwise. Flatten each piece with a cleaver. Rub both sides with butter and garlic.

Put the chopped meats, shallots, garlic and bread into a large bowl. Stir in the eggs, parsley, brandy and sage. Season with salt, pepper, and more sage or savory, if needed. The

Appetizers

mixture must be very pungent. Place some in the center of each flattened piece of pork and roll it as you would a jelly roll. Tie each roll with a string. Rub the surface with lemon, and wrap each roll in bacon strips.

Place the rolls in an oiled dish, top with the bay leaves and bake for 2 hours, basting with ½ cup of broth from time to time. Let cool until the next day and slice before serving.

There is another version of *enchaud* that must be served warm. Open the pork loin in the center, from top to bottom, leaving the sides untouched and creating a pocket in the center of the meat.

Sauté the shallots, salt pork, garlic and parsley in butter for a few minutes. Add the eggs and wrap this stuffing with a slice of ham, then slide it into the pocket in the center of the meat.

Wrap the piece of pork with the caul or slices of bacon and bake for 2 hours in a 350° oven. Meanwhile, peel and core 8 apples. Put 1 clove and 1 teaspoon sweet butter in each apple and place them around the pork after 1 hour of cooking.

Serve warm.

Filets de Harengs

Marinated Kippered Herring Fillets

These are easy to prepare and are used in salads with warm potatoes. They will keep, covered, in the refrigerator for at least one week.

> *3 thick kippered herring fillets*
> *2 onions, peeled and sliced*
> *1 carrot, peeled and sliced*
> *3 bay leaves*
> *10 peppercorns*
> *Olive oil*

Les
Hors-d'Oeuvre

Place the herring fillets in the bottom of a dish. Cover with the onions and carrots, bay leaves, peppercorns and oil. Wrap in foil and refrigerate or leave in a cool place to marinate for at least two days before tasting.

Fricandeau

Chicken Liver, Pork and Herb-Spiced Patties

These are variations on a theme found in each province of France—*gayettes, caillettes, crépinettes,*—each housewife makes her very own creation. These are what I found to be the liveliest *fricandeau* in Burgundy. They are eaten warm but can be kept in an earthenware pot and used cold in summer with a little green salad.

For 8 people:

½ *pound chicken livers (or pork liver)*
2 *tablespoons sweet butter*
3 *shallots, peeled and chopped*
½ *pound lean salt pork, finely chopped*
½ *cup sorrel leaves (or spinach), shredded*
1 *garlic clove, peeled and crushed*
4 *tablespoons finely chopped parsley*
1 *tablespoon thyme*
  Pinch of clove
2 *teaspoons sage*
2 *tablespoons coarsely chopped pistachio nuts*
  About 20 slices of bacon
6 *tablespoons lard, or more if needed*

Sauté the chicken livers for a few minutes in butter, chop them, and set aside. Sauté shallots for a few minutes. Mix all the ingredients except the bacon and lard and form into egg-size balls. Flatten with your hands and tightly wrap each patty in slices of bacon.

Melt the lard in a large skillet and sauté the patties on all sides, using a spatula to turn them. After 5 minutes cover the pan and cook for 1 hour. Serve at once or let cool and put in an earthenware pot. Pour the cooking fat over the patties and store in a cool place. Serve cold with a bitter green salad of dandelion, chicory or watercress.

Appetizers

Sometimes the little dumplings are dipped in beaten egg, rolled in bread crumbs and baked in a 350° oven for 1 hour.

Gâteau de Foies Blonds

Chicken-Liver Soufflé

This light chicken-liver soufflé is at its best when made with fresh Bressan chicken livers; in order to replace that unobtainable treat here, I have decided to marinate the livers. A delicious fresh course served in individual dishes, or a good luncheon main course, it is often served unmolded but then requires ten eggs. I find this version lighter.

For 8 people:

8 fresh chicken livers
½ cup good sherry or port
1 tablespoon vegetable oil
1 teaspoon sweet butter
1 tablespoon flour
Salt
Freshly ground black pepper
3 shallots, minced
½ cup lean salt pork or bacon, finely diced
Thyme
4 tablespoons heavy cream
1 garlic clove, peeled
½ cup finely chopped parsley
3 eggs, separated
Freshly grated nutmeg

Rinse and dry the livers. Put them in a bowl, cover with sherry (or port), and marinate for at least 2 hours.

Heat the oil and butter in a heavy skillet. Drain the livers and sprinkle them with flour, salt and pepper and sauté them in the butter and oil. Add the shallots and salt pork and cook over low heat for 10 minutes, turning the livers with tongs from time to time.

Les
Hors-d'Oeuvre

Sprinkle with thyme and the marinade, add cream, garlic and parsley. Cook a few more minutes, and remove from the heat to cool.

Preheat the oven to 350°.

Put the cooled mixture in a blender or food processor with the egg yolks and nutmeg and make a thick paste. Put into a bowl.

Beat the egg whites until stiff and gently fold them into the liver mixture. Check the seasonings. It must be highly flavored and heavy on pepper and nutmeg.

Pour into a buttered soufflé mold and place the mold in a large ovenproof pan in 2 inches of hot water (halfway up the side of the mold). Cover with foil and bake from 45 minutes to 1 hour.

Serve in its own dish with a bowl of tomato *Coulis* (p. 63) or a bowl of onion purée. A strong red wine or a chilled dry white wine goes well with this.

Petites Brochettes

Little Cubes of Cheese and Ham Dipped in Egg and Bread Crumbs
and Deep-Fried

Wonderful for children or for buffets and prepared in a jiffy, these come from the Jura and should be served with a chilled white wine.

For 8 people:

8 slices country or plain ham, cut into 2-inch strips
1½ pounds Swiss cheese, cut into 1-inch cubes
2 eggs, beaten with 1 tablespoon vegetable oil and 1
*   tablespoon mustard*
1 cup bread crumbs
About 2 cups oil for deep-frying

Wrap the strips of ham over the cheese cubes. Dip into the beaten egg mixture, then roll in the bread crumbs. Using 8 metal skewers, put 6 cubes on each skewer.

Heat the oil until it is very hot and deep-fry for about 1

minute, or until golden. The cheese should be partially melted.

Drain on paper towels, sprinkle with pepper and serve at once with a tossed green salad.

La Gougère

A Seasoned Cheese Pastry

This glorious cheese hors d'oeuvre tastes and smells as wonderful as it looks. It can be made into a fluffy golden crown or individual little cakes.

You can have it as an appetizer with a chilled kir (p. 284), as a main course for lunch, or with a good red wine to start an important meal. It was originally eaten only to enhance the taste of Burgundy wines.

For 8 people:

1½ *cups equal parts warm milk and water*
8 *tablespoons sweet butter*
1¾ *cups unbleached flour*
Salt
Cayenne pepper
Freshly ground white pepper
Freshly grated nutmeg
6 *large eggs*
1½ *cups plus 2 tablespoons Swiss cheese, cut into ¼-inch dice*
1 *tablespoon Dijon-style mustard*
1 *tablespoon milk*

Preheat the oven to 400°.

Bring the milk and water to a boil; add the butter. Remove from the heat and stir in the flour, salt, cayenne, pepper and nutmeg all at once. Stir vigorously with a big wooden spoon.

After a few minutes, the mixture should come away from the sides of the pan and form a ball. Add the eggs one by one, beating after each addition with the spoon. Pour in 1½ cups of the diced cheese and the mustard. The mixture will be shiny and smooth. Taste for seasoning—*it must be highly seasoned.*

Les
Hors-d'Oeuvre

Butter a large, heavy cookie sheet and, with a tablespoon, pile the dough high in the shape of a 9-inch wide crown with a 2-inch hole in the center, or fill buttered muffin tins with 2 tablespoons of dough in each mold, if you prefer individual puffs.

Smooth the top, brush lightly with milk and sprinkle with 2 tablespoons of the diced cheese.

Bake the crown for 45 minutes, the little puffs for 20 minutes. Do *not* open the oven door during the baking.

After baking, open the door and leave the *gougère* in the oven for 5 minutes. It should then be firm to the touch, though it will collapse a little when out of the oven.

Serve with a dry white wine, a strong rosé or a hearty red wine. This is better served warm or lukewarm.

Le Régal Aillé

A Garlic Treat

When cooked, garlic becomes sweet and nutty and adds a superb touch to a first course. (*Régal* means a treat.)

For 8 people:

> 6 *tablespoons vegetable oil*
> 6 *tablespoons sweet butter*
> 50 *garlic cloves (preferably red garlic), unpeeled*
> *Salt*
> *Freshly ground black pepper*
> 1½ *cups dry white wine*
> 8 *slices toasted bread, halved*
> 8 *tablespoons minced parsley and chives*

Heat the oil and butter in a pan and sauté the garlic for 5 minutes.

Add salt, pepper and the wine and bring to a boil. Simmer 15 minutes, uncovered.

Pass the garlic cloves through a Moulinex mill or crush them with a fork, discarding the skins, and spread the paste on the pieces of toast. Quickly reduce the wine sauce and pour over the toast. Sprinkle with the parsley and chives and serve.

Appetizers

41

Jambon Persillé

Aspic of Ham, Parsley, Garlic and Vinegar

A traditional part of New Year's Eve or Easter dinner, this is also glorious for a buffet or a summer lunch. Make large quantities of it, since it will keep a week in the refrigerator.

For 20 to 25 people:

> *1 10-pound mild-cured butt (or ready-to-cook ham), with bone in and most of the fat and rind removed*
> *2 to 3 pounds veal bones (or a 4-inch piece of veal knuckle)*
> *1 calf's foot, split*
> *3 large onions, each studded with 2 cloves*
> *8 carrots*
> *1 garlic clove*
> *10 peppercorns*
> *3 tablespoons tarragon*
> *3 tablespoons thyme*
> *1 quart dry white wine*
> *3 cups broth*
> *3 egg whites, beaten*
> *8 cups parsley, finely cut with scissors*
> *8 tablespoons wine vinegar*
> *8 garlic cloves, peeled and finely chopped*
> *Salt*
> *Freshly ground black pepper*

Place the ham in a large kettle with the veal bones, calf's foot, onions, carrots, garlic clove, peppercorns, tarragon, thyme, wine, broth and enough water to cover by 1 inch. Bring to the boiling point, reduce the heat, and simmer covered for 5 hours. (You may prefer, after it has reached the boiling point, to cover it with a piece of foil and bake it in a 325° oven on a middle shelf for about 4 hours.)

Les Hors-d'Oeuvre   When the ham is cooked and you can easily pierce it with a fork, remove from the heat and let it cool completely in the stock for about 1 hour.

Discard the veal bones and calf's foot. Remove the ham from the kettle and place it on a board or a table. Remove the bone, then tear the meat with your fingers, shredding it in small pieces and discarding any gristle you may find. Put the ham in a bowl, mix it vigorously with a fork and set aside.

Reduce the stock over a high flame to about 3–4 quarts. Skim off the fat. Correct the seasoning; it should be highly flavored. Remove the onions, crush them, and add them to the bowl of ham. Pass the rest of the stock through a sieve covered with 2 or 3 layers of cheesecloth.

Add the beaten egg whites to the stock and bring to a boil, stirring. Simmer for 15 minutes, remove from the heat, and let cool. Stock should be clear. Pour one-third of it into a 5-quart porcelain bowl. Sprinkle with a thin layer of parsley, then add a layer of ham, then vinegar, chopped garlic, salt and pepper. Add a little stock and repeat until all the ham, parsley, vinegar, and garlic are in the bowl, ending with a layer of parsley. Press the mixture hard with your hands, add a little more stock and cover with a plate weighted with a large can. Chill for at least 24 hours. Chill the rest of the stock in a separate bowl.

Serve in its own mold, or if you prefer, unmold it onto a large flat serving dish, slice and serve with some of the chopped aspic (congealed stock) spread around it as garnish.

Note: In Burgundy the rind and outer layer of fat are chopped and added to the dish. I have omitted them from the recipe because I have noticed that in the United States they were always pushed aside by my guests, but you may add them if you like their crunchy texture and taste.

Les Petits Paniers

Warm Dumplings, Some Stuffed with Chopped Beef, Vegetables, Herbs and Eggs, Some with Cream and Onion

A good first course, these little baskets are also perfect for a picnic or a buffet.

Appetizers

For 8 people:

Dough

3 *cups flour*
2 *small eggs*
8 *tablespoons sweet butter, melted*
2 *tablespoons vegetable oil*
  Salt

Filling I

2 *tablespoons vegetable oil*
2 *shallots, peeled and minced*
½ *green pepper, chopped*
5 *mint (or tarragon) leaves, chopped*
½ *pound chopped beef*
2 *small egg yolks*
3 *tablespoons spinach, cooked, drained, and chopped*
1 *tablespoon rice, cooked and drained*
3 *sprigs parsley, minced*

Filling II

6 *onions, peeled and minced*
3 *tablespoons sweet butter*
1 *teaspoon coriander*
4 *tablespoons sour cream*
½ *cup milk*
½ *cup grated Swiss cheese*

Put the flour on a floured surface, add the eggs, melted butter, oil and salt, and mix. Add 3 tablespoons of water and knead until smooth. Cover with a kitchen towel and refrigerate for at least 30 minutes.

Filling I:
Heat the oil and cook the shallots and green pepper for a few minutes. Add the mint or tarragon. In a large bowl, mix together the beef, shallots and green pepper, egg yolks, spinach, rice and parsley.

Filling II:
Sauté the onions in the butter for a few minutes. Add the coriander and stir into the sour cream.
Preheat the oven to 400°.
Roll the dough as thin as you can and cut into 5-inch

Les
Hors-d'Oeuvre

squares. Fill each square with 1½ tablespoons of stuffing. Fold the dough in half over the filling and press with your fingers all around the dumpling. Place on a buttered cookie sheet, sprinkle with a little milk and grated cheese and bake for 15 minutes.

Roulade au Fromage

Cheese and Mint Pork Rolls

A lively spring dish, this is at its best when goat cheese and fresh mint are in season. It can be prepared ahead of time.

For 8 people:

3 pounds potatoes, peeled
½ cup goat cheese (French, Greek, Italian or Spanish)
2 teaspoons peppercorns, coarsely crushed
2 teaspoons thyme
11 tablespoons sweet butter
8 ½-inch-thick slices (about 2½ pounds) of pork shoulder butt (remove as much fat as possible and pound with a cleaver)
Salt
8 tablespoons fresh mint, cut fine with scissors
½ cup warm milk
½ cup cream
3 tablespoons grated Swiss cheese
2 tablespoons chopped fresh mint

Cook the potatoes in salted water. Mix the goat cheese with pepper, thyme and 4 tablespoons of the butter in a bowl. Sprinkle each slice of pork with salt and spread a thick layer of the cheese mixture on it. Roll each slice tightly and secure it with a piece of string. Mix 1 tablespoon of the mint with 4 tablespoons of the butter.

Preheat oven to 375°.

Mash the potatoes into a purée, add the milk, cream and 2 tablespoons of butter. Whip vigorously and put over medium heat. Add the grated cheese, stirring.

Appetizers

45

Butter an ovenproof dish. Pour the puréed potato into it. Place the pork rolls on top, then spread the mint-and-butter mixture on top. Bake for 15 minutes and dot with 1 tablespoon of butter. Bake for 30 minutes more. Serve piping hot in its cooking dish sprinkled with 1 tablespoon of mint.

Roulades au Céleri

Celery Hearts Wrapped in Ham and Baked in a Cheese and Mustard Sauce

This is made in a jiffy and will do for a light lunch or hors d'oeuvre.

For 8 people:

8 *celery hearts, cut in half lengthwise*
6 *teaspoons sweet butter*
4 *tablespoons flour*
2 *cups warm milk*
2 *bay leaves*
  Freshly grated nutmeg
  Salt
  Freshly ground pepper
1 *egg yolk*
3 *tablespoons cream*
1 *tablespoon Dijon-style mustard*
8 *slices good ham (boiled or country), cut in half*
½ *cup shredded Swiss cheese*
2 *tablespoons bread crumbs*
2 *tablespoons sweet butter*

Cook the celery hearts in boiling salted water for 30 minutes. Drain.

Melt the butter in a saucepan and briskly stir in the flour. Stir in the milk, bay leaves, nutmeg, salt and pepper. When the mixture thickens, beat together the egg yolk and cream and add them. Remove from the heat and add the mustard. Preheat the oven to 350°.

Wrap each celery piece with a slice of ham and place them side by side in a buttered ovenproof dish. Pour the warm sauce over the ham, and sprinkle with cheese and bread crumbs. Dot with butter and bake for 20 minutes.

Saucisson Chaud Lyonnais

Sausage with Potatoes Seasoned with White Wine and Mustard

It may be hard to find *saucisson à cuire* in the United States, but the Polish sausage kielbasa and the Italian cotechino make good replacements and are readily available in neighborhood markets.

For 8 people:

> *About 4 pounds kielbasa (or cotechino)*
> *4 pounds potatoes, boiled in their skins*
> *4 tablespoons dry white wine*
> *2 teaspoons Dijon-style mustard*
> *⅔ cup peanut or olive oil*
> *4 tablespoons red wine vinegar*
> *Salt*
> *Freshly ground black pepper*
> *2 tablespoons chopped parsley and chives*

Prick the sausages with a fork, place them in cold water and bring to a boil. Cook for 25 minutes.

Meanwhile, cook the potatoes and then, holding them in a kitchen towel, peel them while warm, and slice them. Place them in a warm shallow serving dish.

Mix the wine, mustard, oil, vinegar, salt and pepper and pour over the potatoes. Toss gently.

Slice the sausages, place on a serving dish, sprinkle with the parsley and chives and serve. You can also serve the sliced warm sausages with a very light *Gratin Dauphinois* (p. 187).

Appetizers

Terrine de Canard

Duck Pâté

This can be made with the addition of truffles, calf's liver, or goose liver, but the following version, though less extravagant to prepare, is one of the finest I have ever tasted.

For about 10 people:

1 5-pound duck
¼ cup cognac (or any other brandy)
½ cup Madeira
1 tablespoon oil
1 tablespoon lard
1 pound lean salt pork (or bacon), chopped
1 pound pork breast, chopped
1 pound chicken livers
1 duck liver
3 garlic cloves, peeled and chopped
4 bay leaves
4 teaspoons thyme (or savory)
3 eggs
Freshly ground black pepper
Strips of bacon

Remove as many bones as you can from the duck with a little sharp knife. Strip away the fat and cut the meat into ½-inch pieces.

Marinate the duck meat in the cognac and Madeira for 2 hours.

Meanwhile, heat the oil and lard in a skillet and sauté the salt pork (or bacon) for 3 minutes, stirring; add the pork breast and cook for 5 minutes; then add the livers and sauté for another 5 minutes. Remove from the heat and add the garlic, bay leaves, and thyme (or savory). Let cool.

Remove the bay leaves, add the egg and pass the mixture through a food processor or blender briefly. It must be smooth but keep some consistency. Correct the seasoning; the mixture should be flavorful.

Les
Hors-d'Oeuvre

Drain the duck from its marinade and sprinkle it with pepper.

48

Line an ovenproof dish with strips of bacon. Place the duck pieces on the bottom and cover them with the liver mixture. Cover everything with more strips of bacon, press hard with your hands, cover with foil and refrigerate overnight.

Preheat the oven to 375°. Place the foil-covered dish in a larger ovenproof dish filled with 1 cup of hot water. Bake for 1 hour and 40 to 50 minutes.

Let cool, then cut a piece of wood or cardboard that will just cover the top of the pâté. Wrap this cover in aluminum foil and place on top of the covered pâté. Weight it down with full cans and refrigerate for at least 8 hours. Serve cold, in slices, from the dish.

Les Salades

Salads

The Romans started it all with their mixed salads, blending green lettuce with onions, eggs and olives or leeks, lettuce and mint, and cooks have not stopped displaying a rich variety in tastes and textures up to today's Nouvelle Cuisine, which has created the most disconcerting marriages—some legitimate, some less so. In fact, too often anything goes in a salad, and it is easy to display virtuosity at the expense of the final taste.

There are cold salads and warm salads. The dressing can be a simple vinaigrette, a mixture of cream and mustard or plain light cream seasoned with herbs.

A cold salad might include lettuce, chopped sautéed chicken livers, and a rich sauce of egg yolk, mustard, oil and vinegar; or sliced potatoes marinated in white wine and tossed with mussels, celery and truffles; or crayfish, green peppers and avocado seasoned with a light tomato sauce; or a cheerful mixture of nasturtiums, dandelion greens and lamb's-tongue lettuce, seasoned with verjuice.

Among the warm salads are shredded white cabbage sautéed with pork and seasoned with warm vinegar, or dandelions seasoned with sautéed brain, garlic and a mixture of mustard and warm vinegar. They also include lentils and white beans in lightly seasoned mixtures.

Cold tossed salads are usually served to refresh the palate between courses or to accompany a meat dish, but lately they, along with the warm salads, are served as a first course or as a main course in a light lunch.

Les Salades

Laitue Bourguignonne

Green Salad Seasoned with Garlic, Butter and Lemon

A delicate, most unusual way of serving fresh greens.

For 8 people:

3 tablespoons sweet butter
1 garlic clove, peeled and crushed
Salt
Juice of 1 lemon
Freshly ground white pepper
3 tablespoons minced parsley
Bibb lettuce or tender leaf lettuce or tender Boston lettuce

Melt the butter until it is soft and lukewarm. Add the garlic, salt, butter, lemon juice, pepper and parsley. Mix thoroughly.

Wash and dry the lettuce leaves carefully. Place them in a large glass or china bowl. Pour the sauce over them, toss gently and serve at once.

Salade aux Griaudes

Crisp Diced Pork Seasoned with Vinegar and Herbs

A delicate border illustration.

For a buffet, a snack or a summer hors d'oeuvre, this is a simple dish to prepare but a very interesting one.

For 8 people:

1 pound lean salt pork, cut into very small dice
½ cup red wine vinegar
Freshly ground black pepper
1 garlic clove, minced
2 tablespoons minced parsley

Slowly heat the pork until all the fat has melted and it is crisp. Put the pork in a bowl and discard the fat. Add the vinegar

Salads

51

to the skillet for 1 minute, then pour it over the crisp pork. Sprinkle with pepper, garlic and parsley and serve as a side dish.

Salade à la Menthe

Lettuce Seasoned with Mint Marinated in Oil, Garlic and Wine Vinegar

Mint is often used in Burgundy for health as well as for flavor. It brings an unusual freshness to this salad, and one quickly becomes addicted to it.

For 8 people:

4 *mint sprigs or about 18 fresh mint leaves, minced*
3 *chive leaves, minced*
8 *tablespoons vegetable oil*
Salt
Freshly ground black pepper
4 *tablespoons wine vinegar*
2 *heads of Boston lettuce, trimmed, washed and dried*
1 *head of escarole, trimmed, washed and dried*
2 *garlic cloves, peeled and minced*

Place the mint and the chives in a bowl with the oil and set aside for 30 minutes. Add the salt, pepper and vinegar, and mix thoroughly.

Place the lettuce leaves in a large bowl, sprinkle with garlic and pour the sauce over them. Toss well and serve.

Salade au Chou

Sautéed Strips of Cabbage Seasoned with Bacon, Vinegar, Oil and Spices

Les Salades

Choose tender cabbage and don't overcook it. This salad has a wonderful taste and texture.

For 8 people:

  2 *heads of Savoy cabbage*
  2 *tablespoons sweet butter*
  7 *tablespoons olive or peanut oil*
  ½ *pound bacon, diced (about 2 cups)*
  4 *tablespoons wine vinegar*
  1 *tablespoon Dijon-style mustard*
    Salt
    Freshly ground black pepper
  2 *garlic cloves, minced*
  2 *tablespoons minced parsley (or chives)*

Trim the cabbage and cut into very narrow strips.

Heat the butter and 1 tablespoon of the oil in a large skillet; add the diced bacon and sauté on all sides until crisp. Add 2 tablespoons of the vinegar, then the cabbage. Cook briefly over high heat, until the cabbage is just wilted.

Meanwhile, mix together the mustard, 2 tablespoons of vinegar, 6 tablespoons of oil, salt and pepper. Pour over the cabbage and bacon and stir carefully.

Add the garlic and parsley to the salad just before serving.

Salade aux Noix

Green Salad with Walnuts, Lemons, Mustard and Cream

For 8 people:

  3 *heads of young Boston (or Bibb) lettuce*
  16 *walnuts, cut in half*
  1 *tablespoon Dijon-style mustard*
    Juice of 1 lemon
    Cayenne pepper
  1 *cup heavy cream*
    Salt

Trim the lettuce, wash and dry them and place them in a glass or china bowl. Sprinkle with the walnuts.

In another bowl, mix the mustard, lemon juice, cayenne, cream and salt. Pour it over the lettuce and serve.

Salads

53

Salade de Céleri

Celery Hearts Seasoned with Walnuts, Cheese, Vinegar and Oil

A very rich salad, perfect for a winter meal.

For 8 people:

4 *celery hearts, finely chopped*
1 *cup coarsely chopped walnuts*
½ *pound Roquefort or blue cheese*
2 *tablespoons brandy*
  Freshly ground black pepper
2 *tablespoons red wine vinegar*
6 *tablespoons walnut (or peanut) oil*
  Salt (optional)

Place the celery hearts in a bowl with the walnuts. Crush the cheese in the brandy, add the pepper, vinegar and oil and beat with a fork. Pour over the celery and walnuts. Check the seasoning and add salt if desired. Stir well and serve.

Salade de Haricots Verts

A Green Bean Salad with Shallots and Mushrooms

This lovely dish is usually made with fresh truffles, but with fresh mushrooms it remains a treat if you don't overcook the beans.

For 8 people:

2½ *pounds green beans, trimmed and washed*
1 *pound white mushrooms, washed, dried and thinly sliced*
3 *shallots (or little white onions), peeled and minced*
3 *tablespoons walnut oil*
1 *tablespoon red wine vinegar*
  Salt
  Freshly ground black pepper

Cook the beans in a large pot of salted water for 10 to 15 minutes. Drain and place them in a large shallow bowl. Sprinkle with mushrooms and shallots.

Vigorously stir together the oil, vinegar, salt and pepper and pour over the vegetables. Mix gently and serve lukewarm or cold.

Salade de Lentilles

A Lentil Salad with Vegetables, Herbs and Bacon

A hearty winter dish, a good buffet dish.

For 8 people:

4 cups dried lentils
4 carrots, peeled and cut in quarters
2 onions, peeled and studded with 1 clove each
1 garlic clove, peeled
3 bay leaves
3 sprigs of thyme
Freshly ground black pepper
Salt
½-pound piece of smoked bacon
3 tablespoons chopped parsley
½-pound piece of smoked bacon
4 slices bread, cut in triangles for croutons
3 tablespoons sweet butter

Sauce

2 tablespoons Dijon-style mustard
8 tablespoons olive or peanut oil
4 tablespoons red wine vinegar
3 tablespoons minced chives
3 garlic cloves, peeled and crushed
3 red onions, peeled and minced
Salt
Freshly ground pepper

Wash and prepare the lentils according to the directions on the package. Place them in a large pot of cold water with the

Salads

carrots, onions, garlic, bay leaves, thyme, salt and pepper. Cover and simmer for about 35 minutes, or until the vegetables are tender.

Prepare the sauce, blending the mustard, oil, vinegar, chives, garlic, onions, salt and pepper in a large bowl. Stir well.

Drain the lentils and carrots, discarding the bay leaves, thyme and onions with cloves. Cut the bacon into thin slices, then cut the slices into strips and fry them. Drain on paper towels. Pour the lentils and carrots into the sauce. Add the bacon strips and stir gently. Sprinkle with parsley and check the seasoning. Fry the triangles of bread in the butter.

Serve lukewarm (in a dome shape) in a shallow dish surrounded with the croutons.

Salade de Lyon

A Tossed Green Salad with Herring and Boiled Eggs

For 8 people:

> 3 herrings, cut in 1-inch pieces
> ⅓ cup oil
> Pepper
> 2 onions, sliced

Dressing

> 2 tablespoons wine vinegar
> 2 tablespoons Dijon-style mustard
> Salt
> Freshly ground black pepper
> 3 tablespoons finely chopped parsley

Greens and Garnish

> Chicory, trimmed and washed
> Watercress, trimmed and washed
> Endive, washed and sliced lengthwise
> Boston lettuce, trimmed and washed
> Celery hearts, cut in thin strips and washed
> 4 hard-cooked eggs, peeled and quartered

A day or so ahead, cut the herrings and marinate them in oil with pepper and onion.

To prepare the dressing, combine in a bowl the oil in which the herrings have marinated with the vinegar, mustard, salt and parsley.

Place the well-drained greens in a large bowl. Place the cut herrings on top and the quartered eggs around. Pour on the dressing and serve. Toss after the dish has arrived at the table.

Salade de Nevers

Green Salad with a Dijon Mustard, Roquefort, Bacon, Garlic, Egg and Vinaigrette Sauce

You need very tender young dandelions or equally tender chicory for this pungent, invigorating salad.

For 8 people:

6 *cups dandelion greens, very carefully washed, trimmed and dried*
2 *tablespoons oil*
1 *cup lean salt pork, diced quite small (½-inch pieces)*
3 *tablespoons wine vinegar*
1 *tablespoon Dijon-style mustard*
2 *tablespoons Roquefort or blue cheese*
Salt
Freshly ground black pepper
3 *garlic cloves*
About 3 slices of good bread cut into ½-inch pieces
2 *tablespoons minced parsley (or chives)*
4 *hard-cooked eggs, shelled and quartered lengthwise*

While you clean and trim the greens, warm a large salad bowl and heat 1 tablespoon of oil in a skillet. Add the salt pork and cook over medium heat until crisp.

Meanwhile, mix the vinegar, the mustard and the cheese into a soft paste.

Place the greens in the warm bowl, add salt, pepper, the

Salads

vinegar-mustard-cheese mixture, and the pork. Sauté the garlic cloves in 1 tablespoon of oil in the skillet for 2 minutes and discard them. Add the pieces of bread to this garlic-scented oil and, when they are golden on all sides, add them to the salad. Stir carefully. Sprinkle with parsley or chives and place the hard-cooked-egg quarters all around the bowl. Serve at once. The salad should be warm.

Note: It is more efficient to use two skillets at once, cooking the salt pork in one and the garlic and croutons in the other. Your dandelion salad will be warmer this way.

Salade de Pommes de Terre

A Warm Potato Salad Seasoned with Wine, Mustard and Herbs

This is served with boiled sausage or kippered herring.

For 8 people:

16 potatoes
6 tablespoons white wine
2 teaspoons dried thyme or chopped fresh thyme
10 tablespoons vegetable oil (walnut or olive oil)
2 tablespoons red wine vinegar
2 tablespoons Dijon-style mustard
2 shallots, minced
1 garlic clove, minced
3 tablespoons fresh herbs (parsley or chives)
Salt
Freshly ground black pepper

Wash and boil the unpeeled potatoes in salted water. Holding them with a thick kitchen mitt or a towel, peel and cut them into thick slices. Bring the wine and the thyme to a boil and pour over the potatoes.

Bring 8 tablespoons of oil and the vinegar to a boil, add the mustard, shallots and garlic and pour over the potatoes.

Les Salades

Sprinkle with the herbs, salt and pepper and dribble 2 tablespoons of oil over the top.

Serve lukewarm or at room temperature.

Salade des Vendangeurs

Green Tossed Salad with Ham, Fresh Herbs and Warm Vinegar

A wonderful salad with a great variety of greens and fresh herbs.

For 8 people:

Dandelion, chicory, watercress and leaf lettuce
Freshly ground black pepper
1 tablespoon lard (or oil)
2 cups bacon (or lean salt pork), cut into ½-inch cubes
2 tablespoons vegetable oil (optional)
3 tablespoons wine vinegar
½ cup thin strips (1-inch by ½-inch pieces) of sliced
    country ham or prosciutto
1 tablespoon minced chives
1 tablespoon minced tarragon
1 tablespoon minced chervil
1 tablespoon minced parsley (or mint or basil)
1 garlic clove, peeled and crushed

Wash, trim and dry the greens and place them in a large bowl. Sprinkle with pepper. Heat the lard in a skillet, lower the heat, and sauté the diced bacon until crisp. Pour the bacon and the fat over the greens. (You can add 2 tablespoons of vegetable oil if the bacon does not yield enough fat.) Add the vinegar to the skillet, heat for 2 seconds and pour over the greens. Add the ham, herbs and garlic and mix thoroughly.
    Serve at once.

Salade Dijonnaise

A Lettuce, Egg, Ham, Celery, Cheese, Walnut, Mustard and Herb
Salad

Superb for a buffet or a picnic, this can be made with olive, peanut or walnut oil.

For 8 people:

6 *hard-cooked eggs, shelled*
1 *pound boiled ham (about 2 cups), diced (½-inch pieces)*
½ *pound salami, diced (½-inch pieces)*
2 *celery hearts, diced (½-inch pieces)*
12 *walnuts, coarsely chopped*
1 *pound Swiss cheese, diced (½-inch pieces)*
4 *Granny Smith apples, peeled and diced (½-inch pieces)*
4 *tablespoons strong Dijon-style mustard*
2 *tablespoons wine vinegar*
8 *tablespoons olive, peanut or walnut oil*
Salt
Freshly ground white pepper
2 *large heads of Boston lettuce or 4 heads Bibb lettuce, washed*
3 *tablespoons chopped chervil*

Separate the yolk from the white of the hard-cooked eggs. Dice the egg white, ham, salami, celery, walnuts, Swiss cheese and apples and mix them together in a large bowl.

Crush the egg yolks with the mustard, vinegar and oil. Stir well and add salt and pepper.

Place the lettuce leaves around the edges of a large glass or white china bowl, add the diced ingredients and pour the sauce over everything. Chill.

Remove from the refrigerator 1 hour before serving. Just before serving, toss gently and sprinkle with chervil.

Salade de Pissenlits

A Dandelion Salad with Bacon and Garlic Croutons

Les Salades

The best dandelions come early in spring, after the snow has melted. The plants should be tender and pale green, but if they are not, use only the young, inner leaves. Wash and dry thoroughly.

For 8 people:

> 2 cups lean salt pork, diced very small or cut in thin
>   strips
> 2½ pounds dandelion greens (or escarole or chicory)
> 4 tablespoons wine vinegar
>   Freshly ground black pepper
> 4 slices good bread, toasted or fried in butter
> 2 garlic cloves, peeled

Melt the salt pork slowly. Place the dandelion greens in a
warm bowl. Pour the pork fat over the leaves. Add vinegar
to the pork in the skillet, and pour over the leaves. Sprinkle
with pepper and serve at once with toasted slices of bread
rubbed with garlic.

Salade Rouge et Verte

A Green Pepper and Red Beet Salad Served with a Celery and Shallot
Salad Seasoned with Oil, Vinegar, Mustard and Fresh Herbs

You must prepare the two salads separately and keep them
refrigerated until ready to use. This is a beautiful dish, full of
flavor and color.

For 8 people:

Green Pepper and Beet Salad

> 2 green peppers, cut in very small strips
> 1 cup cooked red beets, peeled and diced
> 3 tablespoons vegetable oil
> 1 tablespoon red wine vinegar
> 1 garlic clove, finely crushed
> 2 tablespoons minced parsley

Celery Heart and Shallot Salad

> 4 celery hearts, diced
> 1 or 2 shallots (or 1 white onion), minced
> 3 tablespoons vegetable oil
>   Juice of 1 lemon
> 1 tablespoon Dijon-style mustard
>   Salt
>   Freshly ground black pepper

Salads

Garnish

---

3 tablespoons fresh herbs (chives, mint, chervil)

Prepare the two salads in separate bowls, tossing them delicately in their sauces, made by thoroughly mixing all the ingredients except the vegetables.

When you are ready to serve, place the pepper and beet salad on a shallow dish with the celery salad all around. Sprinkle with the fresh herbs and serve.

Salade Verte à la Crème

Green Tossed Salad with a Cream, Egg Yolk, Vinegar and Herb Sauce

For 8 people:

3 teaspoons salt
2 teaspoons freshly ground white pepper
2 egg yolks
2 tablespoons wine vinegar (or lemon juice)
4 tablespoons light cream
3 tablespoons finely chopped fresh herbs (chervil, chives, mint, basil, parsley)
4 lettuce hearts or Bibb or leaf lettuces, washed and dried

Pour all the ingredients for the sauce except the cream and the herbs into a large bowl and mix vigorously. Stir in the cream and herbs.

Place the lettuce leaves in a glass or china bowl and pour the sauce over them. Toss gently and serve at once.

Le Saladier Lyonnais

A Pungent Salad of Chicken Livers, Eggs, Herrings, Meat, Herbs and Vinaigrette Sauce

Les Salades

This is a crowd pleaser from Lyon. Highly seasoned, it is a

wonderful summer lunch, or the core of a country buffet, or the first course of a hearty informal meal.

There are many variations of the *saladier*. Sometimes poached eggs are placed on top. Sometimes the whole salad nests on a bed of endive, watercress and dandelion greens. If you use a mutton foot (a must in Lyon, but not easily available in the United States), split it and carefully remove all the hair growing underneath in the center before you cook it in *court-bouillon,* then dice it.

For 8 people:

4 chicken livers
2 tablespoons sweet butter
1 tablespoon vegetable oil
2 cups cold meat (boiled beef or chicken or ham), diced
4 large herrings, cut in 1-inch pieces and marinated in ⅓ cup oil with pepper and 2 sliced onions
1 mutton foot, trimmed, cooked and diced (optional; see headnote)
2 tablespoons finely chopped chives
4 tablespoons finely chopped tarragon (or chervil)
2 tablespoons finely chopped parsley
8 tablespoons peanut or olive oil
3 tablespoons wine vinegar
3 tablespoons Dijon-style mustard
Salt
Freshly ground black pepper
Pinch of coriander
4 hard-cooked eggs, shelled and quartered lengthwise
1 tablespoon fresh herbs (tarragon or chives)

Sauté the livers in the butter and oil. Quarter or dice them.

Remove the fat (if any) from the cold meat and dice. Put the livers, meat, mutton foot if available, herrings, chives, tarragon and parsley in a large bowl.

Mix the oil, vinegar, mustard, salt, pepper and coriander and pour into the bowl. Stir gently. Place the quartered eggs all around and sprinkle the fresh herbs on top.

It is better to prepare this one hour ahead to increase the flavor.

Salads

Les Sauces

Sauces

Rich, sumptuous sauce recipes have been handed down for generations, but less flour is used now, and heavy cream, vegetables and wine are added to natural juices instead. The sauces are made to enhance flavor, not to mask it.

The red-wine sauces *(bourguignonne, matelote),* the white-wine sauces *(lyonnaise, pauchouse)* and the sauces made with highly seasoned broth are always thickened with vegetables like onions or tomatoes and fresh cream. They use garlic, mustard, coriander, pepper, shallots and vinegar, and embody the spirit of Burgundy.

Beurre Bourguignonne

A Butter, Garlic, Shallot and Parsley Sauce

For snails, mussels, clams or green beans, a wonderful pungent sauce.

Enough for 6 dozen snails:

2 cups sweet butter, softened
6 garlic cloves, peeled and minced
3 shallots, peeled and minced
2 cups chopped parsley
4 tablespoons salt
Freshly ground black pepper

Put all the ingredients in a large bowl. Crush and mix them. Cover in plastic wrap and keep in the refrigerator until ready to use. The butter will remain fresh and tasty for about two weeks.

Coulis de Tomates

A Warm Tomato sauce

The secret here is to cook the sauce briefly to avoid a bitter taste. It can be poured into a jar, covered with a little oil and kept for a week in the refrigerator.

For 2½ cups of sauce:

2 onions, peeled and minced
5 pounds ripe tomatoes
2 tablespoons olive oil
2 garlic cloves, peeled and crushed
½ cup chopped parsley
1 teaspoon dried herbs (oregano, thyme)
Bouquet garni
2 teaspoons sugar
Salt
Freshly ground black pepper

Squeeze the onion in a towel to remove excess moisture. Pass the tomatoes through a Mouli food mill and discard the skins.

Heat the oil in a heavy-bottomed skillet, add the onions, half of the garlic, the parsley, herbs and bouquet garni. Cook for 10 minutes.

Place the tomato purée in a heavy-bottomed pan, add the sugar and simmer, uncovered, for 10 minutes. Pour it into the onion and herb mixture and heat, uncovered, for 5 minutes.

Remove from the heat, add the remaining garlic, salt and pepper. Discard the bouquet garni.

Beurre d'Escargot

What do beef and snails have in common? This lively butter sauce. It makes for a spirited roast beef or turns the simplest steak into a Burgundy treat, especially if you serve it with a *Gratin Dauphinois* (p. 187) or a *Paillasson* (p. 190). You may like to use this *beurre d'escargot* with broiled fish (bluefish or

Sauces

swordfish) as well.

The simplest way to make this butter is to mix everything except the butter in a food processor, then add the butter and mix for one second.

Enough butter for 8 people:

4 shallots, peeled and minced
1 garlic clove, minced
3 tablespoons minced parsley
Salt
Freshly ground black pepper
8 tablespoons butter, softened

Mix all the ingredients, cover and leave at room temperature.

Place dots of the butter between sliced beef or on top of fish and serve at once.

Marinade

For Beef, Pork, Rabbit or Chicken

This can also be made with white wine. Meat should be marinated in this for two days before being cooked.

For 2 quarts of marinade:

1 carrot, peeled and sliced
2 onions, peeled and sliced
2 garlic cloves, peeled and crushed
½ cup parsley, stems and leaves
1 celery stalk
Thyme
2 bay leaves
5 peppercorns
2 cloves
1 quart hearty red wine
1 cup wine vinegar
1 cup brandy
2 tablespoons vegetable oil
Salt

Mix all the ingredients, and it is ready to use.

Sauce à la Menthe

A Warm, Unctuous Sauce Made with Egg Yolks, Vinegar, Butter and
Fresh Mint

This lively sauce is superb with poached trout.

For 2 cups of sauce:

> 6 *egg yolks*
> 1½ *tablespoons wine vinegar*
> *Salt*
> *Freshly ground black pepper*
> 8 *tablespoons sweet butter, melted*
> 2 *tablespoons fresh mint leaves, cut up with scissors*

Place the egg yolks, vinegar and seasoning in a blender.
Blend for a few seconds. Add the butter and blend at top
speed for a few seconds more. Keep the sauce over tepid
water until ready to use. Add the mint just before serving.

This sauce can be made by hand by mixing the egg yolks
and butter together energetically, stirring in the vinegar and
cooking the mixture over low heat for a few minutes.

Sauce au Beurre Rouge

A Red Wine, Vinegar, Shallot and Butter Sauce

This superb, highly flavored sauce is served with poached fish
(cooked in *court-bouillon*).

For 1½ cups of sauce:

> 4 *tablespoons shallots, peeled and minced*
> ½ *cup red wine vinegar*
> ¼ *cup red wine*
> *Salt*
> *Freshly ground pepper*
> 4 *tablespoons water*
> 3 *sticks sweet butter, chilled and cut into sections*

Sauces

Cook the shallots, vinegar and wine over low heat until they become a paste. Season to taste with salt and pepper.

In another pan, heat the water and add the butter, whipping and stirring constantly. It must not reach the boiling point. Add the shallot paste little by little, stirring constantly. Check the seasoning. Transfer to a tepid serving bowl and serve. (If you must keep it for a while, place it over a bowl of barely warm water.)

Sauce Bourguignonne

A Red Wine, Bacon and Onion Sauce

This hearty sauce can be reheated and will improve in the process. Sautéed mushrooms are often added to it.

For 1 bowl of sauce:

> 1 *large chunk bacon with rind removed (or country ham), cut into strips ¼ inch thick and 1½ inches long*
> 1 *carrot, peeled and diced*
> 1 *onion, peeled and diced*
> 1 *tablespoon sweet butter*
> 1 *tablespoon vegetable oil*
> *Freshly ground nutmeg*
> 1 *clove*
> 2 *cups red wine*
> 1 *tablespoon tomato paste*
> 1 *tablespoon flour*
> 1 *tablespoon Dijon-style mustard*
> 5 *peppercorns, crushed*
> 1 *tablespoon sweet butter (optional)*

Sauté the strips of bacon for 3 minutes. Remove from the pan and set aside.

Sauté the vegetables in the hot butter and oil for a few minutes until soft. Add a pinch of nutmeg and the clove, then stir in the wine and the tomato paste. Cook, uncovered, for 20 minutes—until it reduces by half. Put the sauce through a sieve, add flour and return it to the stove. Add the strips of bacon. Allow the mixture to heat for a few minutes, then remove from the heat and add the mustard and peppercorns.

If you want to keep the sauce and reheat it later, add 1 tablespoon butter.

Sauce de Sorges

A Lively Herb Sauce Made with Eggs and Oil and Seasoned with
Mustard and Lemon

A tart sauce to serve with boiled artichokes, asparagus, celery root or a boiled meat.

For ¾ cup of sauce:

1 tablespoon Dijon-style mustard
Juice of 1 lemon
Peel of 1 lemon, grated
Salt
Freshly ground black pepper
3 tablespoons vegetable oil
2 warm hard-cooked eggs, yolks and whites separated
1 tablespoon minced shallots
2 tablespoons chervil, cut with scissors
1 tablespoon finely chopped tarragon
1 tablespoon finely chopped chives

Put the mustard, lemon juice, lemon peel, salt and pepper in a large bowl. Pour the oil in gradually, stirring (as you would for a mayonnaise). Add the egg yolks and the fresh herbs mashing the yolks as you stir. Crush the egg whites through a sieve into the sauce. Check the seasoning.

Sauce Dorée

A Light Mayonnaise Seasoned with Shallots, Wine, Herbs and Cream

Wonderful with boiled beef, boiled poultry, raw fennel or celery root.

Sauces

For 2½ cups of sauce:

- 2 *teaspoons minced shallots*
- 2 *teaspoons sweet butter*
- ½ *cup white wine*
- ½ *cup chopped tarragon leaves*
- 3 *tablespoons light cream*
- 2 *cups homemade mayonnaise (see below)*

Cook the minced shallots in the butter until limp; add, while stirring, the wine, tarragon and cream. Stir the hot mixture into the mayonnaise.

Serve lukewarm or cold.

Sauce Mayonnaise

Homemade mayonnaise is easy and quick to prepare.

For 2 cups of sauce:

- 2 *egg yolks, at room temperature*
- 1 *tablespoon Dijon-style mustard (or 1 teaspoon, according to taste)*
- 2 *cups oil (½ peanut and ½ olive oil, or all peanut), at room temperature*
- 1 *tablespoon red wine vinegar (or 2 tablespoons lemon juice)*
- *Salt*
- *Freshly ground white pepper*

If you make this by hand, slip a kitchen towel under the bowl to prevent it from sliding while you beat the egg yolks and mustard together. Then add the oil in a slow steady stream, whisking constantly until firm.

Bring the vinegar to a boil and stir it into the sauce while beating (or use cold lemon juice instead, according to taste). Add salt and pepper.

If you use a blender, place 1 tablespoon of oil in the bowl with the rest of the ingredients, cover and blend on low speed for 2 minutes; stop, then add the rest of the oil in a steady flow and blend slowly.

Place the mayonnaise in a covered bowl and refrigerate. It will keep three to four days. If the egg yolks separate from the oil, place a fresh egg yolk in a new bowl, add 1 teaspoon of mustard and stir well. Slowly add the curdled mixture, stirring until it is firm and silky. Correct the seasoning.

Sauce Bourguignotte

A Good Sauce for Eggs and Fish

For 2 cups of sauce:

- 4 *tablespoons sweet butter*
- 2 *tablespoons flour*
- 2 *cups hearty red wine*
- 10 *shallots, peeled and minced*
- 2 *tablespoons minced parsley*
- 2 *teaspoons thyme*
- 2 *bay leaves*
- 4 *garlic cloves, peeled and crushed*
- 4 *tablespoons sweet butter*

Heat the butter in a heavy-bottomed pan. Add the flour, stirring, then the wine, shallots, herbs and garlic. Let the sauce reduce for a few minutes, uncovered. Discard the bay leaves and put the sauce through a sieve into a warm bowl. Add the butter bit by bit while stirring; correct the seasoning if necessary and serve.

Sauce Meurette

A Rich Sauce Made with Red Wine and Vegetables and Seasoned with Herbs

This is Burgundy's national sauce, mostly used with eel, pike, trout and carp, although it can also be served with poached eggs or lamb's brains.

Sauces

Enough for 8 servings:

- *2 tablespoons sweet butter*
- *2 large onions, peeled and chopped*
- *3 carrots, peeled and chopped*
- *4 garlic cloves, peeled and crushed*
- *2 whites of leeks, chopped (or 4 shallots, peeled and chopped)*
- *1 quart hearty red wine*
- *2 bay leaves, crushed*
- *2 teaspoons thyme*
  Salt
  Freshly ground black pepper
- *1 teaspoon sugar*
- *3 tablespoons flour thoroughly mixed with 5 tablespoons softened sweet butter*
- *2 tablespoons brandy (optional)*
- *2 tablespoons red currant jelly*

Additional garnishes

- *1 cup sautéed mushrooms*
- *16 pearl onions*
- *8 small croutons sautéed in oil and rubbed with garlic*

Heat the butter and sauté the onions for a few minutes. Add the carrots, garlic and leeks and cook until soft. Add the wine, herbs and seasoning and bring to a boil. Lower the heat and simmer, uncovered, for 40 minutes.

Discard the bay leaves. Pass the mixture through a sieve, crushing the vegetables with a wooden spoon. Add the flour-and-butter paste to the wine-vegetable mixture. Put it back on the stove and simmer for 2 minutes, stirring. Pour in the brandy. Ignite. Beat in the red currant jelly and serve.

Sauce Mousseline Dijon

A Warm, Frothy Egg, Butter, Lemon and Mustard Sauce

Les Sauces

A lovely tart sauce for poached eggs, poached or broiled fish and boiled vegetables.

For 1 cup of sauce:

> *3 egg yolks*
> *Juice of 1 lemon*
> *1 teaspoon cold water*
> *Salt*
> *Freshly ground black pepper*
> *½ cup sweet butter, cut in small pieces*
> *2 tablespoons Dijon-style mustard*

Put everything but the mustard in a pan over simmering water. Whip steadily until frothy and thick. Add the mustard and check the seasoning. Serve lukewarm in a warm bowl.

Sauce Moutarde I

Mustard Sauce

To serve with pork chops, veal or boiled vegetables.

> For 2 cups of sauce:

> *4 tablespoons sweet butter*
> *4 tablespoons flour*
> *1½ cups warm milk (or broth)*
> *2 egg yolks*
> *4 tablespoons Dijon-style mustard*
> *1 tablespoon wine vinegar*
> *2 tablespoons cream*
> *Salt*
> *Freshly ground pepper*

Heat the butter and add the flour, stirring briskly with a whisk, then add the warm milk or broth. Cook, stirring, until the mixture thickens. Remove it from the heat and, stirring vigorously, add the egg yolks. Return the sauce to low heat for a few minutes.

Remove it from the heat and add the mustard, vinegar, cream, salt and pepper. Check the seasoning. Keep warm at a simmer until ready to serve—don't let it come to a boil.

Sauces

Sauce Moutarde II

Mustard Sauce

To be served with broiled meat.

For 2½ cups of sauce:

2 onions, peeled and minced
2 shallots, peeled and minced
3 tablespoons sweet butter
1 tablespoon vegetable oil
1 tablespoon flour
2 cups white (or red) wine
2 tablespoons red wine vinegar
1 tablespoon tomato paste
Salt
Freshly ground pepper
2 tablespoons Dijon-style mustard
2 tablespoons finely chopped parsley

Sauté the onions and shallots in the butter and oil over medium heat until golden. Sprinkle with the flour and cook, stirring, a few minutes longer. Stir in the wine, vinegar, tomato paste, salt and pepper and simmer over low heat, uncovered, for 30 minutes. Check the seasoning.

Just before serving, stir in the mustard and parsley.

Sauce Tomate Crue

A Raw Tomato Sauce

This comes from the South. It is served with cold dishes.

For 2 cups of sauce:

5 pounds very ripe tomatoes, peeled
2 onions, peeled and quartered
2 garlic cloves, peeled
3 tablespoons chopped parsley
3 tablespoons chopped basil (optional)
3 tablespoons olive oil
Salt
Freshly ground black pepper

Put half of the tomatoes in a blender with half of the onions and 1 garlic clove. Blend at high speed for 5 minutes and pour into a bowl. Blend the rest of the tomato, onion and garlic along with the parsley (and basil) and oil. Blend for 5 minutes and add it to the first batch in the bowl. Season with salt and pepper and stir well.

Covered in the refrigerator, this sauce will keep four to five days.

Sauces

Les Poissons

Fish

Because of its many creeks, rivers, ponds, waterfalls and lakes, Burgundy is blessed not only with a vast population of good-natured fishermen adding a peaceful note to its countryside but with an abundance of salmon, eel, trout, pike, carp, barbel, bream, herring, perch, frogs, crayfish and the rarest freshwater treat—*l'omble chevalier.*

Most fish in Burgundy, Lyonnais and Savoy are cooked in wine and herbs, enriched with cream and often with mustard. But the recipes are as varied as they are numerous. In Burgundy the *matelote* is usually called a *pauchouse* when prepared with white wine or a *meurette* when red wine and more than one kind of fish are used. Pike may be larded, broiled with butter, white wine and mustard, or baked with cream and vinegar. It may be served on a purée of sorrel and tarragon, or cooked covered with shallots, garlic and mushrooms and sprinkled with nutmeg. Frogs are sautéed, then cooked gently with snails, garlic, herbs and white wine. Carp are often marinated, then stuffed with their roe, herbs and mushrooms and served with an oil, vinegar and hard-cooked egg sauce.

Trout are sometimes cooked *au bleu,* briskly in a fragrant *court-bouillon* or stuffed with mushrooms, herbs and cream, or made into *quenelles.* Crayfish are cooked with cream, brandy, wine mustard and Spanish saffron or quickly cooked in a highly seasoned *court-bouillon* made of white wine. They are also mixed with cream and cheese for a succulent gratin.

Salmon may be stuffed with vegetables and cooked in wine and mustard, or simply cooked in *court-bouillon* and served with a mustard, egg yolk, spice and chive sauce. It can also be eaten raw with herbs and oil.

Shad is simmered on top of chopped sorrel and shallots and sprinkled with brandy and wine before it is baked, or stuffed with its roe and sorrel to be marinated and broiled.

Snails deserve a whole chapter to themselves, but I have

Les Poissons

included them here in a few delectable preparations.

Crayfish are best from June to fall and must be cooked alive. I have replaced them with shrimps because they are hard to find in the United States, except in New Orleans.

Generally, no seawater fish are used, since, in Burgundy, they were mostly thought of as punishment served only during Lent. The children still sing the little ballad:

> "No more herring
> Bad smelling, foul tasting
> Give us good ham instead!"

I have selected here recipes that appeal to the American palate, represent the main trends of Burgundy cuisine old and new, and can be made with fish currently available in the United States.

Remember, always spend almost as much time *choosing* a fish as when you're cooking it. The eye must be clear and bulging, the gills red, and the scales must adhere firmly to the skin and have a sheen. When you serve lemon—unless it is done only to please the eye—peel and dice it so that its taste is clear and sharp.

Anguille en Matelote

Eel Cooked in Wine and Herbs

Despite their unfortunate resemblance to snakes, eels have refined tastes and a delicate flesh. They love clear water, they hate mud. They feed on snails and grasshoppers when they are on land, and on fish when they swim in rivers. Their flesh is considered a delicacy in Burgundy.

They must be killed in a rather rigorous fashion with a sharp blow on the head; they are then hung on a hook on a wall with a ring tied around the neck. Before cooking an eel, one must grip the skin with a piece of cloth, pull it down and peel it off. The head, fins and tail must also be removed, along with the entrails. Dry the eel carefully with paper towels.

This recipe will reheat well and should be served with plain boiled potatoes.

Fish

For 8 people:

2 onions, peeled and chopped
2 tablespoons sweet butter
1 tablespoon vegetable oil
Salt
Freshly ground black pepper
16 thick slices of eel, trimmed and peeled
6 to 8 cups red (or red and white) wine
Parsley
2 bay leaves
Thyme
1 carrot, peeled and chopped
1 teaspoon fennel seeds
2 garlic cloves, peeled and crushed
2 tablespoons sweet butter
2 tablespoons flour
16 croutons, sautéed in butter

Sauté the onions in the butter and oil. Sprinkle with salt and pepper. Add the pieces of eel and sauté on all sides, then cover with wine. Add the herbs, carrot, fennel seeds and garlic and simmer until the fish is done, about 15 to 25 minutes. If it flakes easily from the bone, it is ready. Discard the bay leaves. Mix the butter and flour and drop this paste into the fish sauce, stirring. Cook for a few minutes. Correct the seasoning. The sauce should be glossy and coat the pieces of fish. For a smoother sauce, pass the fish liquid through a sieve before adding the butter-flour paste, but I rather like the rough texture of the *matelote*.

Serve in a warm serving dish surrounded with croutons. Some people like to add brandy to the sauce and ignite it.

Carpes en Meurette

Sautéed Carp Cooked with Garlic, Onions, Herbs and Wine

Carp are found in ponds or rivers all over Burgundy. When a pond has not been emptied, the fish can reach over five pounds. Carp are usually served stuffed and cooked in wine

Les Poissons

and cream. They can be stuffed with bread, bacon, carp roe, parsley and egg and cooked in white wine and chopped vegetables or red wine. They can be stuffed with a thick cream sauce consisting of mushrooms, thyme, carp roe, and cream, and basted while baking with a mixture of cream and white wine. In Morvan they are stuffed with a light puff pastry enriched with diced Swiss cheese. They can be sautéed in butter and seasoned with garlic, parsley, butter and lemon, or parboiled in herbs and white wine and served with an egg yolk and cream sauce seasoned with chopped gherkins. They can be served baked with wine, fresh spices and butter and seasoned with capers. The following recipe is a classic and can also be done with eel, perch, whitefish or bass.

For 8 people:

   2 *cups (1 pound) lean salt pork, diced*
   2 *teaspoons vegetable oil*
  10 *garlic cloves, peeled and crushed*
   2 *onions, peeled and chopped*
   2 *bay leaves*
   2 *teaspoons thyme*
   2 *2-pound carp, trimmed and cut in slices 1½ inches thick*
   6 *cups red wine*
   3 *tablespoons sweet butter*
   3 *tablespoons flour*
  16 *croutons, sautéed in butter*

Sauté the salt pork in the oil; add the garlic cloves, onions, bay leaves, thyme, slices of carp and the wine, and simmer, uncovered, for 30 minutes, stirring from time to time. Knead the butter and flour together and add to the sauce, stirring for another 30 minutes. Discard the bay leaves.

Serve with croutons sautéed in butter and, if you like, rubbed with garlic.

Fish

Les Escargots

Snails

Snails roam Burgundy throughout spring and summer, chewing fresh grass. In the autumn, when they are plump enough, they close their shell openings with a sand and chalk mixture, which looks like a plaster, and sleep from October to March. This period of hibernation goes roughly from Halloween to Easter and is the best time to eat them.

Snails were always considered a delicacy in Burgundy, and throughout the centuries barges loaded with snails would glide along canals and rivers, bringing their precious cargo to the various castles and monasteries. The Romans, who were fond of snails, kept them and fed them herbs.

In Burgundy during the Middle Ages snail parks were the property of monasteries and convents. The best snails were fed in vineyards. Real gourmets have always been against the practice of making the snails fast just before eating them, because while it may indeed cleanse the snails' stomachs of dangerous weeds, it also makes them dry and hard. So snails should be kept for about eight days in an enclosed place and fed with lettuce, thyme and clean water.

They can be sautéed in olive oil with diced lean salt pork, crushed walnuts and diced anchovy fillets and served on cooked spinach. They can be stuffed in mushroom caps, then covered with *beurre escargot* and broiled.

Dredged with flour, salt, and pepper, they can be lightly sautéed in hot butter, then poured into beaten eggs to make a superb omelet.

Preparation of Snails

You can buy canned snails with a bag of clean shells attached. Leave them overnight in a good broth made of salted water, a clove, a garlic clove and a bouquet garni, and use them in the recipes that follow.

If you use fresh snails, remove the protective membrane at the opening of the shell. Wash them several times and let them stand in clean cold water with salt, vinegar and a pinch of flour for about two hours. Rinse them in cold water and

Les Poissons

blanch them in a large pot of boiling water for six minutes. Drain them and remove them from their shells. Take off and discard the black tip of the tails and replace the snails in their shells. Cook them with carrots, onions and herbs (and a handful of ashes, if you have them) in a mixture of half white wine and half water to cover them completely. Add salt and cook over a low flame for three hours. Let them cool in their liquor and remove them from their shells when cold.

Boil the empty shells in water with a pinch of bicarbonate of soda for thirty minutes to cleanse them, and dry them in a low oven.

Escargots Bourguignonne

Snails Baked with Butter, Garlic, Shallots and Parsley

Allow about one dozen snails for each guest. Serve with a dry white wine.

For 8 people:

> 2 *cups sweet butter*
> 5 *garlic cloves, peeled and minced*
> 2 *shallots, peeled and minced*
> 1 *large bunch parsley, minced*
> *Salt*
> *Freshly ground black pepper*
> *Juice of 1 lemon*
> 100 *snails and their shells, cooked according to the directions under Preparation of Snails (p. 80)*
> ½ *cup dry white wine*

Preheat oven to 400°.

Mix butter, garlic, shallots, parsley, salt, pepper and lemon juice into a soft paste and fill half of each shell with it. Put one snail in each shell and put a little more of the butter mixture on top of it. Place the shells on a snail plate and pour a little wine over each. The wine will mix with the hot butter, which will melt in the bottom of the dish as it cooks.

Bake for 6 minutes and serve hot with bread.

Fish

81

Escargots au Vin Blanc

Marinated Snails Stuffed and Baked

Once the snails are cleaned and cooked according to the directions given under Preparation of Snails, above, they can be prepared in various ways. Snails can be fried and seasoned with oil and vinegar. They can be cooked with cream and garlic in a pastry shell for a *tarte aux escargots*. Chopped with shallots and parsley, they can be used to stuff large mushrooms. They can be sautéed in butter, then covered with cheese and more butter and baked. They can be dipped in butter and bread crumbs and cooked on skewers. They can be cooked with wine, mushrooms and herbs in a casserole. They can be sautéed in butter and put back in their shells with butter, parsley and a little white wine. They can be chopped and sautéed with frogs' legs. They can be deep-fried, then sprinkled with garlic and parsley.

The following recipe is a particularly enticing one.

For 8 people:

8 *dozen snails*
½–1 *cup dry white wine*
2 *tablespoons good brandy*
2 *teaspoons thyme*
3 *bay leaves*
2 *cups sweet butter*
5 *shallots, peeled and minced*
4 *garlic cloves, peeled and minced*
1 *cup hazelnuts, finely chopped*
Parsley, minced
Salt
Freshly ground black pepper
16 *croutons, sautéed in butter and rubbed with 1 clove of garlic*

After preparing the snails according to the directions given under Preparation of Snails (p. 80), marinate them for 24 hours in the wine, brandy, thyme and bay leaves, stirring and basting three or four times.

Knead the butter with the shallots, garlic, hazelnuts, parsley, salt and pepper.

Les Poissons

Twenty minutes before the meal, preheat the oven to 400°
and fill each shell with one snail and some of the butter-and-
herb mixture.

Bake for 10 minutes and serve with the croutons.

Filets au Safran

Baked Fish Fillets, Cooked with Endives and Seasoned with Saffron

Medieval Burgundy cooking used many spices, but this recipe, although high in flavor, is very delicate. You can prepare
it with any light fish such as pike, whiting, sole or bass.

For 8 people:

Head and bones of one fish
1 carrot, peeled and sliced
1 onion, peeled and sliced
2 bay leaves
1 sprig of thyme
1 cup dry white wine
Salt
8 endives, trimmed and sliced
12 tablespoons sweet butter
Salt
Freshly ground pepper
10 sole fillets
Large pinch of Spanish saffron sta-
mens
Juice of 1 lemon
3 tablespoons minced chervil

Bring the fish bones, carrot, onion, bay leaves, thyme, wine
and about 2 cups of water to a boil, add salt, and simmer for
20 minutes.

Sauté the endives in 4 tablespoons of the butter. Sprinkle
with salt and pepper, cover and cook over low heat for 15
minutes, stirring twice.

Slice the endives into a large ovenproof dish. Place the sole
fillets on top. Season with salt and pepper. Pour half of the fish
broth through a sieve into the dish. Bake for 6 minutes.

Fish

Meanwhile, bring the rest of the broth to a boil and reduce by half. Crush and sprinkle the saffron into it. Add the remaining 8 tablespoons of butter cut in large pieces, stirring constantly over low heat. Check the seasoning and add the lemon juice.

Pour over the sole fillets and serve sprinkled with chervil.

Filets de Brochet Mâcon

Marinated Pike Fillets Baked with Mushrooms and Enriched with Cream, Wine and Herbs

Pike have firm, delicate flesh, although they are cruel, gluttonous animals. The following recipe can also be made with bass.

For 8 people:

- *2 good-sized pike fillets*
- *2 cups dry white wine*
- *1 large onion, peeled and chopped*
- *8 shallots, peeled and minced*
- *1 bunch parsley, stems and leaves chopped*
- *2 bay leaves*
- *10 peppercorns, crushed*
- *½ pound mushrooms, trimmed and thinly sliced*
- *Salt*
- *Freshly ground black pepper*
- *1 cup light cream*
- *4 tablespoons sweet butter*

Place the fillets in a dish and cover with the wine, onion, shallots, parsley, bay leaves and peppercorns. Cover with a piece of waxed paper and let marinate overnight.

Drain the fillets and place them in an ovenproof dish. Spread the sliced mushrooms over them.

Pour the marinade into a saucepan, bring it to a boil and reduce for 20 minutes.

Preheat the oven to 350°.

Discard the bay leaves; pass the sauce through a sieve

and dribble it over the fish. Sprinkle with salt and pepper, add the cream and bake for 30 minutes, basting two or three times. Add the butter, stirring a little, just before serving.

Gratin de Morue

A Dried-Codfish Gratin

"Crayfish are fine, and lobsters are fine, but when I prepare a codfish gratin for you, then you will know what fine cooking really means"—so goes the saying. This inexpensive dish can be prepared ahead of time and is a treat.

For 8 people:

> 2 *pounds dried codfish fillets*
> 2 *pounds potatoes, peeled and thinly sliced*
> *Salt (if needed)*
> *Freshly ground white pepper*
> *Freshly grated nutmeg (to taste)*
> 1½ *quarts of milk*
> 3 *egg yolks*
> ½ *cup cream*
> 1 *garlic clove, peeled*
> 4 *tablespoons sweet butter*

Leave the codfish in cold water according to the instructions on the package, or soak in several changes of cold water for 24 hours to remove the salt.

Place the sliced potatoes in a deep saucepan. Season them with salt, pepper and nutmeg, and cover with milk. Bring to a boil and simmer for 20 minutes.

Meanwhile, beat the egg yolks and cream in a bowl. Remove the potatoes from the heat and, while stirring, add the egg mixture. Check and correct the seasoning.

Preheat oven to 350°.

Place the codfish fillets in a large pan of cold water. Bring it to a boil and cook for only 2 minutes. Drain. Remove the skin and bones and shred the fish finely.

Rub an ovenproof dish with the garlic clove, then with butter. Pour half of the potatoes into the dish, cover them

Fish

with shredded codfish and then add the remaining potatoes. Dot with butter and bake for 30 minutes. Serve in its baking dish.

Petits Poissons à la Bourguignotte

Whitebait Broiled, Then Marinated with Herbs, Wine and Vinegar

This is usually made with baby pike, but it can be done with almost any fresh firm-fleshed fish.

For 8 people:

4 pounds whitebait
Salt
Freshly ground black pepper
4 tablespoons vegetable oil
6 onions, peeled and chopped
3 tablespoons parsley
2 teaspoons thyme
3 bay leaves
1 cup red wine vinegar
Salt
Freshly ground black pepper

Garnish

1 bowl of mayonnaise
½ cup chopped walnuts

Sprinkle the fish with salt and pepper and with 2 tablespoons of oil. Broil for a few minutes until it is cooked and flakes easily.

Lay the fish in a shallow dish. Cover it with the chopped onions, parsley, thyme and bay leaves. Heat the vinegar and pour it over the fish. Add salt, pepper and the remaining 2 tablespoons of oil and cover the dish with a lid or a sheet of foil. Let it marinate for three days.

Serve cold with a bowl of mayonnaise and a bowl of chopped walnuts.

Les Poissons

Filets de Poisson aux Pâtes

Fish Fillets Baked with Sherry, Cream and Sorrel
and Served with Noodles

For 8 people:

10 *fillets of any fresh firm fish*
2 *bay leaves*
1 *tablespoon sweet butter*
  Salt
  Freshly ground black pepper
½ *cup dry white sherry*
1 *cup light cream*
1 *cup shredded sorrel*
1 *large dish of homemade noodles, barely cooked (p. 215)*

Preheat the oven to 375°.

Place the fillets side by side in an ovenproof dish with the bay leaves on top of them. Dot the fillets with butter. Bake for 10 minutes; sprinkle with salt and pepper, and turn the oven off. Cover the fish with aluminum foil.

Pour the sherry into a saucepan. Over medium heat, add the cream and let it reduce, stirring until the sauce thickens and coats the spoon. Season with salt and pepper. Add the shredded sorrel and bring to a boil. Place the fillets in a warm serving dish. Spoon the sauce over them and serve with homemade noodles.

Grenouilles au Vin Blanc

Frog's Legs Sautéed and Served with a White Wine, Garlic, Cream
and Herb Sauce

Frog's legs are best in the fall, when they are light. Only the back legs are served. They can be fried, cooked with wine or used in fritters.

Fish

For 8 people:

2 tablespoons flour
48 frog's legs
1 cup sweet butter
2 tablespoons vegetable oil
2 garlic cloves, peeled and crushed
3 tablespoons white wine
6 tablespoons cream
Salt
Freshly ground black pepper
4 tablespoons chives, parsley, and chervil, finely
chopped

Sprinkle the flour on the frog's legs. Sauté them in the butter and oil on all sides. Remove and keep warm. Add the garlic to the skillet, then the wine and reduce by half. Remove from the heat and add the cream, salt and pepper. Pour the mixture over the frog's legs. Sprinkle with the herbs and serve at once.

Morue à la Lyonnaise

Salt Codfish Boiled, Then Sautéed with Onions and Potatoes and
Seasoned with Warm Vinegar

For 8 people:

2 pounds salt codfish, poached and flaked
1 teaspoon thyme
1 bay leaf
7 onions, peeled and sliced
½ cup vegetable oil
8 potatoes, peeled, boiled and sliced ¼ inch thick
½ cup sweet butter
2 garlic cloves, peeled and minced
½ cup parsley, minced
5 tablespoons red wine vinegar
2 teaspoons freshly crushed coriander
Freshly ground black pepper

Les Poissons

Soak the codfish in cold water according to the directions on the package, then poach it in unsalted cold water, with the thyme and bay leaf, boiling it for 5 minutes. Remove all skin and bone and flake the fish.

Sauté the onions in the oil until golden, add the potatoes and the codfish and cook for 5 minutes. Add the butter. Sprinkle with garlic and parsley. Pour into a warm shallow dish. Briefly heat the vinegar in the hot skillet and dribble it over the fish and potatoes. Sprinkle with coriander and pepper and serve at once.

Morue en Beignets

Codfish Fritters

Salt codfish is sold in fillets. Choose the thickest part, near the tail. Since all codfish is not salted to the same degree, follow the instructions on the package.

An overnight soaking is best done in a colander immersed in a large pan of cold water. Change the water often. Usually dried codfish is poached briefly before being used in a recipe. Cover the fish with cold water and place over high heat. As soon as it comes to a boil, lower the heat and leave the fish for 10 minutes in the water. Remove the bones and skin with tweezers.

For 8 people:

2 *pounds salt codfish, trimmed, boiled and finely shredded*
1 *pound potatoes, boiled and puréed*
4 *eggs*
Salt
Freshly ground black pepper
Parsley
Oil for deep-frying

Blend the shredded cod and puréed potatoes in a blender. Add the eggs, salt, pepper and parsley and make little balls 2 inches wide. Flatten them and deep-fry them.

Serve with fried fresh parsley all around.

Fish

Saumon en Papillotte

Salmon Cooked with Fresh Mint and Tomatoes

The Loire Valley has delicious salmon, and lots of mint grow on its banks. This is a superb dish, but make sure both the salmon and the mint are very fresh.

For 8 people:

3 pounds skinless, boneless fillets of salmon
8 tomatoes (fresh or canned), thickly sliced
2 cups mint leaves
Salt
Freshly ground black pepper
Freshly ground coriander
1 cup Béarnaise sauce (optional)

Blanch the salmon in a *court-bouillon* for 5 minutes. Let it cool in its juice.

Preheat the oven to 350°.

Put 8 10-inch squares of aluminum foil on an oiled oven-proof baking sheet. On each square place 3 slices of tomato sprinkled with a few mint leaves, then a fillet of barely cooked salmon. Sprinkle with salt, pepper and coriander, add more tomato slices and, finally, the rest of the mint leaves.

Close each square of foil, leaving as much air space inside as possible. Bake for 15 minutes.

When you are ready to serve, slide each foil pouch onto a warm serving dish, then open and roll down the sides of the pouches.

Béarnaise sauce is a good though not essential accompaniment for this dish.

Poisson à la Moutarde

Slices of Fish Seasoned with a Mustard, Wine and Cream Sauce

Les Poissons

Served with spinach or sorrel, a light dish.

For 8 people:

3 tablespoons flour
8 thick slices of any lean firm-fleshed fish (about ½ pound each)
4 tablespoons oil
2 tablespoons butter
4 tablespoons Dijon-style mustard
1 teaspoon dry white wine
2 cups light cream
4 tablespoons sweet butter
Salt
Freshly ground white pepper

Sprinkle the flour on the slices of fish and sauté them in oil and butter for 4 minutes on each side. Set them aside, but keep them warm.

Mix the mustard with the wine and heat until reduced by half. Add the cream and reduce by two-thirds. Remove from the heat and add the butter, whipping briskly. Season to taste.

Pour the sauce over the slices of fish and serve at once.

Perche à la Charollaise

Fish Baked with a Wine and Cream Sauce

This is the easiest way I know to prepare a firm-fleshed fish and transform it into a Burgundy treat.

For 8 people:

1 4-pound perch or any firm-fleshed fish, cleaned and trimmed
6 shallots, peeled and chopped
2 cups dry white wine
Salt
Freshly ground black pepper
1 cup light cream
2 tablespoons sweet butter
½ cup sour cream

Fish

Preheat the oven to 400°.

Place the trimmed fish on top of a layer of chopped shallots. Pour the wine over it. Sprinkle with salt and pepper and add the light cream. Dot with butter and bake for 25 minutes.

Test for doneness. Add the sour cream and stir it into the juices lightly. Bake for 5 more minutes and then serve.

Poisson en Meurette

Fish Cooked in a Red Wine, Vegetable and Bacon Sauce

This is also called a *matelote* and is made with a hearty red wine and freshwater fish.

> 4 *pounds freshwater fish (carp, pike, eel, trout, perch)*
> ½ *cup bacon (or lean salt pork), cut into small dice*
> 1 *cup red wine*
> 2 *garlic cloves, peeled and crushed*
> 2 *large onions, peeled and sliced*
> 2 *cloves*
> 3 *teaspoons thyme*
> 2 *bay leaves*
> *Salt*
> *Freshly ground black pepper*
> 3 *tablespoons brandy*
> 4 *bread slices, cut into triangles*
> *Butter*

Scale, clean and chop the fish. Sauté it in oil with the bacon for a few minutes and set aside. Bring the red wine, garlic, onions, cloves, thyme and bay leaves to a boil and reduce by half over medium heat. Run the wine through a sieve into a heavy-bottomed pan. Add the fish, salt and pepper and bring to a boil. Remove from the heat, add the brandy, and ignite. Place over low heat and simmer, uncovered, for 30 minutes. Check and correct the seasoning.

Prepare the slices of bread and fry them in butter. Rub them with a clove of garlic.

Place the fish in a warm shallow dish, pour the sauce over it, and place the bread triangles all around.

Some people like to add 3 tablespoons of butter kneaded

Les Poissons

with 2 tablespoons of flour to thicken the sauce, but I think a light pungent sauce is better.

Saumon aux Herbes

Raw Salmon Marinated with Herbs, Lemon and Oil

The salmon from the Loire Valley is usually stuffed with sorrel or coated with cream sauce, but this is a lighter dish—perfect as a luncheon dish or as part of a summer buffet.

For 8 people:

1½ pounds salmon
6 tablespoons good olive oil
2 teaspoons crushed green peppercorns
2 teaspoons freshly ground black pepper
Juice of 1 lemon
3 tablespoons minced chervil

Remove all skin and bones from the salmon with tweezers and cut paper-thin fillets.

Brush the surface of the fillets with olive oil and place them in the refrigerator for two hours to make the flesh firmer. Cut 2-inch strips widthwise and spread them on a large serving plate. Sprinkle with green and black pepper, lemon juice and the chervil.

Serve with warm, buttered toast or a green tossed salad.

Truite Farcie aux Herbes

Trout Stuffed with Greens, Cream, and Shallots and Baked with Wine, Herbs and Cream

The fresh trout of the Morvan region are famous in Burgundy. They can be stuffed with salmon and cream and cooked in red wine, or sautéed with butter. The following recipe is a truly delicious way to prepare this fish.

Fish

93

For each person:

1 *trout, about 8 ounces*
1 *tablespoon chopped sorrel or spinach*
1 *tablespoon sweet butter*
4 *tablespoons cream*
  Freshly grated nutmeg
  Salt
  Freshly ground black pepper
2 *tablespoons finely chopped shallots*
⅓ *cup dry white wine*
1 *teaspoon mustard*
1 *teaspoon lemon juice*

Open the trout at the back, slicing it all along to clean it, and clip the backbone at each end with scissors to remove it. Place the sorrel or spinach and the butter in a saucepan and cook over low heat. Add 1 tablespoon of the cream and the nutmeg. Season the trout with salt and pepper and stuff it with the sorrel or spinach mixture. Lay it on its side in a buttered ovenproof dish.

Preheat the oven to 375°.

Spread the chopped shallots on the trout. Add the wine and heat on the top of the stove, then cover with a sheet of waxed paper and bake for 10 minutes, or until the flesh flakes easily.

Pour the cooking liquid into a saucepan. Reduce it by half, then add the remaining cream, mustard and lemon juice. Check the seasoning. Place the trout on a warm serving dish and spoon the sauce over it.

Les Poissons

Les Oeufs

Egg Dishes

If *les oeufs en meurette* is one of the most celebrated dishes, there are also, in most regions of Burgundy, elegant and imaginative variations on fried, poached, stuffed and baked eggs. From poached eggs covered with a crayfish sauce to scrambled eggs prepared with wild mushrooms and cream, or hard-cooked eggs stuffed with snails and shallots, the repertory is rich.

There are delicious omelets as well. The Romans used to season theirs with honey and pepper, and since then imagination has never lacked in that realm. There are flat omelets made with onions, parsley, garlic and fresh pork blood. There are mountain omelets made with potatoes, chervil, cream and Swiss cheese, or with rich wild mushrooms, country ham and herbs. Then there are the fancier rolled omelets—some stuffed with walnuts and snails, some with dandelion greens and onion, a favorite at Easter time. There are elaborate omelets stuffed with calf's brains and sweetbreads and some with the tender flesh of crayfish.

There are omelet cakes—several omelets piled high, filled with chives, sorrel, goat cheese, and coated with a cream, herb and lemon juice sauce.

I have chosen here the recipes I thought would be most likely to please the modern palate. I will not dwell on how to make an omelet, since one should not have to think twice about the technique. Remember only that for four eggs you must use a 10-inch skillet, heavy-bottomed, well greased and very hot, and that the eggs should be beaten for only a few seconds before being poured into the skillet.

Egg Dishes

Faux Escargots

Fake Snails

An easy way to serve eggs Burgundy style. If one-half garlic clove per person seems too much, use one-third. Allow one ramekin per person.

For each person:

½ garlic clove, peeled and crushed
1 tablespoon softened sweet butter
1 tablespoon minced parsley
Salt
Freshly ground black pepper
1 or 2 eggs
1 teaspoon sweet butter

Crush the garlic and add the butter, parsley, salt and pepper to make a paste.

Preheat the oven to 350°.

Butter each ramekin. Break 1 or 2 eggs into each and bake for 7 to 10 minutes (or for 3 minutes on top of the stove). Top with the garlic-butter mixture and serve at once.

Oeufs en Cocotte

Shirred Eggs with Shallots, Mushrooms and Cream

For 8 people:

6 tablespoons sweet butter
6 shallots (or white onions), peeled and minced
½ pound mushrooms, washed, dried, and chopped
1½ cups light cream
Salt
Freshly ground white pepper
5 tablespoons chives, finely chopped
8 large fresh eggs

Heat 3 tablespoons of the butter in a heavy-bottomed skillet. Add the shallots and cook over low heat for 2 minutes. Add the mushrooms and cook over low heat, stirring with a wooden spoon, for 3 minutes. Pour in 1 cup of the cream and let it thicken, stirring from time to time with a wire whip. Season with salt, pepper and 1 tablespoon of the chives.

Preheat the oven to 350°.

Butter 8 individual china ovenproof ramekins and pour the mixture into them evenly. Carefully break one egg into each dish. Divide the remaining ½ cup cream among them and sprinkle with 3 tablespoons of the chives.

Place the ramekins in a large ovenproof dish, adding enough hot water to the larger dish to reach half the height of the ramekins. Bake 10 to 15 minutes, or until the egg whites are opaque. Sprinkle with the remaining tablespoon of the chives and serve.

Oeufs à la Dijonnaise

Baked, Stuffed Eggs

Dijon mustard made with dry white wine transforms this classic stuffed-egg recipe into a pungent dish.

For 8 people:

> 8 *hard-cooked eggs*
> 2 *tablespoons Dijon-style mustard*
> 3 *tablespoons heavy cream*
> 1 *tablespoon wine vinegar*
> 2 *shallots, minced*
> 3 *tablespoons minced fresh herbs (chives, chervil and*
>   *tarragon)*
> *Salt*
> *Freshly ground white pepper*
> 2 *tablespoons sweet butter, softened*
> 1 *tablespoon wine vinegar*

Preheat the oven to 350°.

Shell and halve the hard-cooked eggs lengthwise. Mix the egg yolks, mustard, cream, vinegar, shallots, herbs, salt and

Egg Dishes

97

pepper into a paste and fill the white halves of the eggs with it. Place in an ovenproof porcelain dish. Dot with butter and 1 tablespoon vinegar and bake for 10 minutes. Serve warm.

Oeufs au Nid

Eggs Baked in a Nest of Mashed Potatoes and Sprinkled with Cheese

This is a good dish for children. You can add leftover chicken or meat or simply prepare it with mashed potatoes and grated cheese.

For 8 people:

1 cup minced ham and/or leftover chicken
6 cups mashed potatoes, whipped with milk and butter
Salt
Freshly ground black pepper
Freshly grated nutmeg
2 tablespoons sweet butter
8 eggs
4 tablespoons grated cheese

Preheat the oven to 400°.

Add the meat to the mashed potatoes, mixing in salt, pepper and nutmeg. Arrange the mixture in a buttered baking dish, making a deep hole for each egg. Place a dab of butter in each hole and break an egg into it. Add salt and pepper. With a fork, make a deep groove circling each egg to make a nest. Sprinkle with cheese and bake for 15 minutes.

Oeufs Crémés

Shirred Eggs with Cheese

Les Oeufs

Prepared in a jiffy, this mountain recipe is a children's favorite. Choose a pretty ovenproof dish, since it will be brought to the table.

For 8 people:

> *4 tablespoons sweet butter*
> *½ pound Swiss cheese, thinly sliced*
> *8 large eggs*
> *¼ pound Swiss cheese, grated*
> *3 tablespoons heavy cream*
> *Freshly ground nutmeg*
> *Freshly ground white pepper*
> *Salt*

Preheat the oven to 375°.

Butter an ovenproof dish and cover the bottom with the sliced cheese. Bake for 4 minutes until the cheese starts melting. Remove from the oven and carefully break the eggs into the dish, side by side. Sprinkle with the grated cheese. Dribble cream over the top and sprinkle with nutmeg, pepper and a little salt. Bake for 10 to 12 minutes, until the whites are set and the yolks are still moist.

Oeufs au Civet

Fried Eggs Seasoned with Onions, Wine and Herbs

This treatment of fried eggs is truly inspired.

For 8 people:

> *3 tablespoons sweet butter*
> *2 tablespoon vegetable oil*
> *8 onions, peeled and thinly sliced*
> *1½ cups dry white wine*
> *Salt*
> *Freshly ground black pepper*
> *4 tablespoons wine vinegar*
> *Juice of 1 lemon*
> *8 eggs*
> *3 tablespoons finely chopped parsley*

Heat 1 tablespoon of butter and 1 tablespoon of oil in a thick skillet. Add the sliced onions and cook until golden. Add the wine, salt, pepper, vinegar and lemon juice and, stirring occa-

Egg Dishes

99

sionally, cook, uncovered, for 20 minutes. The liquid should be reduced by half.

Meanwhile, heat 2 tablespoons of butter and 1 tablespoon of oil in another skillet and fry the eggs. Pour the onion-and-wine mixture into a warm serving dish and slide the fried eggs on top.

Sprinkle with chopped parsley and serve at once.

Oeufs en Cassolette Dijonnaise

Poached Eggs Covered by a Shallot, Lemon, Cream and Butter Sauce and Seasoned with Herbs

A lovely luncheon dish, quick to prepare and most elegant.

For 8 people:

2 tablespoons Dijon-style mustard
4 tablespoons heavy cream
2 tablespoons lemon juice
6 tablespoons dry white wine
4 shallots, peeled and minced
2 tablespoons minced tarragon (or chervil or chives)
8 eggs
6 tablespoons sweet butter
Salt
Freshly ground white pepper
2 tablespoons minced parsley

Preheat the oven to 250°.

Pour the mustard, cream, and lemon juice into a bowl with the white wine and stir well. Add the shallots and tarragon. Pour into a saucepan and cook over low heat, stirring, for 10 minutes. Remove from the heat.

Meanwhile, heat a wide, shallow pot of salted water to the boiling point. Reduce the heat to a gentle boil and, breaking each egg into a saucer, gently slide it into the water. Cook for 3 minutes. Trim the whites of the eggs so that each egg looks pretty and place them in individual buttered ramekins. Cover with a sheet of foil and leave the ramekins in the oven to keep warm.

Cut the butter into small pieces and add to the warm sauce. Stir vigorously off the heat. Add salt and pepper and pour this thick sauce over the individual eggs.

Sprinkle with parsley and serve very hot.

Oeufs en Meurette

Eggs Poached in a Wine, Onion and Herb sauce

This traditional dish has a questionable name in Burgundy; it is called "donkey's balls." It is a hearty dish. I tried to make it lighter for modern appetites, and since I did not want to thicken the sauce with flour and could not thicken it with pork blood, I reduced the wine and the onions. Prepared a day ahead, *meurette* sauce improves greatly. Cooled, it is also easier to degrease.

These tangy, light *oeufs en meurette* are high in flavor and should be served with a bitter dandelion or watercress tossed salad.

For 8 people:

2 *tablespoons butter*
1½ *cups bacon (or lean salt pork), cut into 1-inch*
    pieces
3 *large onions, peeled and minced*
2 *or 3 shallots, peeled and minced*
2 *garlic cloves, peeled and minced*
1½ *quarts hearty red wine*
1 *clove*
1 *lump of sugar*
  Salt
  Freshly ground black pepper
2 *bay leaves*
2 *teaspoons thyme (or a large sprig of fresh thyme)*
8 *slices of stale bread, with crusts removed*
3 *tablespoons sweet butter*
1 *tablespoon vegetable oil*
8 *large eggs*
8 *tablespoons chopped parsley*

Egg Dishes

Heat the butter in a heavy-bottomed skillet, add the bacon (or lean pork) and cook for 5 minutes. Add the onions, shallots, and garlic and cook over low heat for 5 minutes. Add the wine, clove, sugar, salt, pepper, bay leaves and thyme and cook, uncovered, for 40 to 60 minutes, reducing and thickening the sauce.

Discard the bay leaves and thyme. Remove the bacon and set aside. Pass the hot sauce through a Mouli mill or a food processor and check the seasonings. Remove as much fat as possible from the sauce.

Put the puréed sauce in a large skillet and bring it to a boil. Reduce the heat to very low and slip in the eggs, two or three at a time. Cook for about 3 minutes. Meanwhile, fry the slices of bread in the butter and oil. Drain the eggs and place them on the slices of bread. Add the bacon to the sauce and pour over the eggs. Sprinkle with the parsley and serve.

Omelette à la Crème

A Fluffy Cream Omelet

A glorious, soufflé-like omelet, perfect for an elegant luncheon. Sour cream is more interesting than American heavy cream; you may want to try it both ways.

For 4 people:

6 egg whites
6 egg yolks
3 tablespoons sour cream (or 2 tablespoons sour cream
    and 1 tablespoon heavy cream)
Salt
Freshly ground black pepper
Heavy pinch of freshly grated nutmeg
4 tablespoons sweet butter
1 tablespoon vegetable oil
1 tablespoon chervil (or any fresh herb), minced

Les Oeufs

Whip the egg whites until stiff. Beat the egg yolks, cream, salt, pepper and nutmeg. Heat 3 tablespoons of the butter and the oil in a 9-inch skillet and pour in the egg-and-cream mixture. Lower the heat and delicately fold in the beaten egg whites. Cover and cook for about 7 minutes on one side. Invert the omelette onto a flat plate and return it to the skillet. Cook the other side for 3 minutes longer.

Spread 1 tablespoon of softened butter over the top, sprinkle with herbs and serve on a warm dish.

Oeufs Savoyard

Eggs Baked on a Layer of Sliced Potatoes and Cheese with Cream

For 8 people:

> 3 *pounds potatoes, peeled and sliced*
> 2 *tablespoons sweet butter*
> 1 *tablespoon vegetable oil*
>   *Salt*
>   *Freshly ground black pepper*
> 1½ *cups grated Swiss cheese*
> 8 *eggs*
> 8 *tablespoons light cream*

Preheat the oven to 350°.

Sauté the sliced, dried potatoes in the butter and oil in a large skillet for 15 minutes. Place them in an ovenproof dish and sprinkle with salt, pepper and cheese. Break the eggs, one by one, on top of the potatoes and sprinkle with salt and pepper. Pour the cream over the eggs and bake for 10 to 15 minutes. Serve in the baking dish.

This recipe can also be made by substituting sautéed sliced mushrooms for half the amount of potatoes.

Egg Dishes

Omelette à la Mie

A Bread-crumb, Cream and Herb Omelet

For each person:

½ *cup bread crumbs*
½ *cup light cream*
2 *eggs, beaten*
Salt
Freshly ground black pepper
1 *tablespoon chopped fresh herbs*
1 *tablespoon butter*
1 *tablespoon oil*

In a bowl, mix all ingredients except the last two. Heat the butter and oil in a skillet and pour in the mixture. Lower the flame and cook for about 5 minutes on one side. Invert the omelette on a flat plate, slide it back into the skillet and cook for about 3 minutes.

Omelette à la Moutarde

Mustard, Cream and Chive Omelet

This is an invigorating omelet that would make for a cheerful lunch served with a tart green salad. It's truly interesting in both texture and flavor.

For 4 people:*

4 *tablespoons sweet butter*
2 *tablespoons minced chives*
8 *eggs*
2 *tablespoons Dijon-style mustard*
2 *tablespoons light cream*
Salt
Freshly ground white pepper

Heat 1 tablespoon of the butter in a skillet and cook the chives over low heat for 2 minutes.

Preheat the oven to 350°.

Whip 3 egg whites until stiff. Pour the remaining eggs and yolks into a bowl, add the mustard, cream and cooked chives, and stir until lightly foamy. Add the egg whites, salt and pepper.

Heat 2 tablespoons of the butter in the skillet, pour in the eggs and heat for 1 minute. Put the skillet in the oven for 3 to 4 minutes.

Gently place the omelet on a warm serving dish, spread the remaining tablespoon of butter on it and serve at once.

*For eight people, use two skillets after doubling the ingredients.

Omelette de Savoie

A Baked Swiss Cheese, Country Ham and Cream Omelet

This is the best omelet in the world for luncheons or first courses. One quickly becomes totally addicted and fiercely loyal to it.

For 4 people:

  8 eggs
¼ pound Swiss cheese, grated
¼ pound country ham, Virginia ham or prosciutto, diced
3 tablespoons light cream
  Salt
  Freshly ground black pepper
3 tablespoons sweet butter
1 tablespoon vegetable oil

Beat the eggs in a large bowl. Add half the grated cheese, the diced ham, cream, salt and pepper.

Preheat the oven to 350°.

Heat the butter and oil in the skillet and pour the egg mixture into it. Cook over high heat for 3 minutes. Fold the omelet in half and slide it onto an ovenproof dish.

Sprinkle it with the rest of the grated cheese and bake for 2 minutes.

Egg Dishes

Serve at once. The top should be golden and crisp and the inside creamy.

Omelette aux Croûtons

A Crouton Omelet

For each person:

1 slice of bread
3 tablespoons sweet butter
2 eggs
Salt
Freshly ground black pepper
1 tablespoon oil

Dice and sauté the bread in 2 tablespoons of the butter. Beat the eggs in a bowl and add salt and pepper and the croutons. Heat the oil and 1 tablespoon butter in a skillet and pour in the egg-crouton mixture. Lower the flame and cook for about 5 minutes on one side. Invert the omelette onto a flat plate, slide it back into the skillet and cook for about 3 minutes.

Omelette aux Foies

A Chicken Liver Omelet

For each person:

½ cup chicken livers
2 tablespoons sweet butter
2 tablespoon vegetable oil
Salt
Freshly ground black pepper
2 eggs

Sauté the livers in 1 tablespoon each of the butter and oil. Season with salt and pepper. Beat the eggs in a bowl and add the livers. Heat the remaining butter and oil in a skillet and pour in the egg-liver mixture. Lower the heat and cook for about 5 minutes on one side. Invert the omelette onto a flat plate, slide it back into the skillet and cook for about 3 minutes.

Les Oeufs

Omelette d'Escargot

A Snail Omelet

For each person:

1 garlic clove, peeled and minced
6 snails, cooked according to directions under Preparation of Snails (p. 80)
2 walnuts, chopped
3 tablespoons sweet butter
2 eggs
1 tablespoon oil
1 teaspoon minced parsley

Sauté in a skillet the garlic, snails and walnuts in 2 tablespoons of the butter. Beat the eggs in a bowl and add the contents of the skillet. Wipe the skillet and heat the oil and the remaining butter in it. Pour in the mixture. Lower the heat and cook for about 5 minutes on one side. Invert the omelette onto a flat plate, slide it back into the skillet and cook for about 3 minutes. Sprinkle the parsley on top and serve.

Omelette du Morvan

A Country Ham and Mushroom Omelet

For each person:

½ cup country ham, diced
½ cup mushrooms, quartered
3 tablespoons sweet butter
2 tablespoons vegetable oil
2 eggs
Salt
Freshly ground black pepper

Egg Dishes

Sauté the ham and mushrooms in 2 tablespoons of the butter and 1 tablespoon of the oil. Beat the eggs and add salt and pepper and the ham-mushroom mixture. Wipe the skillet and heat the remaining oil and butter in it. Pour in the omelette mixture. Lower the heat and cook for about 5 minutes on one side. Invert the omelette onto a flat plate, slide it back into the skillet and cook for about 3 minutes.

Omelette Machon

An Onion, Cream and Vinegar Omelet

The *machon* (a Lyon word for something to chew on) is a little snack, eaten midmorning or midafternoon.

For 4 people:

2 *tablespoons sweet butter*
1 *tablespoon vegetable oil*
3 *large onions, chopped*
6 *eggs*
Salt
Freshly ground black pepper
1 *tablespoon light cream*
4 *tablespoons chopped parsley*
3 *tablespoons red wine vinegar*
1 *tablespoon chopped chives or scallions*

Heat the butter and oil in a skillet. Add the chopped onions and cook over low heat until soft. Meanwhile, beat together in a bowl the eggs, salt, pepper and cream. Add the parsley and pour the egg mixture over the cooked onions. Stirring gently, cook the omelet on one side for 5 minutes, then gently slide it (cooked side down) onto a plate. Brush the skillet with a little oil and replace the omelet (raw side down) in the skillet and cook for 2 minutes.

Slide the omelet onto a warm serving dish. Pour the vinegar into the hot skillet and bring it to a boil. Pour it over the omelet, sprinkle with pepper and chives and serve at once.

Les Oeufs

Les Viandes

Meats

Meat is abundant and of the highest quality in Burgundy: superb Charolais cattle in the South, chicken and ducks from Bresse, pigs and game from Morvan.

Some of the dishes rely on beef and tenderloin, but most regional treats use rather inexpensive cuts carefully prepared, enhanced by wine, vegetables and herbs. Beef, lamb, rooster and even turkey are often sautéed, then cooked with red wine, brandy, herbs and garlic as in the heady *boeuf bourguignon* or the pungent *coq au vin* described here. Chicken, goose, duck and veal are often sautéed, then cooked with white wine, herbs, mustard and cream.

I have not chosen many wild boar, hare, partridge or wild duck recipes, since game is not available everywhere in the United States, but I have selected many pork recipes. Pork is fatter and less tasty in the United States than it is in Burgundy, so I have modified seasonings, and the results are pleasant. In Burgundy all of the pig is used. The casing for its intestines —washed in vinegar and water, brushed, stretched and shredded—is eaten cooked with shallots and white wine; the casing is also used for making sausages. The pig's blood is collected and mixed with onions, spices, herbs, diced fat and chestnuts and put in a piece of intestine casing. Ears, feet (the front ones are more tender because they support less weight) and tail are all prepared with great care. Hams kept forty-five days in brine and three days in a well to become desalted are simmered with shallots and vinegar or cooked with mustard and cream. Pork is boiled, broiled, cooked with prunes or leeks and prepared in a hundred ways. It is perhaps Burgundy's main meat, and there is no end to the variations in its preparation.

Blanquette de Veau

Veal Simmered with Vegetables, Wine and Herbs, Egg Yolks, Cream and Lemon Juice

A delicious Lyon treat to serve with plain rice or noodles. Make sure it is lemony and quite heavily seasoned.

For 8 people:

- 4 *pounds veal shoulder and breast, cut into 2-inch pieces, some with bones, some without*
- 2 *quarts dry white wine*
- 2 *onions, peeled, with 1 clove stuck in one of them*
  Bouquet garni
- 4 *carrots, peeled and cut in sticks*
- 4 *leeks (only the white part), peeled and sliced (optional)*
- 2 *celery stalks*
  Salt
  Freshly ground pepper
- 6 *tablespoons sweet butter, softened*
- 1 *cup flour*
- ½ *cup light cream*
- 4 *egg yolks, beaten*
  Juice of 2 or 3 lemons
  Capers

Place the pieces of meat in a pan and cover with wine and about 2 quarts of water. Bring to a boil. Remove the foam on top and add the onions, the bouquet garni, carrots, leeks, celery, salt and pepper and simmer for 1 hour. Pass the stock through a sieve.

Meanwhile mix the soft butter and flour into a paste. In another pot, over low heat, slowly add three-quarters of the cooking stock and simmer, stirring, for 15 minutes. Pour into the meat pan.

Stir the cream into the beaten egg yolks. Add the lemon juice, stirring, then slowly add a ladle of the warm sauce, stirring all the time, and pour into the meat pan. Don't let it boil. Check the seasoning.

Sprinkle with a few capers and serve at once.

Les Viandes

Boeuf à la Mâcon

A Gratin of Cooked Meat Baked with Onions, Wine, Herbs and Mustard

An old recipe that comes from Mâcon to be made whenever the *potée,* the *pot-au-feu* or the boiled ham has been too abundant and you are faced with leftovers.

For 8 people:

4 tablespoons sweet butter
1 tablespoon vegetable oil
4 onions, peeled and thinly sliced
Salt
1 tablespoon flour
1½ cups white wine
Freshly ground black pepper
Pinch of freshly ground nutmeg
2 bay leaves
3 pounds boiled meat (beef, pork, poultry, ham),
    diced or sliced
3 tablespoons wine vinegar
2 tablespoons Dijon-style mustard
3 tablespoons minced parsley (or chives)
Juice of 1 lemon (optional)

Preheat the oven to 350°.

Heat 2 tablespoons of the butter and the oil in a large skillet. Add the onions, sprinkle with salt and sauté over low heat for 10 minutes, until soft. Sprinkle with flour, stirring, then add the white wine, salt, pepper and nutmeg and cook over low heat for 15 minutes.

Butter an ovenproof dish and line it with half of the onion mixture. Sprinkle with crumbled bay leaves. Layer the boiled meat on top, sprinkle with salt and pepper and cover with the rest of the onions. Dot with the remaining butter and bake for 15 minutes.

Meanwhile, mix the vinegar and mustard. Dribble it over the dish just before serving. Sprinkle the top with parsley (or chives). You may also sprinkle lemon juice over the parsley.

Meats

Boeuf à la Sauvage

Marinated Slices of Beef Served with a Rich Wine and Vegetable
Sauce

This turns an ordinary piece of beef into an interesting dish.
It is good for a dressy dinner, and you can prepare almost
everything at the last minute. Serve with *Gratin Dauphinois*
(p. 195) or *Gâteau de Pommes de Terre* (p. 185). The beef must
marinate for three days to be properly enhanced by the flavor
of all the herbs.

For 8 people:

1 fillet of beef or 1 large blue-point sirloin tip, sliced (1
inch thick)
Salt
Freshly ground black pepper
2 carrots, peeled and minced
2 onions, peeled and sliced
1 tomato, quartered
1 garlic clove, unpeeled, crushed
2 bay leaves
2 teaspoons thyme
Hearty red wine, enough to cover the
meat
2 tablespoons vegetable oil
7 tablespoon sweet butter
1 tablespoon red wine vinegar
4 tablespoons minced chervil

Sprinkle the slices of beef with salt and pepper and place them
in a shallow dish. Add the carrots, onions, tomato, garlic, bay
leaves and thyme and cover with red wine. Let the meat,
covered with a sheet of foil, marinate for 3 days on the lowest
shelf of your refrigerator.

An hour before you are ready to serve your meal, preheat
the oven to 300° and drain the carrots, tomato and onions.
Heat 1 tablespoon of the oil and 1 tablespoon of butter in a
large skillet and sauté the vegetables for 10 minutes, stirring
with a wooden spoon. Add the vinegar and two-thirds of the
marinade and simmer until the vegetables are tender and the

Les Viandes

marinade is reduced to 1 cup. Pass through a sieve, pressing hard, and set aside.

While the marinade simmers, dry the pieces of meat with paper towels and sauté them in 4 tablespoons of the butter and 1 tablespoon of the oil on both sides. Place them in a warm serving dish, cover with a sheet of foil, and leave them in the oven with the door slightly open as you finish the sauce.

Pour the remaining one-third of the marinade into the skillet, scrape up the juices coagulated on the bottom, add 2 tablespoons of butter and stir vigorously. Add the vegetable purée and pour it over the slices of meat. Sprinkle with pepper and chervil before serving.

Boeuf aux Légumes

Sautéed Beef Baked with Vegetables, Herbs, Wine and Spices

An easy dish, since it can be entirely prepared ahead of time, and ingredients are available everywhere all year round.

For 8 people:

1 tablespoon sweet butter
1 teaspoon vegetable oil
4 pounds rump pot roast (or lean boneless chuck or sirloin tip), cut into 2-inch cubes
1 onion, chopped
1 celery heart, coarsely chopped
3 carrots, sliced
Salt
Freshly ground pepper
4 pink turnips, peeled and sliced (optional)
½ cup chopped parsley
3 cups red wine
2 teaspoons tomato paste
1 garlic clove studded with 2 cloves
3 bay leaves
2 tablespoons minced chives (or parsley or basil)

Meats

Heat the butter and oil and sauté the pieces of meat on all sides. Add the onion and sauté for 5 minutes longer, then add the celery heart, carrots, salt and pepper and, after 5 minutes, the turnips.

Preheat the oven to 350°.

Cook over medium heat for 10 minutes, stirring once. Check the seasoning and pour the mixture into an ovenproof dish.

Blend the parsley, wine, tomato paste, garlic with cloves, and bay leaves; pour over the meat and vegetables. Cover with foil and bake for 2 hours.

Remove the foil and, with a ladle, skim off the fat floating on the top. Sprinkle with fresh herbs and serve in the baking dish, along with noodles or rice or any vegetable purée.

This is better prepared a day ahead because it is easier to remove the fat. If the dish is to be used the next day, bake only 1½ hours in the oven; reheat for 30 minutes before serving.

Boeuf en Daube Charollaise

A Beef Stew

Daube was a festive dish often served at Easter or at weddings. It was also carried by the grape pickers for their lunch and eaten cold in thick slices.

As a child, I remember quarters of beef marinating in large barrels with fowls and herbs and vegetables before special family gatherings. The mere sight was intoxicating.

In a sixteenth-century archive, I found a staggering recipe served for a wedding. It included 30 pounds of Charolais beef, 8 large fowls, 2 veal heads, 40 pigs' feet, 20 quarts of red wine, a quart of old brandy and a variety of herbs and spices.

Les Viandes

This lighter and more appropriate version of *daube* is for 8 persons. Prepare it ahead. It is always better reheated.

For 8 people:

1½ quarts red wine
½ cup brandy
1 onion, peeled and quartered
3 bay leaves
20 peppercorns
2 2-inch-wide pieces of orange peel
6 pounds of top round (or bottom round, chuck shoulder or tip of roast beef), cut into 2-inch cubes
1 teaspoon oil
1 cup diced lean salt pork
1 piece of pork rind (about 1 pound), cut into pieces
1 veal knuckle
3 carrots, peeled and quartered
3 onions, peeled and studded with 2 cloves each
6 garlic cloves, peeled
3 tomatoes, fresh or canned
2 teaspoons thyme
Nutmeg
Salt
1 lump sugar

Mix the first six ingredients together to make the marinade. Put the beef in a large bowl with the marinade, cover and let stand a few hours (or overnight on the lowest shelf of the refrigerator).

Dry the meat carefully. Heat the oil in a heavy-bottomed pot and add the salt pork, sautéeing on all sides for 5 minutes. Remove the salt pork and set aside. Add the meat and sauté on all sides for 5 minutes.

Line a *doufeu** with the pork rind. Add the beef, veal knuckle, carrots, onions, garlic cloves, tomatoes, thyme, nutmeg, salt and sugar and cover with one-half of the marinade. Cover and let stand for 2 hours.

Add the rest of the marinade and cook on top of the stove (or in a 325° oven) for about 2 hours. Remove the herbs, orange peel, rind and cloves. Let cool overnight.

Remove as much fat as possible from the top. Check the seasoning. Reheat over low heat and serve with noodles or boiled potatoes or Fennel Purée (p. 206).

---

*The *doufeu* is the best of cast-iron casseroles. It comes either round or oval, and has a recessed cover, which is filled with a little water. The even distribution of heat makes it perfect for stews and dishes such as *boeuf bourguigonon* and *coq au vin.* it is available in most department and hardware stores throughout the United States.

Meats

Boeuf Beaujolais

T-Bone Steak Sautéed with a Shallot, Herb and Wine Sauce

A quick, pungent way to prepare a plain steak. Cooked on the stove and kept warm in the oven, it is served with a sharp sauce. A *Gratin Dauphinois* (p. 195) would be lovely with this; also a *Flan de Pommes de Terre* (p. 180) and *Champignons de Dijon* (p. 177).

For 3 people:

2 tablespoons sweet butter
1 tablespoon vegetable oil
1 thick T-bone steak
2 shallots, minced
1 tablespoon peppercorns
Finely chopped parsley
Thyme
2 bay leaves
1 celery stalk, finely chopped
1 cup good red Burgundy wine
1 garlic clove, minced
1 tablespoon good cognac
2 teaspoons sweet butter

Preheat the oven to 300°.

Heat the butter and oil in a heavy skillet and cook the steak for 4 minutes on both sides over high heat. Place it in a dish, cover with foil and put it in the oven.

Over high heat, add the shallots, peppercorns, parsley, thyme, bay leaves, celery and red wine to the skillet and cook, uncovered, for 10 minutes, until the sauce has reduced by two-thirds. Add the minced garlic, the cognac and the butter.

Cut the meat and pour the sauce over it. Serve at once.

Note: For a smoother sauce, pass it through a sieve before pouring over the meat.

Boeuf Blond

Beef Cooked with a Sweet White Wine and Large Whole Yellow
Onions

This blond beef comes from the Charolais region, where the
large cream-colored cattle are bred. It is simmered with a
sweet white wine and large yellow onions.

Choose a Sauterne-like sweet wine and serve it with the
meal along with Fennel Purée (p. 206), or Cabbage Purée (p.
196) or homemade noodles (p. 215).

For 8 people:

>   2 *tablespoons oil*
>   *About ¼ pound lean salt pork (or*
>   *bacon), cut into thin narrow strips*
>   *About ¼ pound lean veal, cut into*
>   *thin, narrow strips*
>   1 *4-pound piece of rump pot roast, as lean as possible,*
>   *tied with a string to keep its shape*
>   20 *whole yellow onions, peeled*
>   2 *cups sweet white wine (or sweet white vermouth)*
>   2 *garlic cloves, each studded with 1 clove*
>   3 *bay leaves and 2 sprigs thyme (or 3 sprigs thyme)*
>   1 *quart (approximately) hot broth or hot water*
>   *Salt*
>   *Freshly ground black pepper*
>   2 *tablespoons arrowroot, blended with 2 tablespoons*
>   *sweet white vermouth*
>   3 *tablespoons finely chopped chives*
>   2 *tablespoons finely chopped parsley*

Preheat oven to 350°.

Heat the oil in a large, heavy-bottomed pan on top of the
stove. Add the lean salt pork (or bacon) and stir for 3 minutes.
Add the veal, lower the heat, and add the beef. Sauté on all
sides over low heat for 15 minutes. Add the yellow onions,
then the sweet white wine, and cook, uncovered, over medium heat for 20 minutes.

Add the garlic cloves, bay leaves and thyme and place
everything in a deep ovenproof dish. The meat should be

Meats

surrounded by the whole onions and covered with the white wine and herbs. Add enough water (or broth) to cover it almost completely. Sprinkle with salt and pepper and cover with a lid or sheet of aluminum foil. Bake for 3 hours.

Remove as much fat from the top as you can, discard the bay leaves and garlic cloves (and the cloves, if you find them).

Place the meat and onions, covered with foil, in the turned-off oven while you reduce the cooking stock to about 1½ cups. Then add the cornstarch-vermouth mixture to the liquid and simmer for 5 minutes.

Slice the meat and the onions delicately with a very sharp knife and place them in a warm serving dish. Pour the reduced, thickened stock over them. Sprinkle with chives, parsley and pepper and serve at once with sweet white wine.

This dish can, of course, be prepared ahead of time. Cover and keep in the refrigerator. Degrease and reheat for about 20 minutes prior to serving.

Boudin Blanc et Pruneaux

White Sausages Cooked in Butter and Served with Stuffed Prunes and Tart Apples

You will find these veal or chicken white sausages in any German market and in most large supermarkets. Serve this dish with a rich red wine or a chilled dry white wine.

For 8 people:

20 *large prunes*
2 *cups warm tea*
1 *cup sweet butter*
4 *pounds Granny Smith or other tart apples, peeled, cored and sliced*
  Freshly grated nutmeg
  Salt
  Freshly ground white pepper
11 *white sausages* (Weisswurst)
1 *cup almonds, finely chopped*
2 *tablespoons minced dill (optional)*

Leave the prunes in the warm tea for one hour, then drain them and carefully remove the pits so that the prunes retain their shape.

Melt 2 tablespoons of the butter in a skillet and add the apples. Sprinkle them with nutmeg, salt, and pepper, and cook them, shaking them from time to time. Keep warm.

Preheat the oven to 450°.

Prick the sausage skins with a fork. Remove the skins of 3 sausages and slice them so you have twenty pieces. Roll the pieces in the almonds and stuff the prunes with them.

Brown the other sausages in butter in a large skillet for a few minutes, then place them with the stuffed prunes in an ovenproof dish. Dot with butter and bake for about 10 minutes.

The sausages are very delicate, so be careful not to bake them too long. Place them on a warm serving dish with the cooked apples in the center and serve at once. You may sprinkle the dish with dill.

Côte de Boeuf Bourguignonne

Rib Steak with a Shallot, Wine and Herb Sauce

Wonderful with a *Gâteau de Pommes de Terre* (p. 185), a *Gratin d'Oignons* (p. 186) or a *Flan de Pommes de Terre* (p. 180).

For 4 people:

2 *thick rib steaks*
2 *tablespoons vegetable oil*
9 *tablespoons sweet butter*
Freshly ground pepper
Freshly ground coriander
4 *shallots, peeled and minced*
1 *garlic clove, peeled and minced*
Salt
5 *tablespoons dry white sherry (or other wine)*
4 *tablespoons minced chives (or parsley)*

Take the steaks out of the refrigerator 1 hour before you intend to use them.

Meats

Preheat the oven to 350°.

Heat 1 tablespoon of the oil and 3 tablespoons of the butter in two heavy skillets (or prepare in two batches). Sear the steaks quickly on each side, then lower the heat and continue cooking for 6 to 8 minutes, depending on their thickness.

Turn off the oven. Sprinkle the steaks with pepper and coriander. Slide them onto a large baking dish, cover with foil and leave in the oven while you prepare the sauce.

Heat 2 tablespoons of the butter and 1 tablespoon of oil in one of the skillets, add the shallots and cook for 5 minutes. Add the garlic, then the sherry, and cook for another 5 minutes. Add coriander, salt and the chives.

Remove the meat from the oven. Sprinkle it with salt and pepper and turn it over.

Add 4 tablespoons of butter to the sauce, stirring vigorously. Cut the meat into individual portions and pour the sauce over it so the flavor will penetrate the meat.

Côtes de Porc au Vinaigre

Pork Chops Cooked with Garlic, Herbs, Onions, Vinegar and Mustard

A lively way to deal with pork chops and make them both digestible and delicious. Serve with *Purée de Choux* (p. 196) or braised endive, or *Terrine de Navets* (p. 212).

For 8 people:

1 tablespoon vegetable oil
2 tablespoons and 2 teaspoons sweet butter
8 pork chops, at least 1 inch thick
1 tablespoon flour
Salt
Freshly ground black pepper
2 garlic cloves, peeled and crushed
2 bay leaves
4 onions, peeled and finely chopped
8 shallots or green onions, finely chopped
3 tablespoons wine vinegar
3 tablespoons Dijon-style mustard
½ cup chopped cornichons

Les Viandes

Heat the oil and 2 tablespoons of the butter. Sprinkle the chops with flour, salt and pepper and sauté them on both sides for about 10 minutes in several batches, turning them twice. Add the garlic and bay leaves and cook over low heat, uncovered, for 10 minutes. Remove the chops to a dish and cover with foil to keep them warm.

Add the onions, shallots, vinegar, 2 teaspoons of butter and mustard to the skillet, scraping up the coagulated juices with a fork. Simmer, uncovered, for a few minutes. Add the chops and pickles for a few minutes and slide onto a warm serving dish.

You may want to add 2 tablespoons of tomato purée for a thicker sauce.

Boeuf Marinière I

For centuries, before the railroad came, bargemen would go down the Rhone River carrying fishing boats to the South and would come back home, up the river, drawn by twenty or more horses. They gave Burgundy the famous *matelote* and these two versions of *boeuf marinière.*

This recipe is better done a day or so ahead and reheated.

For 8 people:

4 pounds of beef, cut into 2-inch cubes
2 tablespoons sweet butter
2 tablespoons vegetable oil
5 onions, peeled and thinly sliced
Salt
Freshly ground black pepper
1 tablespoon arrowroot
1 teaspoon coarsely crushed coriander
3 bay leaves
3 teaspoons thyme
1 cup white wine
5 garlic cloves, peeled
2 anchovy fillets, trimmed and washed
3 tablespoons sweet butter
¼ cup chopped parsley (or chives)

Meats

Preheat the oven to 400°.

Dry the cubes of beef thoroughly with paper towels.

Heat the butter and oil in a heavy skillet and sauté the meat on all sides for 5 minutes, using a pair of tongs. Do it in three batches and put the sautéed meat aside in a large bowl.

Add the onions to the skillet, sprinkle with salt and pepper and cook over low heat for 5 minutes, stirring from time to time. Add the meat to the onions, sprinkle with arrowroot and put the skillet in the oven for 15 minutes to brown the arrowroot.

Remove from the oven, add the coriander, bay leaves, thyme and wine. Cover and simmer for 2½ hours.

Crush the garlic, anchovies and butter together into a paste and stir in with a long wooden fork just before serving. Sprinkle with parsley or chives.

Boeuf Marinière II

This is a splendid dish for a large family dinner. It can be served with homemade noodles (p. 215), or *Purée de Haricots Blancs* (p. 208) or *Pommes de Terre aux Herbes* (p. 203).

For 8 people:

4 *pounds lean beef*
3 *tablespoons sweet butter, at room temperature*
2 *tablespoons arrowroot or flour*
2 *tablespoons oil*
3 *pounds onions, thinly sliced*
    Salt
    Freshly ground black pepper
2 *tablespoons wine vinegar*
5 *anchovy fillets, crushed*
5 *garlic cloves, peeled and crushed*
2 *tablespoons Dijon-style mustard*
4 *tablespoons finely chopped parsley*

Les Viandes

Slice the meat into thin 2-inch strips. Mix the butter and arrowroot into a paste. Put the oil in a heavy-bottomed pot, add a layer of sliced onions, salt and pepper, a layer of sliced meat, salt and pepper, and dot the top with the butter-arrowroot paste.

Cover tightly and cook very slowly for 2 hours, checking from time to time.

Put the vinegar, anchovies, garlic, mustard, parsley and pepper into a blender, food processor or mortar and make a paste.

Just before serving, add the anchovy paste to the pot, stir and pour it into a warm shallow serving dish after checking the seasoning. The onion and meat must be almost melted when you add the paste.

Variation:
Another way to prepare this recipe is to omit the paste made with garlic, anchovies and mustard and gently stir 2 tablespoons of brandy into the sauce before serving.

Côte de Veau Dijonnaise
Veal Chops Baked with Onions and Wine

This elegant and light luncheon dish can be prepared ahead of time. I have used Parmesan to replace the dry strong sheep or goat cheese generally used in Burgundy.

For 8 people:

8 *veal chops (¾ inch thick)*
1 *tablespoon vegetable oil*
4 *tablespoons sweet butter*
6 *cups onions, peeled and finely chopped*
Salt
Freshly ground black pepper
2 *tablespoons thyme*
2 *teaspoons coriander*
1 *cup freshly grated Parmesan cheese*
1 *cup dry white wine*
½ *cup broth*

Meats

Preheat the oven to 350°.

Sauté the chops on both sides in a skillet in the oil and 2 tablespoons of butter until brown. Remove and set aside. Add 2 tablespoons of butter to the skillet and cook the onions until soft.

Butter an ovenproof dish and cover the bottom with half of the cooked onions. Sprinkle with salt, pepper and 1 tablespoon of the thyme. Place the chops on the layer of onions. Sprinkle with salt, pepper and coriander and cover with the rest of the onions. Sprinkle with salt, pepper, the remaining thyme and grated cheese.

Pour the wine and broth into the dish, dot with butter and bake for 25 minutes.

Check the seasoning and serve in the baking dish.

Boulettes Dorées de Montagne

Beef, Cheese, Onions and Herbs—Little Balls Sautéed and Seasoned with Coriander

Wonderfully easy and perfect for a buffet or for children's parties. Cook in two skillets at the same time.

For about 8 people:

½ cup and 5 tablespoons vegetable oil
1 tablespoon sweet butter
3 onions, finely chopped
2 pounds chopped beef
2 thick slices of bread, moistened in milk and squeezed
2 eggs
1½ cups finely chopped parsley (and any fresh herbs you can find—chervil, basil, mint, etc.)
Salt
Freshly ground black pepper
Pinch of nutmeg
2 teaspoons thyme or savory
Flour for dredging
½ pound Swiss cheese, sliced and cut into small pieces
2 tablespoons crushed coriander

Les Viandes

Heat 1 tablespoon of the oil and the butter in a heavy skillet, add the onions and cook slowly for 5 minutes. Remove and set aside.

Mix the meat, onions, bread, eggs, parsley, salt, pepper, nutmeg and thyme with your hands. Divide into about twenty little balls and roll them in 4 tablespoons of the oil, then in flour.

Heat ½ cup of the oil in the skillet and sauté the balls on all sides for 10 minutes, turning with kitchen tongs or two wooden spoons.

Press a piece of cheese, carefully, on top of each ball. Cover the skillet and cook for 3 minutes.

Sprinkle with coriander and serve at once.

Croquettes aux Herbes

Pork, Bacon and Herb Patties

These used to be cooked in summer over open fire pits. Baked in an oven, they are made in a jiffy. Serve them with *Purée de Choux* (p. 196), endives or *Crozets* (p. 214).

For 8 people:

> *3 pounds pork, chopped*
> *8 teaspoons thyme*
> *2 bay leaves, crushed*
> *Salt*
> *Freshly ground black pepper*
> *2 teaspoons sage*
> *16 to 24 slices smoked bacon*

Preheat oven to 375°.

Mix the pork, herbs and spices. Shape the mixture into 8 large flat patties. Wrap each patty in bacon slices and place it on a square of oiled foil. Fold carefully and bake for 35 to 40 minutes.

Meats

Boeuf en Gelée Vézulienne

Marinated Beef Braised with Vegetables and Served Cold in Its Aspic

〰〰〰〰〰〰〰〰〰〰〰〰〰〰〰〰〰〰〰〰〰〰

A spectacular country treat, which must be prepared two days ahead of time but is well worth it.

For about 8 people:

3½–4 *pounds rump of beef, cubed*
1½ *pounds lean salt pork, diced*
2 *tablespoons brandy*
Dry white wine, enough to cover the beef and salt pork
1 *onion*
Bouquet garni
2 *tablespoons vegetable oil*
5 *carrots, peeled, sliced and cooked (about 20 minutes)*
3 *onions, peeled and sliced*
2 *garlic cloves, peeled and crushed*
Parsley
1 *onion stuck with 2 cloves*
Salt
Freshly ground pepper
1 *calf's foot*
1 *pig's foot*
2 *2-inch-square pieces of pork rind*
3 *tablespoons finely chopped chives*

Put the meats in a large bowl, add brandy and cover with the wine. Add the onion and the bouquet garni and marinate for 12 hours.

Preheat the oven to 300°.

Heat the oil in a heavy-bottomed pan. Dry the beef and lean salt pork and sauté them on all sides for 10 minutes.

Place a layer of beef, pork, about half of the carrots and onions, garlic, parsley, salt and pepper in an ovenproof dish. Add the calf's and pig's feet, then another layer of meat and vegetables.

Les Viandes

Meanwhile, add the clove-studded onion to the marinade and bring the marinade to a boil and cook, uncovered, for 20 minutes. Pass through a sieve onto the meat and vegetables. Sprinkle with salt and pepper and put the pork rind on top. Cover and bake for 5 hours, adding water two times, as needed.

Remove the meats. Discard the bones and pork rind. Strain the cooking juices. Chill, then scrape the fat off the top. Reheat.

Decorate the bottom of a large shallow dish with the remaining sliced carrots. Place the pieces of meat on top. Pour in the degreased juices and place in the refrigerator.

Serve unmolded, sprinkled with chives.

Civet de Dinde

A Turkey Stewed in Red Wine and Herbs

In Burgundy this dish brings luck: "Such a good civet for dinner, fate can't harm me." Curiously, in Nivernais a chopped eel is often added to the stew for a more velvety sauce.

Serve with *Terrine de Navets* (p. 212), steamed rice, *Pouti*, which is a potato and chestnut purée (p. 204), or homemade noodles (p. 215).

For 8 people:

1 12-pound turkey, cut into serving pieces (about 16
pieces)
3 tablespoons vegetable oil
1 tablespoon sweet butter
6 onions, peeled and chopped
½ cup chopped lean salt pork (or bacon)
3 garlic cloves, peeled and crushed
1 tablespoon flour
Enough red wine (preferably a hearty
Burgundy) to cover the meat
Salt
Freshly ground black pepper
3 tablespoons thyme
2 bay leaves
3 tablespoons chopped fresh tarragon or parsley

Meats

Preheat oven to 325°.

Sauté the pieces of turkey in the oil and butter on all sides until golden. Add the onions, then the pork and, 5 minutes later, the garlic. Sprinkle with flour. Pour in enough red wine to cover the meat and bring to a boil on top of the stove. Add salt, pepper, thyme and bay leaves; cover and bake for 1½ hours.

Check the meat. If the joints are still pink, continue cooking. Remove pieces (thighs last) as they complete cooking and place in a warm serving dish. Cover and keep warm in the oven while you degrease the cooking juices. Discard the thyme and bay leaves. Crush the garlic with a fork, check the seasoning, add salt and pepper. Pour the sauce over the turkey. Sprinkle with tarragon or parsley and serve at once.

Daube d'Agneau

A Lamb Stew

A tasty stew to serve with a *Purée de Choux* (p. 196) and homemade noodles (p. 215) or *Purée de Haricots Blancs* (p. 208).

For 8 people:

1 large shoulder of lamb, cut in 2-inch cubes
3 cups red wine
3 garlic cloves, peeled and crushed
  Thyme
  Bay leaves
  Parsley
1 carrot, peeled and sliced
1 onion, peeled and sliced
3 tablespoons lard
1 onion, peeled and chopped
  Salt
  Freshly ground black pepper
2 garlic cloves
3 tablespoons minced parsley
1 tablespoon sweet butter

Les Viandes

Marinate the cubes of lamb in wine with the garlic, herbs, carrot and sliced onion for a few hours.

Heat the lard in a thick-bottomed pan. Add the chopped onion. Dry the meat well and sauté it on all sides. Pour in the marinade and bring it to a boil. Season with salt and pepper, cover and lower the heat. Cook for 2 hours. Discard the bay leaves.

Sauté the garlic and parsley in butter for 1 minute and sprinkle on the dish just before serving.

Canard à la Menthe

Duck Roasted with Mint and Apples

There are three main varieties of duck in France. The Nantais is the fleshiest, the Rouennais is close to the Long Island duck and the Peking duck, and Canard de Barbarie is similar to the mallard.

This is a fresh, lively way to prepare a Long Island duck. Very tart apples and fresh mint make it a splendid dish. Serve with fresh new peas or apple purée, *Petits Navets en Ragoût* (p. 202), *Purée de Choux* (p. 196) or *Raisiné* (p. 270).

For 8 people:

2 ducks, about 4 pounds each (if you can find only larger ducks, you will need to cook them longer)
1 lemon, halved
Salt
Freshly ground pepper
3 teaspoons thyme
4 tablespoons sweet butter
1 cup finely chopped fresh mint (in winter you may use dried mint)
8 large crisp apples (preferably Granny Smith), peeled, cored and quartered
2 tablespoons sweet butter
½ cup sweet white wine (or sherry)
Juice of 1 lemon
½ cup chopped fresh mint

Meats

Preheat the oven to 425°.

Pull out as much fat from the ducks as you can near the neck and tail and in the cavity. Discard it. Prick the wings, thighs, back and under the wings with a fork.

Wipe the ducks with paper towels and rub them with the cut lemon, salt, pepper and thyme. Stuff the inside with butter and chopped mint. Truss the birds and place them in a shallow baking dish. Bake for 15 minutes and remove the fat.

Reduce the temperature to 375° and turn the ducks on their sides. After 30 minutes, turn them on the other side and remove the fat once more. Cook for another 30 minutes.

Place the apples in the baking dish. Dot them with butter and let them cook around the ducks for one-half hour.

Prick the thighs of the ducks; the juices should be yellow (or rosy, if you like your duck undercooked).

Cut the ducks into serving pieces, place in a warm serving dish and surround with the apples. Add wine (or sherry) to the cooking pan, scraping the coagulated brown juices with a fork. Add the mint-and-butter stuffing and stir. Check the seasonings and pour over the pieces of duck. Sprinkle the lemon juice, mint and a little pepper over both ducks and apples and serve.

Canard Sauvage à la Diable

Wild Duck Baked with Lemon, Mustard, Shallots and Wine

Better choose a grain-fed shallow-water duck than a wild diving duck that feeds on fish and has too strong a taste. The majority of wild ducks coming into the market are mallards. But canvasback and Muscovy ducks are sometimes available in winter. Frozen ducks can turn very dry, and to keep them moist you will have to lay strips of bacon over their breasts and thighs.

This recipe comes from Franche-Comté and uses sharp seasonings for a truly devilish effect. Serve with rice or a vegetable purée or *Paillasson* (p. 190), along with *Raisiné* (p. 270).

Les Viandes

For 8 people:

2 *wild ducks, fresh or defrosted (reserve the livers)*
Salt
Freshly ground black pepper
Sage
4 *tablespoons sweet butter*
Peel of 1 lemon, chopped
Juice of 1 lemon
2 *tablespoons Dijon-style mustard*
8 *shallots, minced*
3 *tablespoons chopped parsley*
½ *cup red wine*
Thyme
Savory
2 *tablespoons minced parsley*

Preheat the oven to 400°. Season the cavity of the birds with salt, pepper and sage. Spread half of the butter all over the outside of the ducks and sprinkle with salt and pepper. Truss the ducks.

Bake in a shallow dish for 20 minutes (if you have defrosted birds, lay strips of bacon on top to keep them moist). The flesh should be pink and underdone when you remove it from the oven. Let it stand for 5 minutes before cutting it into serving pieces.

Reduce the oven heat to 350°.

Mix the chopped lemon peel with the lemon juice and the mustard. Put the duck livers through a sieve and add to the lemon-mustard mixture.

Heat the remaining butter and sauté the shallots until soft. Add the parsley and spread in an oven-proof dish. Place the pieces of duck on top. Sprinkle with salt and pepper. Cover with a sheet of foil and bake for 10 minutes. Transfer onto a warm serving dish, and cover with the foil to keep warm.

Pour the wine into the oven dish and scrape the coagulated juices with a spoon. Season with salt, pepper, thyme and savory. Bring to a boil on top of the stove and simmer for 10 minutes. Add the mixture of liver, mustard and lemon, stir vigorously and pour over the pieces of duck.

Sprinkle with parsley and serve.

Meats

Civet de Porc

Pork Slowly Cooked with Onions, Red Wine and Herbs

This old recipe used to be made often in Burgundy, and the sauce was thickened with fresh pork blood. Since one can't get blood in the United States, I have chosen other thickeners, but it is a rich, tasty dish, superb with a purée of fresh apples, a purée of celery, a *Paillasson* (p. 190) or a *Gratin de Chou* (p. 210).

For 8 people:

4 *pounds pork shoulder, boned and cut in 2-inch cubes*
2 *tablespoons sweet butter*
1 *tablespoon vegetable oil*
⅔ *cup (about 4 ounces) bacon, cut into small dice*
5 *large onions, minced*
2 *cups red Burgundy wine*
  Salt
  Freshly ground black pepper
1 *tablespoon sage*
2 *teaspoons thyme (or a sprig of fresh thyme)*
3 *bay leaves*
1 *tablespoon arrowroot mixed with 1 tablespoon water to make a paste*
2 *tablespoons finely chopped chives (or parsley, or any other fresh herb)*

Dry the cubes of pork with paper towels. Sauté them for about 5 minutes in butter and oil in a large skillet, turning them on all sides until golden. Add the bacon and onions and sauté for 10 minutes more.

Drain off all excess cooking fat. (You may wish to save it for other dishes.) Add the wine and vigorously scrape the bottom of the pan. Sprinkle the meat with salt, pepper, sage and thyme. Add the bay leaves, cover and simmer for 1½ hours, stirring from time to time. Stir in the arrowroot paste 10 minutes before the end of the cooking time.

Check the seasonings. Remove as much fat as you can with a long-handled spoon and pour the *civet* into a warm serving dish. Sprinkle with fresh herbs.

Les Viandes

Cochon de Lait Vigneron

Stuffed Suckling Pig Cooked with Vegetables and Herbs

A glorious festive dish. In Burgundy, grape pickers love to eat it cold after the harvest, but I prefer it hot and crispy. It is best served with cooked apples, baked tomatoes, *Gratin d'Oignons* (p. 186), *Gâteau de Pommes de Terre* (p. 185) or *Paillasson* (p. 190).

Suckling pig can be ordered in many markets, especially in Cuban, Puerto Rican and Mexican neighborhoods, where it is a traditional dish.

For about 10 people:

> *1 pork liver (or 1 cup chicken livers)*
> *1 tablespoon vegetable oil*
> *4 cups onions, peeled and chopped*
> *1 cup diced lean salt pork (or boiled ham)*
> *5 teaspoons thyme*
> *2 teaspoons sage*
> *3 eggs*
> *2 tablespoons cream*
> *Salt*
> *Freshly ground black pepper*
> *3 garlic cloves, peeled and crushed*
> *1 cup chopped parsley*
> *2 tablespoons dry white wine*
> *½ cup pork blood (optional)*
> *1 suckling pig (about 10 pounds)*
> *2 tablespoons sweet butter*
> *1 garlic clove, peeled*
> *Salt*
> *Freshly ground black pepper*
> *2 carrots, peeled and sliced*
> *2 onions, peeled and sliced*
> *2 bay leaves*
> *2 teaspoons thyme*
> *½ cup white wine*

Soak the pork liver in cold water for a few hours. Drain and chop.

Meats

Preheat the oven to 375°.

Heat the oil in a pan and sauté the onions, then the liver, then the salt pork. Add the thyme, sage, eggs, cream, salt and pepper, garlic and parsley and cook for about 10 minutes, stirring. Add the wine and pork blood (if available).

Fill the suckling pig with the cooked stuffing and sew it up carefully. Tie the legs with a string and rub the entire pig with butter and a garlic clove. Put a piece of wood in its mouth to keep it open.

Place the suckling pig in an uncovered, buttered ovenproof dish. Wrap the ears and tail with foil, sprinkle with salt and pepper and scatter the carrots, onions, bay leaves and thyme around it. Bake for 15 minutes. Reduce the oven heat to 350° and bake for 3 hours or more. Baste every 15 minutes with pan drippings. During the last half hour, add ½ cup of white wine.

Place the pig on a warm platter. Remove the foil from the ears and tail and replace the wood in its mouth with a small apple or lemon.

Serve whole, surrounded by the vegetables. Slice at the table, removing forelegs and hams, then dividing the meat down the center of the back. Make sure everyone has a piece of crackling skin. Degrease the cooking juice and pour it over the cut slices.

Coq au Vin Bourguignon

Sautéed Chicken Cooked with Onions, Herbs, Red Wine and Mushrooms

A very old treat in Burgundy. There are as many versions as there are cooks, and it all started with the Gauls, who, being attacked by the Romans, sent a rooster to Julius Caesar carrying the ironic message *"Bon appétit!"* Caesar answered with a concoction made from their rooster cooked with herbs and Roman wine. This was, perhaps, the beginning of a great friendship and of interesting culinary exchanges.

Les Viandes

For this *coq au vin bourguignon,* the wine should be as hearty and tasty as possible.

For 8 people:

24 *small white onions (or 12 larger white onions)*
6 *tablespoons sweet butter*
1 *teaspoon sugar*
  Salt
1 *cup lean salt pork, cut into small dice*
6 *tablespoons vegetable oil*
3 *cups mushrooms, halved or quartered*
1½ *quarts red wine (hearty Burgundy type)*
3 *3-pound broiling chickens, each cut into 6 to 8 pieces*
  Freshly ground pepper
2 *large onions, peeled and finely chopped*
2 *tablespoons finely chopped parsley*
¼ *cups cognac*
2 *bay leaves*
2 *garlic cloves, peeled and left whole*
2 *teaspoons thyme*
3 *carrots, chopped*
4 *slices of bread, cut into triangles*
2 *tablespoons minced parsley*

Peel the white onions and cook them for about 10 minutes with 2 tablespoons of butter, sugar and a pinch of salt in enough water to cover them. Remove from the heat and set aside. (If you use large onions, cook for 20 minutes, until soft.)

Sauté the salt pork in 1 tablespoon of the oil on all sides until crisp. Remove and set aside. Sauté the mushrooms in the hot fat on all sides, sprinkle them with salt, remove and set aside.

Bring the wine to a boil and let it reduce, uncovered, for 10 minutes.

Sprinkle the pieces of chicken with salt and pepper. Heat 3 tablespoons of butter and 2 tablespoons of oil in a large skillet and sauté the chicken pieces on all sides until golden. After 10 minutes, add the chopped onions and cook for 20 minutes more. Add the parsley, then pour the cognac over the

Meats

chicken, turn off the flame and ignite. Then pour the hot wine over the chicken. Add the bay leaves, whole garlic cloves, thyme and carrots; cover and simmer for 1 hour. Then uncover and continue cooking for 15 minutes.

Meanwhile, heat 3 tablespoons of oil and 1 tablespoon of butter in a skillet and, when it is very hot, sauté the triangles of bread until crisp and golden.

Warm a large serving dish.

When the chicken is ready, remove the bay leaves and the thyme. Check the seasoning, add the onions and mushrooms and pour into the serving dish. Dip the croutons in the sauce, then in the minced parsley, and place around the dish. Serve at once.

Côtes de Porc Farcies

Pork Chops Stuffed with Ham, Cheese and Sage and Served with a Cabbage Purée

This is an easy way to transform plain pork chops into a surprisingly fancy and flavorful dish. Serve this with cabbage-and-potato purée and a dry white wine.

For 8 people:

- *8 slices country ham (or good boiled ham), finely chopped*
- *1½ cups Swiss cheese, grated or shredded*
- *3 teaspoons sage*
- *Freshly ground black pepper*
- *8 large, thick pork chops*
- *3 tablespoons flour*
- *4 tablespoons vegetable oil or lard*
- *Salt*
- *2 whole garlic cloves, peeled*
- *1 green cabbage, trimmed and quartered*
- *3 potatoes, peeled*
- *2 tablespoons sweet butter*

Les Viandes

Mix the chopped ham, cheese, sage and pepper.

Trim the loose fat from the chops. Pat them dry. Make a

slit in each chop until the tip of your knife reaches the bone. Fill this little pocket with some of the ham-cheese mixture. Push the filling in and secure it with wooden toothpicks if necessary. Dredge the chops with flour.

Heat the oil in a large skillet. Sauté the chops and sprinkle them with salt. Add the garlic cloves, lower the heat, cover and cook for 40 to 45 minutes.

Meanwhile, cook the cabbage and potatoes in a large pot of salted water for 30 minutes. Pass through a Mouli mill or food processor. Season with salt, pepper and butter.

Place the stuffed chops around a warm serving dish and put the vegetable purée in the center.

Épaule d'Agneau Farcie

Stuffed Shoulder of Lamb

For 8 people:

4 large onions, peeled and chopped
4 tablespoons sweet butter
2 tablespoons vegetable oil
½ pound ham (or lean salt pork), chopped fine
2 slices of bread, dipped in ½ cup milk
1 tablespoon rosemary
1 tablespoon thyme
1 whole egg, beaten
Salt
Freshly ground black pepper
1 garlic clove, peeled and chopped
1 4-pound shoulder of lamb, boned
2 tablespoons lard
3 tablespoons thyme
6 carrots, peeled and chopped
3 turnips, peeled and chopped

Sauté half of the chopped onions in 2 tablespoons of the butter and 1 tablespoon of the oil, then mix with the ham and moistened bread. Add the rosemary, thyme, egg, salt, pepper and garlic and spread on the boned shoulder of lamb. Roll it

Meats

lengthwise as tightly as you can, and tie it with a long piece of string.

Preheat the oven to 350°.

Heat the lard in a large cooking pan. Add the lamb and brown on all sides. Sprinkle with some of the thyme and cover with aluminum foil or a lid. Bake for 1 hour. Turn it twice.

Heat the remaining butter and oil in a heavy skillet and cook the carrots, turnips and the remaining onions until tender. Sprinkle with salt, pepper and the rest of the thyme and place around the lamb for its last 20 minutes of cooking time to soak in some of the roasting juices.

Sprinkle with salt and pepper before serving.

Foie de Porc Bourguignonne

Marinated Pork Liver Seasoned with Sage, Wrapped in Bacon and Cooked in White Wine

In Burgundy each family celebrated the killing of the pig with a large meal and offered the pork liver to the neighbors as a ritual present. In America, pork livers are not considered a delicacy, but they are readily available at pork stores.

This is a wonderful dish for a buffet or a summer meal, but pork liver can also be delicious simply sliced and sautéed with onions, then sprinkled with vinegar and sage.

For 8 people:

2 *pounds pork liver*
Dry white wine, enough to cover
6 *sage leaves, fresh or dried*
Salt
Freshly ground black pepper
Slices of bacon, enough to wrap around
   the liver

Place the pork liver in a bowl, cover it with the wine and add the sage. Let it stand overnight in the refrigerator.

Remove the liver and let it dry. Sprinkle it with salt and

Les Viandes

pepper, place the sage leaves around it and wrap it with the bacon slices.

Reduce the marinade over high heat for 30 minutes and then place the wrapped liver in the pan. Lower the heat and simmer, half covered, for 30 minutes.

Remove the liver from the pan. Let it cool. Remove the slices of bacon.

Place the cooking liquid in the refrigerator to thicken and congeal a little and then put the liver in it. Cover with plastic wrap and refrigerate for a few hours.

Unmold and serve, sliced, on lettuce leaves, as a first course or a lunch main course with a salad. You may want to spread the congealed liquid on the lettuce and place the slices of liver on it.

Fricot d'Oie

Goose or Duck Fricassee with Turnips

Because young fowl was unusually good and profitable in Burgundy, the peasants kept the tough birds for themselves. They devised endless ways to prepare them, so *fricots* and *fricassées* have more imaginative recipes than roasted poultry in the Burgundy cuisine's repertory.

For 8 people:

½ pound lean salt pork (or bacon), diced
3 large onions, peeled and sliced
1 tablespoon vegetable oil
2 tablespoons sweet butter
1 goose or duck, cut into serving pieces
2 tablespoons flour
3 garlic cloves, peeled
1 bunch parsley
2 bay leaves
Salt
Freshly ground black pepper
2 pounds small pink turnips, peeled

Meats

Sauté the salt pork and onions in the oil and butter for a few minutes, stirring. Set aside.

Add the pieces of fowl to the pan. Sauté on all sides. When golden, sprinkle flour over each piece and cook for a few minutes. Add the salt pork and onions, ½ cup of water, garlic cloves, parsley, bay leaves, salt and pepper and cook for 45 minutes over medium heat. Add the turnips, cover and cook over low heat for 1 hour. Serve the pieces of goose surrounded by the turnips.

Gigot Boulangère

A Baked Leg of Lamb Cooked with Onions and Potatoes and
Seasoned with Thyme and Wine

This is called "a baker's roast" because in every village housewives would bring some of their dishes to the neighborhood baker on festive days. After his last batch of bread had been baked, and while the oven was still hot, he would cook the leg of lamb, geese and casseroles they had prepared.

For about 8 people:

1 *leg of lamb*
1 *cup sweet butter*
1 *tablespoon thyme*
2 *garlic cloves, cut in slivers*
3 *tablespoons dry white wine*
4 *large onions, peeled and sliced*
8 *potatoes, peeled and thinly sliced*
  Salt
  Freshly ground black pepper
2 *bay leaves, crumbled*
  Parsley

Preheat the oven to 450°.

Rub the lamb with butter and thyme. Insert the garlic slivers into various parts of the lamb. Bake for 30 minutes, then add the wine, scraping the coagulated juices.

Meanwhile, sauté the onions in butter for 5 minutes, stirring. Pour into a large ovenproof dish. Add the potatoes. Season with salt, pepper and the bay leaves. Place the leg of

Les Viandes

lamb on top and pour the cooking juices over it. Sprinkle with salt and pepper and bake for about 30 minutes.

Serve in a warm serving dish with the sliced lamb on one side, the onions and potatoes on the other and little bunches of parsley in the center.

Jambon à la Saulieu

Slices of Ham Cooked with Shallot, Wine, Cream and Tomato Sauce, Sprinkled with Cheese and Broiled

With its delicate yet tangy sauce, this easy dish embodies all the flavors of Burgundy. Serve with noodles (p. 215), *Purée de Fenouil* (p. 206), *Gâteau de Pommes de Terre* (p. 185) or *Gâteau au Céleri* (p. 183).

For 8 people:

1½ pounds mushrooms, sliced
2 tablespoons vegetable oil
1 tablespoon sweet butter
1 cup dry white wine
6 tablespoons minced shallots (or scallions)
3 cups heavy cream
3 tomatoes, peeled, seeded and chopped
Salt
Freshly ground black pepper
2 tablespoons sweet butter mixed with 2 tablespoons flour to make a beurre manié
10 slices cooked ham (about 3 ounces per slice)
Freshly ground coriander
⅔ cup grated Swiss or Parmesan cheese
1 tablespoon sweet butter

Sauté the mushrooms in the oil and butter for 5 minutes. Set aside.

Reduce the wine and shallots in a saucepan for 5 minutes. Add the cream, tomatoes, salt and pepper and simmer for another 5 minutes. Add the *beurre manié* and remove from the heat, stirring. Cover and keep warm.

Butter a deep ovenproof dish. Cover the bottom with the

Meats

ham slices. Sprinkle with pepper and coriander. Cover with the mushrooms and coat with the wine sauce. Sprinkle the grated cheese on top, dot with butter and run under a hot broiler for a few minutes. It shouldn't boil, so don't put it too close to the flame.

Jambon Chaud Chablisienne

Spinach and Ham Baked in a Wine, Cream and Herb Sauce

Easy to prepare all year round, this is a wonderful dish you can make ahead of time. Perfect for a children's meal, too.

For 8 people:

6 *pounds spinach (or 6 packages frozen chopped spinach)*
1 *large onion, peeled and finely chopped*
1 *tablespoon sweet butter*
2 *tablespoons flour*
1 *cup white wine*
¾ *cup chicken broth (or water)*
1 *teaspoon tomato paste*
Salt
Freshly ground black pepper
4 *tablespoons tarragon*
Freshly grated nutmeg
4 *tablespoons cream*
8 *slices (1 pound) cooked ham, shredded*
3 *tablespoons grated Swiss cheese*

Blanch the fresh spinach in salted water for 10 minutes. Drain and chop.

Sauté the onion in butter. Sprinkle with flour and cook over low heat for a few minutes. Add the wine, broth (or water) and tomato paste and stir. Sprinkle with salt and pepper. Add the tarragon, spinach, nutmeg and cream and cook for 5 minutes.

Preheat the oven to 350°.

Les Viandes

Butter an ovenproof dish and spread with one-half of the spinach mixture. Cover with the ham, sprinkle with nutmeg and pepper and cover with the rest of the spinach mixture. Sprinkle with cheese, dot with butter and bake for 15 minutes. Serve hot.

Jambon Grand-Mère

Fresh Ham Rubbed with Herbs and Baked Slowly

There is nothing better than this fresh ham baked for five hours with herbs and garlic and served with a *Paillasson* (p. 190), *Crépinette aux Marrons* (p. 32) and *Purée de Choux* (p. 196). The cold leftovers can be used in a variety of dishes.

> *5 garlic cloves, peeled and sliced*
> *1 12- to 14-pound fresh ham or leg of pork, trimmed of some of its fat*
> *5 tablespoons thyme and sage (or as much as needed)*
> *Salt*
> *Freshly ground black pepper*
> *5 tablespoons dry white wine*

Preheat the oven to 350°.

Insert the garlic slices in the ham in various places. Rub it with the herbs, salt and pepper all over the surface, pressing with your hands.

Bake, fat side up, for 3 hours. Sprinkle more herbs on the surface. Turn it over and pat more herbs on it. Cover with foil and bake for 2 hours.

Remove the ham to a large dish. Add the wine to the coagulated juices in the pan, scraping the bottom vigorously. Slice the meat and pour the juice over it.

Jambon au Torchon et au Foin

Ham Boiled with Herbs and Spices

There is nothing better than this fresh ham baked for five

The flavor of ham depends on the diet of the pig—whether it is fed on sugar beets, chestnuts, cheese or acorns—and on the preparation of the meat. Ham is cured in so many ways

Meats

and cooked in so many ways in Burgundy that there is no monotony in using it often.

Rubbed with salt, it is kept in deep boxes full of ashes, then wrapped in canvas rags and hung on a bar across a fireplace for two hours a day for about three to four weeks while sage, juniper and green hardwood branches provide a fragrant smoke. It can also be covered with salt and hung to dry in the mountain air for six months, rubbed with pepper and eaten raw; it acquires a tangy flavor and a deep rusty color. For a less refined but quicker treatment, it can be kept in brine, then cooked with vegetables.

The following is an old-fashioned way to prepare ham, using the butt portion you can buy in your market that is uncured, uncooked and labeled "Cook before eating."

The original recipe calls for a handful of hay to be spread on the bottom of the pot as a bed for the ham. But since hay is unlikely to be found in the average kitchen, you could use dried herbs of any kind as a substitute—or, because the ingredient isn't essential, omit it altogether.

For 20 people:

1   10- to 20-pound uncooked ham
    A handful of dried herbs (optional)
5   bay leaves
3   tablespoons thyme
2   tablespoons rosemary
10 peppercorns
    Salt
    Dry white wine
1   cup bread crumbs

Wash the ham and leave it in cold water for 6 hours. Wrap it in a large piece of clean cloth and tie it with a string. Scatter a handful of dried herbs on the bottom of a large pot. Place the wrapped ham on top of the herbs and cover with cold water.

Add the herbs, peppercorns and salt and bring to a boil. Simmer for 4 hours. Add the wine (about one-third of the amount of water in the pot) and simmer for 1 hour.

Let the ham cool in its cooking liquid overnight.

Remove from the liquid, cut the cloth and remove the skin and part of the fat. Rub with bread crumbs, pressing down with the palm of your hand. Eat the ham warm or cold.

Les Viandes

Lièvre de Pâques

Hare (or Turkey) Marinated, Then Cooked with Cream and Grapes

A traditional Easter dish—feudal lords let the people shoot on their land on that special holiday in order to have a festive meal. It has to be prepared two days ahead and can be done with turkey as well as hare.

For 8 people:

2 *saddles of hare or 1 large breast of turkey*
½ *cup brandy*
8 *shallots, peeled and chopped*
½ *cup chopped celery*
2 *bay leaves*
1 *tablespoon thyme*
Freshly ground pepper
Salt
4 *tablespoons sweet butter*
1 *cup light cream*
1 *cup fresh grapes*

Marinate the hare or turkey in a bowl with the brandy, shallots, celery, bay leaves, thyme and pepper for two days on a low shelf in the refrigerator or in a cool place. Turn the meat a few times.

Preheat the oven to 350°.

Drain the meat and place it in an ovenproof dish. Spread the top with salt, pepper and butter. Cover with a sheet of foil and bake for 30 minutes. Turn the meat over with tongs, pour the marinade over the top, cover and cook for 30 minutes longer.

Remove the bay leaves. Add the cream and grapes to the sauce and cook for 5 minutes.

Check the seasoning and serve with *Pouti* (p. 204) or *Gratin de Chou* (p. 210) or *Gratin Forestière* (p. 193).

Meats

Meurette de Poulet

A Chicken Cooked with Wine, Vegetables and Herbs

Meurette, or stew, is, with snails, one of the cornerstones of Burgundy cooking. Its main ingredient can be eel, pike, carp or poached eggs. With chicken it is lighter than *coq au vin* and is often prepared with white wine instead of red.

Serves 8 people:

20 *very small pearl onions, peeled*
 5 *tablespoons sweet butter*
   Salt
   Freshly ground black pepper
 1 *teaspoon sugar*
½ *pound bacon, diced (½-inch pieces)*
½ *pound mushrooms, quartered*
 1 *tablespoon vegetable oil*
   Slices of bread, cut into triangles
 4 *yellow onions, peeled and minced*
 2 *4-pound chickens, each cut into 8 pieces*
 3 *scallions, peeled and minced*
 5 *garlic cloves, peeled and minced*
 3 *tablespoons flour*
 3 *cups red wine*
   Salt
   Freshly ground black pepper
 2 *bay leaves*
   Thyme
 1 *garlic clove, peeled and left whole*
   Minced parsley

Place the pearl onions, 1 tablespoon of water, 2 tablespoons of the butter, salt, pepper and sugar in a saucepan and cook, covered, for 10 minutes. Remove the cover, cook for 3 minutes and set aside, covered.

Heat 2 tablespoons of butter in a skillet and sauté the diced bacon for a few minutes. Remove and set aside.

Add the mushrooms to the fat and sauté on all sides until cooked. Remove to another bowl and keep covered.

Add the oil to the skillet and fry the triangles of bread on

Les Viandes

both sides. Place the bread on a cookie sheet and keep warm in a 200° oven until ready to serve.

Add 1 tablespoon of butter to the skillet and sauté the minced yellow onions for 5 minutes, then add the chicken. Sauté on all sides, turning each piece with a pair of tongs, for 10 minutes. Add the scallions and garlic, sprinkle with flour and stir. Cook for 5 minutes, then add the wine, salt, pepper, bay leaves and thyme. Cover and simmer for 50 minutes. Add the pearl onions, bacon and mushrooms. Pour the mixture into a warm serving dish and surround with the croutons (rubbed with a clove of garlic). Sprinkle with parsley.

Oie à la Moutarde

Braised Goose with Mustard and Wine

Braised goose is more tender, has more flavor, and has less fat than roasted goose. Enhanced by a lively sauce, this is a truly festive dinner. The recipe can also be done with a duck (cook only 90 minutes). Serve with braised lettuce, a celery purée, *Pouti* (p. 204) or *Pommes de Terre aux Herbes* (p. 203).

For 8 people:

- 2 *onions, peeled and minced*
- 2 *tablespoons vegetable oil*
- 1 *tablespoon butter*
- 1 *large goose (fresh or frozen), cut into serving pieces*
  Salt
  Freshly ground black pepper
- 1 *cup dry white wine*
  Chicken broth to cover the meat
- 2 *bay leaves*
- 2 *sprigs of thyme*
- 1½ *cups light cream*
- 3 *tablespoons Dijon-style mustard*
- 3 *tablespoons minced tarragon (or any other fresh herb)*

Sauté the onions in the oil and butter for 5 minutes. Add the pieces of goose, skin side down. Sprinkle with salt and pepper.

Meats

Cook over low heat for 5 minutes, turning each piece on all sides. Add the wine, enough chicken broth to cover the meat, the bay leaves and the thyme. Cover and simmer for about 2½ hours, or until the meat can be easily pierced with a fork and its juices run clear.

Place the pieces of goose in a warm serving dish, cover with a sheet of foil and keep in a 200° oven until ready to serve.

Spoon out as much fat as possible from the cooking juice. Scrape up the brown coagulated juices with a fork. Stir in the cream. Reduce by stirring constantly over medium heat for a few minutes. Remove from the heat, add the mustard and check the seasoning.

Spoon the sauce over the pieces of goose. Sprinkle with fresh herbs.

Porc au Vermouth

A Loin of Pork Cooked with Vegetables and Seasoned with Orange and Lemon Juice and Vermouth

In Burgundy this dish is usually prepared with a sweet "cooked" wine (to which sugar and brandy have been added). I have tried sweet dessert wine but have found that the best thing is to use a good-quality sweet vermouth and ignite the meat with brandy. It can be served with *Purée de Choux* (p. 196), braised endives, *Purée de Fenouil* (p. 206) or *Terrine de Navets* (p. 212).

For 8 people:

3 teaspoons thyme
6 teaspoons sage
Salt
Freshly ground pepper
1 5-pound center-cut loin of pork (bone in)
5 tablespoons sweet butter
6 onions, thinly sliced
3 carrots, thinly sliced
3 tablespoons brandy (cognac, preferably)
Juice and skin, minced or grated, of 1 orange

Les Viandes

Juice of 1 lemon
1 cup good sweet vermouth
Salt
Freshly ground black pepper

Sprinkle the thyme, sage, salt and pepper all over the piece of pork and press them down.

Heat 3 tablespoons of the butter in a heavy-bottomed pan and add the onions and carrots. Stir, then add the pork. Sauté for 25 minutes over low heat, uncovered.

Add the brandy and ignite. Add the orange juice, lemon juice, one-half of the vermouth and 2 tablespoons of water. Scrape the bottom of the pan and turn the meat. Cover and simmer for 1½ hours.

Put the meat on a dish and cover with foil to keep warm. Pour the rest of the vermouth into the hot pan and scrape with a fork. Add the orange skin and cook for 5 minutes, uncovered. Add 2 tablespoons of butter, cover, and turn off the heat.

Meanwhile, slice the meat and arrange it on a warm serving dish. Sprinkle with salt and pepper. Pour the hot sauce over the slices of meat and serve at once.

Poule-au-Pot Bourguignon

Stuffed Chickens Boiled with Vegetables and Herbs

Each region in France claims to own the genuine *poule-au-pot* recipe. Henry IV may have spoken about it in the Pyrenees; the dukes of Burgundy were fond of it and gave it its "letters of nobility." Then various chefs embellished the dish with such necessary ingredients as goose livers, but it was the housewives of Burgundy who brought to it a perfect balance of flavors.

Since large flavorful hens are hard to find, the secret here is to cook an extra chicken at the same time to make a *very* concentrated broth. Keep the extra fowl for making a salad. Serve with plain rice.

This must be prepared one day ahead for the best results.

Meats

For 8 people:

Court-bouillon

3 large chickens (including gizzards, feet and necks)
2 carrots, peeled
2 onions, peeled
2 turnips, peeled
  Freshly ground black pepper
  Salt
1 bay leaf
1 sprig of thyme
1 garlic clove, peeled
1 celery stalk

Stuffing

2 slices bread, soaked in ½ cup milk
2 thick slices country ham, chopped
3 onions, chopped and sautéed in butter
4 chicken livers, chopped
2 garlic cloves, minced
1 tablespoon minced parsley
2 eggs, beaten
  Salt
  Freshly ground black pepper

Vegetables

4 carrots, peeled
4 turnips, peeled
1 celery stalk
4 onions, peeled
2 garlic cloves, peeled

Put all the ingredients for the *court-bouillon* in a large kettle, cover with water and cook for 1½ hours. Let it cool. Remove the chickens.

Degrease the broth thoroughly. (When it is cold, the fat will congeal at the top and should be easy to remove. It is better to make the broth a day ahead.) Discard the vegetables.

Prepare the stuffing. Mix all the ingredients well and season.

Stuff two of the chickens (save the third chicken for another use). Sew the openings. Place the chickens in the degreased broth and bring it to a boil. Simmer, covered, for 1 hour. Skim often.

Les Viandes

Add the carrots, turnips, celery, onions and garlic and cook for 30 minutes.

Place the stuffed chickens on a large warm plate and cut them into serving pieces. Put the stuffing in the center of the plate and surround with the vegetables. Pour a ladle of hot broth over everything, sprinkle with salt and pepper and serve.

Serve the rest of the broth separately at the beginning of the meal, or, on another day, over buttered toasted slices of whole-wheat bread spread lightly with mustard.

Porc aux Haricots Rouges

Pork Spareribs Cooked with Onions, Red Wine, Herbs and Red Beans

The herbs, wine and garlic give this dish its rich distinctive flavor, and the red beans are the right complement for it. A good accompaniment is a dandelion-green tossed salad (p. 60).

For 8 people:

2 pounds red beans
1 whole onion, peeled and stuck with 1 clove
1 garlic clove, peeled and left whole
2 bay leaves
Sprigs of thyme
4 pounds spareribs, cut in large serving pieces
1 pig's ear (or pig's knuckle or large piece of pork rind)
3 tablespoons sweet butter
½ pound lean salt pork, diced
3 onions, peeled and chopped
1 tablespoon flour
2 cups hearty red wine
Freshly ground black pepper
3 tablespoons minced parsley

Soak the beans in cold water overnight. On the day of cooking, rinse them well and place them in a large saucepan, covered with the water they have soaked in. Bring to

Meats

a boil. Add the onion with the clove, the garlic clove, bay leaves and thyme. Cover and simmer for 1½ hours, or until tender.

Place the spareribs and the pig's ear (or pig's knuckle or rind) in a large saucepan of boiling water. Boil for 5 minutes. Drain.

Heat the butter and sauté the salt pork and onions. Stir until the onions turn golden. Sprinkle with the flour. Stir while adding the wine, then add the spareribs and the ear. Bring to a boil and cook for 1 hour.

Drain the beans and add them to the pork. Season with pepper, cover and simmer for 15 minutes.

Just before serving, cut the pig's ear (or knuckle or rind) into thin strips and mix with the red beans. Discard the bay leaves and the onion with the clove. Put the beans in a warm serving dish, place the spareribs around them, and sprinkle with parsley. Serve very warm.

Porc Dijonnaise

Pork with Vegetables and a Shallot, Cream and Mustard Sauce

You may use part of a whole ham; the butt portion is more flavorful, leaner and also more expensive (7 pounds will serve 10 people). A smoked shoulder of pork is less expensive but less flavorful with more waste (you need about one pound per person). This highly seasoned dish is superb with a celery purée, *Purée de Fenouil* (p. 206) or *Purée de Choux* (p. 196).

> 2 *tablespoons oil*
> 4 *tablespoons sweet butter*
> 3 *leeks (white part only) or 3 onions, peeled and chopped*
> 4 *carrots, peeled and chopped*
> 1 *quart dry white wine*
> 2 *bay leaves*
> 2 *teaspoons thyme*
> 1 *7- to 10-pound smoked shoulder of pork (or a ham butt)*

Les Viandes

> Broth (or water), enough to cover the
>   meat
> 5 shallots, peeled and minced
> 5 tablespoons light cream
> 2 tablespoons Dijon-style mustard
> Salt
> Freshly ground black pepper

Heat the oil and 2 tablespoons of the butter, and sauté the
leeks (or onions) and the carrots until soft but not brown. Add
the wine, bay leaves and thyme. Cook for 15 minutes, uncovered.

Place the pork on top of this vegetable mixture. Add
enough broth (or water) to cover the meat and cook for about
2 hours, or until very tender.

Meanwhile, cook the shallots in the remaining 2 tablespoons of butter. Add a few tablespoons of the cooking juices.
Reduce the liquid by cooking, uncovered, for 5 minutes.

Drain the meat, place it on a warm serving dish and slice.
Add the cream and mustard to the shallots, correct the seasoning with salt and pepper and spoon the sauce over the slices
of pork. Serve at once.

Poulet à la Crème Charollaise

Chicken Cooked in Sweet White Wine with Herbs and Enriched with
Cream, Egg Yolks and Lemon

A succulent dish served with rice or homemade noodles and
mushrooms. It can be prepared either with sweet white wine
or with sweet sherry.

> For 8 people:

> 2 tablespoons vegetable oil
> 5 tablespoons sweet butter
> 2 4-pound chickens, each cut into 8 pieces
> Salt
> Freshly ground white pepper
> Nutmeg

Meats

153

> 1 garlic clove, peeled
> 2 bay leaves
> Thyme
> 1½ cups sweet white dessert wine (or sweet sherry)
> 3 cups light cream
> 4 egg yolks
> Juice of 2 lemons
> Cayenne pepper
> Salt

Heat the oil and butter in a heavy pan and sauté the pieces of chicken on all sides for 15 minutes, turning with a pair of tongs. Sprinkle with salt, pepper and nutmeg. Cook for 5 minutes, then add the garlic clove, bay leaves, thyme and wine. Cook, covered, for 30 to 40 minutes, until tender. Remove the chicken to an ovenproof serving dish, cover with a sheet of foil, and keep it in a 250° oven.

Add the cream to the wine sauce, scrape up the coagulated juices and cook for 10 minutes, uncovered. Beat the egg yolks in a bowl. Gradually add the sauce to the yolks, stirring constantly. Stir in the lemon juice, cayenne and salt and pour over the chicken. The sauce should be smooth and thick enough to coat the pieces of chicken. Keep the chicken in the oven for 5 to 10 minutes, then serve.

Poulet à la Moutarde

Broiled Chicken Spread with Onion, Mustard and Bread Crumbs and Served with a Shallot, Wine and Herb Sauce

A superb Lyon treat, this must be made with young, plump chickens and is best served with a dry white wine, *Estouffade de Carottes* (p. 179), *Galette aux Pommes de Terre* (p. 182) or *Gratin Forestière* (p. 193).

For 8 people:

> 4 plump tender chickens
> Salt

Les Viandes

Freshly ground black pepper
1½ *to 2 sticks sweet butter, melted*
  2 *tablespoons vegetable oil*
  5 *onions, minced*
  3 *tablespoons Dijon-style mustard*
  1 *cup bread crumbs*
  8 *shallots, finely chopped*
⅔ *cup red wine vinegar*
    Salt
 10 *peppercorns, crushed*
  6 *tablespoons fresh herbs (tarragon, chervil, chives).*
      cut with scissors
    Watercress

Split the chickens down the back. Flatten them with the side of a cleaver or a mallet. Sprinkle both sides with salt, pepper and melted butter. Cook the chickens, skin side up, under a broiler for 15 minutes, basting them with more butter.

Meanwhile, cook the onions in butter and oil until soft and mushy. Place them in a bowl and mix them with the mustard.

Preheat oven to 350°.

Spread the onion-mustard purée on the chickens, then sprinkle the bread crumbs all over them, pressing with your hands so that they hold well. Bake for 35 minutes.

Cook the shallots with the vinegar, uncovered, over high heat. Reduce the sauce to about 10 tablespoons. Add salt, peppercorns and fresh herbs and pass the sauce in a separate bowl along with the chicken, surrounded with watercress.

Poulet au Fromage

Chicken Baked with a Wine, Mustard and Cheese Sauce

A classic in Burgundy gastronomy. Serve with a chilled white or good rosé wine. Superb with *Gâteau de Pommes de Terre* (p. 185), *Paillasson* (p. 190) or *Purée de Fenouil* (p. 206). It can be prepared ahead of time and reheated.

Meats

For 8 people:

3 *broiler chickens, each cut into 6 to 8 pieces*
3 *tablespoons vegetable oil*
5 *tablespoons sweet butter*
  Salt
  Freshly ground black pepper
  Cayenne pepper
2 *cups shredded Swiss cheese*
1 *cup dry white wine*
2 *tablespoons Dijon-style mustard*
1 *cup light cream*
1 *2-inch piece of fresh ginger, grated (optional)*
  Pinch of nutmeg
  Bread crumbs
3 *tablespoons grated Swiss cheese*

Sauté the pieces of chicken on all sides for 5 minutes in the oil and 4 tablespoons of the butter in a large skillet. Sprinkle with salt, pepper and cayenne and cook, uncovered, over low heat for 45 minutes.

Preheat the oven to 375°.

Place the pieces of chicken in an ovenproof dish. Stir the shredded cheese into the cooking juices which are left in the skillet and add the wine, mustard and cream (and ginger, if desired). Heat gently, stirring, while adding salt, pepper, and nutmeg. Pour over the pieces of chicken, sprinkle with bread crumbs and grated cheese. Dot with the remaining butter and bake for 20 to 30 minutes. Serve golden and sumptuous in its baking dish.

Note: After the pieces of chicken are sautéed, you may want to cook 4 leeks (white part only) in 3 tablespoons of sweet butter until soft, and add them to the sauce around the chicken before baking. It thickens the sauce, and I find the dish becomes truly superb that way.

Les Viandes

Poulet au Vinaigre

Sautéed Chicken Seasoned with Vinegar, Garlic, Wine, Mustard and
Cream

One of Burgundy's oldest treats, when sweet-and-sour flavoring was commonly used and wild boar was cooked with a honey sauce.

For 8 people:

- 6 *tablespoons sweet butter*
- 1 *tablespoon vegetable oil*
- 3 *broilers, each cut into 8 pieces*
  Salt
  Freshly ground pepper
- 10 *garlic cloves, unpeeled*
- ½ to ⅔ *cup red wine vinegar*
- 1 *cup dry white wine*
- 5 *teaspoons Dijon-style mustard*
- 2 *tablespoons tomato paste*
- 3 *tablespoons heavy cream*
- 2 *tablespoons cognac*
- 2 *tablespoons fresh herbs (chives, parsley or dill), finely chopped*

Preheat the oven to 275°.

Heat 2 tablespoons of the butter and oil in a heavy-bottomed pan. Dry the chicken pieces with a kitchen towel and add them to the pan. Sauté on all sides, turning with tongs, for about 10 minutes, or until each piece is golden. Add salt and pepper and the garlic cloves, cover, lower the heat and cook for 25 minutes. Remove from the stove, discard the cooking fat and put the garlic cloves aside. Keep the pieces of chicken, covered, in the oven.

Pour the vinegar into the pan and scrape up the coagulated juices from the bottom with a fork. Add the wine, mustard and tomato paste to the pan, stirring with the fork, and cook over medium heat for 3 minutes—no longer. Add the cream, the remaining butter and cognac, stirring all the time. Peel the garlic cloves and mash them into the sauce. Add the chicken and reheat for 3 to 5 minutes, stirring from time to time.

Meats

Check the seasoning. Sprinkle with fresh herbs and serve on a warm shallow dish.

Poulets aux Écrevisses

Sautéed Chicken Cooked with Shallots, Carrots, Wine, Cream and Shrimp

I found shrimp to be a perfectly acceptable substitute for the crayfish traditionally used in Burgundy with chicken. This is a dressy, festive dish and should be served accompanied by a green tossed salad only.

For 8 people:

- 2 *bay leaves*
  Thyme
- 24 *shrimps*
- 6 *tablespoons sweet butter*
- 2 *tablespoons vegetable oil*
- 2 *4-pound chickens, each cut into 8 pieces*
  Salt
  Freshly ground black pepper
- 3 *shallots, peeled and minced*
- 2 *carrots, peeled and diced*
- 2 *onions, peeled and minced*
- 2 *tablespoons cognac*
- ⅔ *cup dry white wine*
- 5 *tablespoons tomato paste*
- 1 *teaspoon saffron*
- 2 *garlic cloves, peeled*
- 6 *tablespoons thick cream*
- 2 *tablespoon tarragon (or other fresh herbs), chopped or whole*
  Cayenne pepper (if needed)

Put a large pot of salted water over high heat and add the bay leaves and thyme. Add the shrimp as soon as the water reaches the boiling point. Cook for 2 minutes. Let them cool in the broth, then peel them.

Meanwhile, heat 3 tablespoons of the butter and the oil in

a heavy skillet or *doufeu* pan and sauté the pieces of chicken in three batches. Season with salt and pepper and cook each piece on all sides by turning with kitchen tongs. Remove and set aside.

Add the remaining 3 tablespoons of butter, shallots, carrots and onions to the pan. Cook over low heat for 15 minutes. Add the cognac and wine and scrape the bottom of the pan vigorously. Add the tomato paste, saffron, garlic cloves and pieces of chicken. Cover and cook over medium heat for 30 minutes.

Add the shrimp and the cream and stir vigorously. Add half of the chopped herbs and cook, uncovered, for 5 to 10 minutes.

Check the seasoning and add more salt and pepper if necessary. (This dish should be highly seasoned.) Add cayenne if needed.

Transfer to a warm shallow dish. Sprinkle with the remaining chopped herbs and serve with plain rice.

Poulet Surprise

Chicken Breasts Baked with Onions, Tomatoes, Herbs, Sherry and Cream under a Crisp Crust of Cheese

Easy to prepare, this is delicious with homemade noodles (p. 215) or endives gratin or *Tomates au Fromage* (p. 211).

For 8 people:

2 *tablespoons vegetable oil*
4 *tablespoons sweet butter*
1 *pound onions, peeled and minced*
1½ *pounds tomatoes, skinned and seeded*
2 *chicken livers, chopped*
3 *teaspoons thyme*
3 *tablespoons sherry*
    Salt
    Freshly ground black pepper
4 *chicken breasts, split in half*
1 *cup light cream*
5 *tablespoons grated Swiss cheese*

Meats

159

Heat the oil and 2 tablespoons of the butter and cook the onions slowly until soft, then add the tomatoes, the chicken livers, thyme and sherry and simmer over very low heat for 1 hour. It will have the consistency of a purée. Add salt and pepper.

Sauté the chicken breasts on all sides for 1 or 2 minutes in the remaining butter. Place them in an ovenproof dish and cover with the purée. Pour the cream over the top and sprinkle with the grated cheese.

Place under the broiler until the cheese turns crisp and serve piping hot.

Poulet aux Noix

Sautéed Chicken Cooked with Mushrooms, Shallots, Garlic, Walnuts and Vermouth

This tasty dish is usually made with fresh walnuts in the eastern part of Burgundy. It is equally interesting prepared with dry walnuts or pecans, and served with *Purée de Fenouil* (p. 206), a green bean purée, *Gratin Trois* (p. 197) or *Gâteau au Céleri* (p. 183).

For 8 people:

2 teaspoons walnut or peanut oil
2 cups smoked lean salt pork, diced (½-inch pieces)
2 4-pound chickens, each cut into 8 pieces
Salt
Freshly ground black pepper
4 tablespoons brandy
Thyme
2 tablespoons vegetable oil
2 tablespoons sweet butter
3 pounds mushrooms, washed, dried, and cut in half
2 cups shelled, halved walnuts
4 shallots, peeled and minced
6 garlic cloves, peeled and minced
½ cup minced parsley
1½ cups dry white vermouth

Les Viandes

Heat the walnut or peanut oil in a heavy-bottomed pan and sauté the pork for 5 minutes, tossing. Remove the pork and set aside. Add the chicken pieces. Sprinkle them with salt and pepper and cook them on all sides for 10 minutes. Add the brandy and ignite, sprinkle with thyme, cover and cook over medium heat for 40 minutes.

Sauté the mushrooms in the vegetable oil and butter in another skillet, season them and add them along with the nut halves, pork, shallots, garlic and parsley to the chicken. Check the seasoning. Add the vermouth and cook for 15 minutes.

Spoon the chicken into a large, warm, shallow dish. Scrape the bottom of the skillet with a fork, reduce the sauce over very high heat and pour it over the chicken. Serve at once.

Le Steak à la Moutarde

T-bone Steak with a Mustard, Sherry and Cream Sauce

Any good T-bone prepared this way will acquire a Dijon accent and taste like Charolais.

This is splendid served with a *Gratin Dauphinois* (p. 187), a *Gâteau de Pommes de Terre* (p. 185), *Haricots Verts à la Crème* (p. 198) or *Petits Légumes* (p. 201).

> For each person:
>
> *1 tablespoon coarsely crushed black peppercorns*
> *1 good-size T-bone steak (about 1 inch thick)*
> *Vegetable oil*
> *Salt*
> *2 tablespoons sherry*
> *2 tablespoons heavy cream*
> *1 tablespoon Dijon-style mustard*

About 2 hours before cooking, press the peppercorns into both sides of the meat.

Preheat the oven to 300°.

Heat just enough oil in a skillet to coat the bottom and sear the meat on both sides over rather high heat. Turn the oven off, put the steak on a platter and put in the oven to keep warm.

Meats

Add salt and sherry to the coagulated juices in the skillet. Add the cream and mustard and scrape and stir vigorously. Bring to a boil while stirring and lower the heat. Cook for 5 minutes. Check the seasoning and pour the sauce over the steak.

Poulet aux Pruneaux

Chicken Cooked with Prunes and Wine

This superb dish comes from the north of Burgundy. It must be prepared a day in advance. The unctuous wine-and-prune sauce is rich in flavor yet lean (since you have time to degrease it thoroughly). An easy dish to serve. Reheat it over low heat just before the meal. It will need very little accompaniment: a crisp watercress or dandelion-green tossed salad and a hearty red wine.

For 4 people:

1 tablespoon peanut or olive oil
½ cup red wine (hearty Burgundy type)
2 tablespoons red wine vinegar
2 onions, sliced
2 garlic cloves, crushed and peeled
2 bay leaves
About 12 black peppercorns
2 teaspoons thyme
1 4-pound chicken, cut into 8 serving pieces
Salt
Freshly ground black pepper
2 teaspoons savory or marjoram
1 tablespoon peanut oil
½ cup diced lean salt pork
3 large onions, thinly sliced
1 teaspoon flour
1 cup red wine (hearty Burgundy type)
1 bay leaf
12 prunes

4 slices of bread
3 tablespoons sweet butter
2 tablespoons chopped parsley

Prepare a marinade by mixing together the first 8 ingredients. Pour it over the chicken. Sprinkle with salt and pepper, cover and leave in the refrigerator overnight, turning it once.

The next morning, lift the pieces of chicken from the marinade, dry them with paper towels and sprinkle them with savory.

Heat the oil in a large heavy skillet or a heavy-bottomed pan and sauté the pork over moderate heat. Add the chicken and sauté for about 10 minutes, turning each piece once with tongs. Transfer the chicken to a plate and add the onions to the pan. Sauté for 10 minutes, then add the chicken to the onions, sprinkle with flour, and let the chicken pieces brown for about 5 minutes, turning them once. Add the wine and the strained marinade. Cook, uncovered, over medium heat for 10 minutes, then add the bay leaf and the onions and herbs from the marinade and cook, uncovered, for 30 minutes.

Meanwhile, soak the prunes in tea or water for about 30 minutes and remove the pits. Add them to the chicken and cook for 15 minutes. Remove from the heat and let cool. Remove the pieces of chicken from the sauce. Skim the fat from the top of pan. Remove the skin of the chicken. Pass the sauce through a Moulinex mill or a blender.

The dish is now ready to be served whenever you need it. It can be kept in the refrigerator and will improve with reheating.

When ready to serve, place the pieces of chicken in a heavy-bottomed pan, taste the sauce and add salt, pepper, thyme or savory if needed and pour over the chicken. Cover and heat over low heat for 20 to 25 minutes.

Prepare the croutons by frying the slices of bread in butter or drying them in a hot oven. Rub them with a garlic clove. Place the chicken in a shallow dish, pour the sauce over it and place the golden croutons all around. Sprinkle with chopped parsley.

Meats

Poulet aux Raisins

Marinated Chicken Cooked with Cream and Grapes

A lovely fall dish, this chicken served with grapes must be marinated overnight for a richer flavor. Serve with *Gâteau de Pommes de Terre* (p. 185), *Gratin de Verdure* (p. 192), *Paillasson* (p. 190) or *Riz aux Herbes* (p. 216).

For 8 people:

1 cup dry white wine
1 tablespoon brandy
2 shallots, minced
2 garlic cloves, peeled
3 teaspoons thyme
2 bay leaves
10 peppercorns
4 tablespoons sweet butter
1 tablespoon vegetable oil
2 chickens, each cut into 8 pieces
Salt
Freshly ground black pepper
1 cup grapes (white or red), peeled with a sharp knife
1 cup cream

Prepare the marinade by mixing together the first 7 ingredients. Simmer it for a few minutes, then cool. Marinate the pieces of chicken overnight (or at least a few hours) on a lower shelf of the refrigerator.

When you are ready to prepare the dish, heat the butter and oil in a heavy-bottomed pan and sauté each piece of carefully dried chicken on all sides for 30 minutes. Sprinkle with salt and pepper and cover with a large sheet of foil to keep warm. Meanwhile, simmer the marinade, uncovered, in a saucepan for 20 minutes. Add the cream and simmer 5 minutes longer to make a sauce.

Preheat the oven to 375°. Place the pieces of chicken in an ovenproof dish, add the peeled grapes and pour the sauce over it. Heat in the oven for 10 to 15 minutes and serve.

Les Viandes

Rôti de Porc de Beaune

Marinated Pork Roast Baked with Spices, Mustard and Wine and
Served with Mushrooms and Cranberry Sauce

This splendid dish includes such a variety of flavors and textures that it is better to serve it with little accompaniment—perhaps only sliced apples sautéed in butter or cabbage purée (p. 196) or homemade noodles (p. 215). The chicken livers add texture to the sauce, but you may prefer to use simply a flour-and-butter paste. The pork must be marinated for twenty-four hours.

For 8 people:

    1 5-pound boneless roast of pork
      Salt
    2 cups red wine
    1 cup port (or good sweet red vermouth)
    5 peppercorns
    5 juniper berries
    1 clove
    1 bay leaf
      Peel of 1 orange, finely chopped
      Peel of ½ lemon, finely chopped
    3 tablespoons Dijon-style mustard
   10 chicken livers (or a mixture of 2 tablespoons flour
         and 2 tablespoons butter)
    6 tablespoons sweet butter
    2 tablespoons vegetable oil
    1 pound mushrooms, trimmed and sliced
      Salt
      Pepper
    4 tablespoons cranberry sauce
    1 teaspoon cinnamon

Rub the pork with salt. Mix all the marinade ingredients (salt, wine, port, peppercorns, juniper berries, clove, bay leaf and orange and lemon peel) and pour over the pork. Cover and keep in a cool place for 24 hours, basting the pork at least five times.

Preheat the oven to 375°.

Meats

Remove the pork from the marinade and place it in a shallow baking pan. Spread the mustard over the entire surface of the roast. Pour the marinade into the bottom of the pan. Bake for 2 hours, uncovered, basting from time to time.

When the roast is almost done, sauté the chicken livers in 3 tablespoons of the butter in a skillet for a few minutes. Crush them with a fork and set aside. Heat the remaining butter, add the oil and sauté the mushrooms, stirring with a wooden spoon. Add the marinade in the baking pan (discard the bay leaf and the orange and lemon peel), the chicken livers, salt, pepper, the cranberry sauce and the cinnamon. Stir well. Cook over low heat for 2 minutes, or until smooth.

Place the pork roast on a warm serving dish. Slice it and season with salt and pepper. Pour some of the sauce over the slices and pass the rest of the sauce in a bowl.

Tarte Bourguignonne

A Meat, Vegetable and Herb Pie

A tasty dish served on most festive occasions in Burgundy. Serve it with a large bowl of strongly seasoned green salad and a hearty red wine. It is better cold on the third day than it is on the first—a perfect picnic or buffet dish, but it is lighter when served warm.

For 8 people:

Pastry (a 10-inch shell)

2½ cups unbleached flour
Pinch of salt
9 tablespoons sweet butter
3 tablespoons lard

Filling

---

1 pound lean salt pork (or country ham), diced
1 pound boneless veal shoulder, diced
1 cup dry white wine
4 onions, peeled and thinly sliced

Les Viandes

4 garlic cloves, peeled and minced
½ cup brandy (cognac, if possible)
3 tablespoons thyme
2 bay leaves
8 tablespoons finely chopped parsley
Salt
Freshly ground pepper
1 egg yolk, beaten together with 1 tablespoon water

The night before:

Prepare the pastry in a food processor or else place the flour, salt, butter and lard in a large bowl and rub them together between the tips of your fingers very lightly and quickly. Add 6 tablespoons (or less) cold water and blend well. Place the dough on a table and press with the heel of your hand away from you three or four times. Gather the dough with a spatula, place it in a bowl, cover with a towel and store in the refrigerator overnight.

Marinate the pork and veal in the wine with the onions, garlic, brandy, thyme and bay leaves overnight in a large covered bowl.

Two hours before the meal:

Roll out the dough as thin as possible (¼ inch). Cover the bottom and sides of a buttered pie dish with half of the pastry.

Preheat the oven to 400°.

Drain the contents of the marinade and set aside. Discard the bay leaves. Pass the meat and onions briefly through a grinder or a food processor. (The mixture should not be too thin.) Add the chopped parsley and salt and pepper and place in heaping tablespoonfuls on the pastry shell approximately ¼ inch apart. Cover with the remaining pastry and close the edges of the pastry with moistened fingers.

With a pair of kitchen scissors, open a hole about 2 inches wide in the center of the top crust and place a little chimney made of waxed paper about 2 or 3 inches high into it, so the steam will escape during cooking.

Brush the pastry surface with the egg yolk mixture and bake for 10 minutes. Reduce the heat to 350° and bake for 40 minutes more.

Meanwhile, bring the marinade to a boil and reduce it to about ¼ cup. Pour this into the little chimney after the pie has been in the oven for 20 minutes.

Remove the chimney and serve the pie warm.

Meats

Travers de Porc aux Herbes

Spareribs with Fresh Herbs

A lively way to prepare spareribs—they will be delicately crisp and fragrant. Serve with a tossed salad and a purée of celery, cabbage or turnip and potatoes, a *Gratin Dauphinois* (p. 187) or a *Galette aux Pommes de Terre* (p. 182).

For 8 people:

8 *pounds of spareribs (preferably the country-style back ribs, which are meatier), cut into bite-sized pieces with a pair of scissors*
Salt
Freshly ground pepper
2 *tablespoons lemon verbena, fresh or dried (or lemon pepper, sold in supermarkets)*
2 *tablespoons thyme*
2 *tablespoons minced fresh coriander*
3 *tablespoons minced fresh herbs*

Preheat the oven to 400°.

Place the spareribs in a shallow roasting pan and pierce all over with a fork. Cover with a sheet of aluminum foil and bake for 35 minutes. Remove the foil; skim and discard all fat. Reduce the oven heat to 375°. The ribs should be crisp. While they are steaming hot, sprinkle with salt, pepper, lemon verbena (or lemon pepper), thyme and coriander and press them into the meat with the back of a spoon. Continue to bake, uncovered, until crispy brown and well done—about 45 minutes. Place the ribs on a warm serving dish, sprinkle with herbs and serve at once.

Les Viandes

Veau à la Moutarde

Veal Sautéed with Shallots, Wine and Mustard

A sharp and fragrant dish, quick to prepare and easy to serve, it can be accompanied by steamed rice, sprinkled with melted butter and a few drops of lemon juice, and a green tossed salad.

For 8 people:

> 8 *thin slices of veal cut from the leg (⅓-inch-thick scallops or cutlets cut in 2-inch strips)*
> *Salt*
> *Freshly ground black pepper*
> 2 *tablespoons sweet butter*
> 3 *tablespoons vegetable oil*
> 8 *shallots, peeled and finely chopped*
> 1 *cup dry white wine*
> 1½ *cups heavy cream*
> 2 *tablespoons (or more) Dijon-style mustard*
> *Juice of 1 lemon*

Sprinkle the veal scallops with salt and pepper and sauté them on both sides in butter and oil. Remove them and set aside. Add the shallots and then the wine to the skillet and cook until the shallots are soft. Add the cream and cook, stirring, until the cream is heated through. Remove the pan from the heat and add the mustard. Stir well and add the veal to the skillet. Continue stirring and heat for 2 minutes. Pour into a warm shallow serving dish. Sprinkle with lemon juice and serve at once.

Meats

Viande aux Baies

Marinated Poultry Cooked with White Wine, Vegetables and Herbs

This can be prepared with chicken, turkey or rabbit. Serve with homemade noodles (p. 215), chestnuts or sautéed mushrooms, *Gratin d'Oignons* (p. 186) or *Gratin Rouge* (p. 195).

For 8 people:

3 *broilers, cut into 8 serving pieces each (or an equal amount of rabbit or turkey)*
3 *cups white wine*
2 *carrots, peeled and chopped*
2 *onions, peeled and chopped*
2 *teaspoons thyme*
2 *bay leaves*
10 *peppercorns*
3 *tablespoons vegetable oil*
1½ *cups bacon, cut in small dice*
Salt
Freshly ground black pepper
1 *cup blackberry jelly (or raspberry jelly)*
Juice of 1 lemon
½ *cup ripe blackberries (or blueberries or any berries available)*

Marinate the pieces of chicken (or rabbit or turkey) in the wine with the carrots, onions, thyme, bay leaves and peppercorns overnight.

Heat the oil in a large skillet, add the bacon and, after a few minutes, sauté the pieces of chicken on all sides for about 10 minutes, or until golden. Add the vegetables, then the marinade. Season with salt and pepper and cook for 1 hour, or until the meat is done. Remove the meat and keep it warm in a low oven (200°).

Remove the bay leaves and pass the marinade through a sieve, crushing the vegetables with a wooden spoon, into a saucepan. Bring to a boil and let it reduce, uncovered. Stir in the jelly, lemon juice and berries. Put the meat back into the sauce and pour into a warm serving dish at once.

Les Viandes

If you can't find the fresh berries, omit them. The dish is interesting enough without them.

Veau Meurette

Sautéed Veal Cooked with Herbs, Onions and Red Wine

A delectable version of an old Burgundy favorite. It is high in flavor, yet light. It can be served with homemade noodles (p. 215), braised endives or celery purée.

For 8 people:

3 pounds veal breast, boned and cut into 1½-inch pieces
5 pounds veal shoulder, cut into large pieces
Salt
Freshly ground black pepper
2 tablespoons sweet butter
2 tablespoons vegetable oil
1½ cups diced lean salt pork
2 garlic cloves, peeled and crushed
2 bay leaves
2 teaspoons thyme
5 cups hearty red wine
12 small, whole white onions, peeled (or 4 big onions, sliced)
3 tablespoons minced fresh herbs (chives, parsley, tarragon)

Preheat the oven to 350°. Sprinkle the veal with salt and pepper and brown it on all sides in the butter and oil for 5 minutes. Set it aside. Sauté the diced pork and garlic, then put the veal back in the pan, add the bay leaves, thyme, wine and onions. Cover and bake for about 2 hours. Remove the veal and keep it warm in a serving dish.

Degrease carefully. Reduce the sauce, and if you wish, pass it through a sieve. Correct the seasoning. Pour the sauce over the veal. Sprinkle with herbs and serve at once.

Meats

Les Légumes

Vegetables

The sample of vegetable recipes I have discovered in Burgundy dating from the Middle Ages to today is wide and rich. Vegetables have always been used with imagination and ingenuity. They are not the center of a meal as they are in Provence, but they enhance or complement every meat, fish or poultry dish.

There is a quaint *fricot,* a medieval dish made with pears and potatoes sautéed in butter to accompany blood sausage. There are chestnuts and onions cooked with red wine to serve with pork or wild boar.

Sorrel purée thickened with eggs and cream does wonders with fish, in omelets, as soup. There are twenty-two ways of preparing potatoes—at least one for every occasion, although, to my taste, *gratin dauphinois* can be served with meat, fish and fowl with equal success.

Vegetables also mingle to enhance their individual taste. There is *ganèfle,* a gratin of grated potatoes, flour and eggs, covered with onions, cheese and truffles, cooked in butter, mixed with chestnuts, goose liver, brandy, cream and Madeira wine.

But there are also simpler dishes—*crosnes* (the Chinese artichokes) sautéed in butter; cardoons (the top stalks have a delicious flavor) prepared with cream or beef marrow and cheese, and for New Year's Eve cooked with onions and anchovies; stews of lima beans, sorrel, spinach and Swiss chard; gratins of zucchini with Swiss cheese, cream, eggs and garlic; white onions cooked unpeeled, then puréed with cream and mustard; dandelion greens cooked with lard; pumpkin prepared in all kinds of ways; and, finally, mushrooms.

In Burgundy, mushrooms come in all colors, tastes and

Les Légumes

sizes. There are sautéed *mousserons* seasoned with herbs and lemon juice or cooked with dry white wine and enriched with cream. There are *cèpes* and *bolets* mixed with garlic, parsley and diced country ham and cooked under the ashes for five hours. There are *chanterelles, girolles* and *morilles* (morels), mushrooms sautéed with shallots and enriched with cream. There are marinated mushrooms kept in walnut oil and herbs, stuffed with shallots and garlic, and a curious dish made of cooked leeks and *morilles,* bacon, shallots, thyme and red wine. The mushroom dishes I have selected can all be prepared with the white variety easily available fresh in all American supermarkets and vegetable markets, since canned or dry mushrooms have never proven satisfactory. Make sure the mushrooms are firm and creamy, and use them the very day you buy them. Freshness is always important and, ideally, all vegetables should be prepared within a few hours of the time you pick or buy them. Select them carefully and give proper attention to their color and texture.

The following are the vegetables most commonly used in Burgundy that are available in the United States.

Artichokes *(les Artichauts)*
It is mainly the globe variety that is used in Burgundy. They must be eaten fresh or the choke will be too large and the leaves too leathery. Fresh firm artichokes squeak when you squeeze them. Artichokes are stuffed with artichoke bottoms, country ham, sorrel, mushrooms and cream, then cooked in butter. Wine tastes awful with artichokes, so serve only cold water or cold beer with them.

Asparagus *(les Asperges)*
They must have closed tips and firm stalks. They are served parboiled, seasoned with cream that has been reduced with herbs and pepper, or in a thick custard garnished with a bowl of cream seasoned with lemon and herbs.

Beans—Dried Beans *(les Haricots Secs)*
The white beans are used in purées with milk and butter, warm in salads, with tomatoes and pork; the red are often cooked with red wine.

Beans—String Beans *(les Haricots Verts)*
They snap between your fingers when they are fresh. The flat green beans are used in soups; the round plump ones and the yellow ones, in warm salads with cream or in gratins. Always cook them by putting them into a pan with a large amount of salted boiling water; bring to a second boil, uncover and simmer until tender.

Vegetables

Cabbage *(le Chou)*
Head cabbage or Savoy varieties are used in purée with pork, in soups and stuffed. They must not be overcooked.

Cardoons *(les Cardons)*
Only the tender stalks of the cardoons are eaten. Trim the strings as for celery. They are parboiled, then cooked with butter and anchovies or used in soups, sautéed with shallots and white wine and enriched with slices of zucchini and chopped parsley.

Celery *(le Céleri)*
Use it in soups, raw in salad, braised with pork or puréed.

Chestnuts *(les Châtaignes; les Marrons)*
They are used in soups, in *crépinettes,* sautéed with truffles and goose livers or with diced potatoes, and in pastry. In America it is easiest to buy them in a can, already blanched and peeled, but they don't taste the same as the fresh kind.

Chinese Artichokes *(les Crosnes)*
These are available in Chinese markets. They must be carefully cleaned, then blanched before you sauté them in butter with herbs or simmer them with cream and parsley.

Dandelion Greens *(les Pissenlits)*
Crisp and fresh, they make a delicious tossed salad seasoned with warm vinegar and crisp dices of bacon.

Endives *(les Endives)*
They must be as small as possible and should be blanched in a large amount of salted water. Cooked, they accompany fish as well as pork or poultry. Raw, they make crisp, lively salads.

Garlic *(l'Ail)*
Garlic has been used in both cooking and medicine since the Chinese, the Egyptians and the Hebrews discovered it. It must be firm and fresh. Do not use a clove of garlic that is yellow and soft and has a green sprout in the center. Buy garlic in a wreath in Italian or Spanish markets and hang it in a dry place.

Burgundy cooking uses a lot of garlic, mostly cooked. Whereas raw garlic is potent, cooked garlic tastes sweet and light.

Les Légumes

Leeks *(les Poireaux)*

They are called "the asparagus of the poor." In the United States they are not available in every supermarket but are well worth looking for. Delicious in soups; with crisp diced ham; in gratins with herbs, nutmeg and cream; in *flamiche,* a pie enriched with cream and eggs; or slowly cooked and puréed to thicken fish or meat dishes; or served as a side dish.

Mushrooms *(les Champignons)*

There is a wide choice of mushrooms in Burgundy. Morels grow in the spring, chanterelles in the summer, and *cèpes* later, but there are endless varieties. They can be sautéed with garlic and parsley; creamed with dry white wine, herbs and cream; deep-fried and sprinkled with herbs; stuffed with country ham and broiled; stuffed with snails; sautéed with chestnuts; or cooked in a gratin with potatoes.

The cultivated variety, sold in supermarkets, will be delicious in the following recipes, but you must choose firm, plump mushrooms with a smooth creamy cap and cook them the day you buy them. You can always reheat them later. Never use canned or dried mushrooms.

Onions *(les Oignons)*

Onions are the basis of Lyon cooking and are also widely used in Burgundy. Yellow onions are for omelets and tarts; little white onions, for *meurette* sauce and with fresh vegetables as garnish; red Spanish onions, for *court-bouillon* and marinade. Onions are used in purée to thicken meat or fish sauces or in stews.

Potatoes *(les Pommes de Terre)*

These were indeed brought to Europe from America for the benefit of the poor, but they have come a long way in Burgundy and are now the basis of many sumptuous dishes. A *paillasson* is as elegant as it is delicious. Stuffed with ham, shallots and herbs and cooked in a rich beef broth, or sliced with onions and sautéed in butter in the Lyonnaise way, potatoes become truly refined treats.

The *rapée,* a rich mixture of grated potatoes, fresh cheese, cream and brandy, cooked in walnut oil, and the various *gratin dauphinois* and *savoyard* have given superior status to this vegetable.

Pumpkin *(la Citrouille, le Potiron)*

Used in the famous Lyon soup, in gratins with cream and

Vegetables

eggs, puréed with garlic, in cake, in custard, in preserves, pumpkin is one of the staples of Burgundy cooking. Acorn, Hubbard or butternut squash can be used in the following recipes, but remember they all need a lot of salt.

Shallots *(les Échalotes)*
Not available in every supermarket, but they are well worth looking for. They keep well and are truly compulsory if you want to cook *bourguignon.* They have a pungent light flavor, and are used in practically every dish.

Spinach *(les Épinards)*
One of the few vegetables you can buy frozen without regretting it. Four ten-ounce boxes will do for eight people. Spinach can be used in soups, omelets and stuffing.

Turnips *(les Navets)*
The little purple or pink ones are blanched, then cooked with cream, herbs and a pinch of sugar and are used in many gratins and soups.

Bonnet de Chou

Baked Cabbage Leaves with Sausages, Apples and Sage

A perfect treat for a cold winter night.

For 8 people:

2 *large heads of cabbage*
½ *pound sliced bacon*
8 *country sausages (Polish or Italian, highly seasoned), sliced*
3 *large Granny Smith apples, peeled, cored and quartered*
2 *teaspoons sage*
3 *tablespoons lard*
1 *spicy dried sausage, sliced*

Preheat the oven to 325°.

Cook the cabbage in a pot of boiling salted water for 20 minutes. Drain well.

Cover the bottom of a large mold or a large ovenproof bowl with the sliced bacon, then spread with half of the cab-

Les Légumes

bage leaves. Cover with the sausages and apples, then with the other half of the cabbage leaves. Sprinkle with sage and dot with lard. Bake for about 4 hours. Unmold and serve surrounded by the sliced sausage.

Champignons de Dijon

Mushrooms in a Dijon Sauce

A sumptuous dish to serve with a good smoked or Virginia-style ham sliced paper-thin or with a roast, it can also be an elegant hors d'oeuvre.

For 8 people:

2 pounds small whole white mushrooms, trimmed, washed and dried (or simply well cleaned)
Juice of 2 lemons
Salt
Freshly ground black pepper
8 tablespoons sweet butter
2 tablespoons vegetable oil
4 shallots, peeled and minced
2 egg yolks
1 cup light cream
2 tablespoons Dijon-style mustard
½ cup dry white wine
3 tablespoons finely chopped parsley

Prepare the mushrooms and sprinkle them with the lemon juice, salt and pepper.

Heat 7 tablespoons of the butter and the oil in a large, heavy-bottomed skillet and add the mushrooms over medium heat. Cook for 5 to 6 minutes. Remove them and their liquid and set aside.

Add the minced shallots to the skillet with 1 tablespoon of butter. Cook for 5 to 6 minutes over low heat.

Mix the egg yolks, cream and mustard in a bowl. Stir in the wine and the mushroom liquid and pour this mixture over the shallots. Add the mushrooms and cook over medium heat, stirring, for 5 minutes.

Vegetables

177

Pour into a warm shallow dish, sprinkle with parsley and serve at once.

Chou Farci

Cabbage Stuffed with Apples, Prunes and Herbs and Cooked with Wine and Sausages

A light and sophisticated Burgundy version of the traditional stuffed cabbage. Serve with a cabbage purée (p. 196) and a chilled white wine.

For 8 people:

1 large head of cabbage, trimmed
½ pound cooked ham, chopped
½ pound lean salt pork or bacon, chopped
½ cup cooked rice
2 garlic cloves, peeled and crushed
2 Granny Smith apples, peeled and chopped
1 whole egg, beaten
Freshly ground black pepper
6 prunes, pitted and chopped
3 teaspoons thyme
1 teaspoon freshly grated nutmeg
Salt
8 slices thickly cut bacon (or fatback)
8 whole prunes, pitted
2 cups dry white wine
2 large, highly seasoned sausages (preferably Polish)
3 tablespoons chopped parsley

Put the cabbage in a large pot of boiling salted water and cook for 20 minutes. Drain.

Remove the tough core with a small sharp knife and discard it. Cut out the center of the cabbage. Chop it and place it in a large bowl. Add the chopped meats, rice, garlic, apples, egg, pepper, chopped prunes, thyme and nutmeg. Stir carefully and check the seasoning before adding the salt. (This mixture is the stuffing.) Set aside the outer portion of the cabbage.

Preheat oven to 375°.

Les Légumes

Place four 20-inch-long pieces of string flat on a table in a cross (+) pattern. Cover them with the strips of bacon. Place the cabbage in the center. Open the leaves (at the bottom) with your fingers. Spoon most of the stuffing mixture into the center and the rest between the leaves of the cabbage, pushing with your fingers. Close the cabbage leaves and tie the string around it. It should be a neat package. (The bacon strips around the strings will prevent them from cutting through the leaves.)

Place the cabbage, tied end up, in a deep narrow pan barely wider than the cabbage. Place the whole prunes around it and cover with the wine. Cover the pan with a lid or heavy sheet of aluminum foil and bake for 1½ hours. Add the sausages and cook for 30 minutes longer.

Holding the string, lift the cabbage from the pan, and place it on a warm serving dish. Remove and discard the strings and bacon strips. Slice the sausages. Cut the cabbage into wedges like a pie and serve it surrounded with prunes and sausages. Pour 3 tablespoons of the cooking juice over it. Sprinkle with pepper and parsley and serve with a separate bowl of cabbage purée.

Estouffade de Carottes

Carrots Seasoned with Mustard and Butter

A lovely accompaniment to a roasted piece of meat or a broiled chicken. Best if you can find fresh young carrots.

For 8 people:

- 3 *pounds small carrots, peeled and thinly sliced*
- ¾ *cup sweet butter*
- 1 *tablespoon vegetable oil*
  Salt
- 1 *teaspoon sugar*
- 4 *slices homemade bread*
- 2 *tablespoons flour*
- 2 *tablespoons Dijon-style mustard*
- 3 *tablespoons broth (or meat or chicken juices)*
- 3 *tablespoons minced parsley*

Vegetables

Bring a large pot of salted water to the boil. Add the carrots and cook for 4 to 6 minutes. Drain.

Heat ¾ cup of the butter and the oil in a heavy skillet. Add the carrots, salt and sugar and stir with a wooden spoon. Cook slowly for 10 minutes. Add 6 tablespoons of water and cook, uncovered, until all the water has evaporated.

Meanwhile, make the croutons: Fry the slices of bread on both sides in a skillet with 1 tablespoon butter, then cut each into 4 triangles.

Mix 1 tablespoon butter with the flour and add to the carrots. Add the mustard and broth. (Meat juices may be used here, previously obtained by scraping the bottom of a pan used for cooking a roast or chicken and adding 3 tablespoons of water or wine.) Stir with a wooden spoon and cook for 3 minutes.

Pour into a warm serving dish. Sprinkle with parsley, place the croutons around, and serve.

Flan de Pommes de Terre à la Bourguignonne

Sautéed Potatoes Baked with Crisp Pork, Onions, Spices, Cream and Eggs

A true wonder.

For 8 people:

¾ *cup diced lean salt pork (or shredded slices of prosciutto ham or Virginia or country-type ham)*
3 *tablespoons vegetable oil*
8 *or 9 onions, peeled and thinly sliced*
4 *tablespoons sweet butter*
8 *or 9 potatoes, peeled, sliced, rinsed in cold water and dried*
 Salt
 Freshly ground white pepper
 Pinch of nutmeg
2 *teaspoons ground coriander*
2 *cups light cream*
4 *eggs, well beaten*

Les Légumes

If you use salt pork, place it in a heavy skillet and sauté it over low heat for 5 minutes with 1 tablespoon of oil. If you use ham, sauté for 1 minute only. Add 2 tablespoons of oil and the onions and cook over low heat for 15 minutes. Then remove with a slotted spoon into a large bowl. Add the butter to the skillet and sauté the potatoes over medium heat for about 30 minutes, tossing them from time to time. Remove with a slotted spoon into the bowl with the onions.

Preheat the oven to 400°.

Spread the salt pork or ham and the onions in an oiled ovenproof dish. Sprinkle with salt, pepper, nutmeg, and coriander, then add the potatoes and sprinkle again with pepper, nutmeg and coriander. Beat the cream and the eggs together and pour over the onion-potato dish. Place it in the oven and cook for about 20 minutes. It should be golden crisp and smell delicious.

Frites à la Crème

French-Fried Potatoes and Sautéed Mushrooms Seasoned with a
Garlic, Egg, Vinegar and Cream Sauce

Truly delicious. The original recipe calls for wild mushrooms, but ordinary mushrooms will do.

> For 8 people:
>
> *Oil for deep-frying*
> *9 potatoes, peeled and cut into sticks*
> *2 pounds fresh mushrooms, cleaned and sliced*
> *3 tablespoons sweet butter*
> *1 tablespoon vegetable oil*
> *2 garlic cloves, peeled and minced*
> *2 eggs*
> *1 tablespoon wine vinegar*
> *3 tablespoons light cream*
> *Salt*
> *Freshly ground black pepper*

Deep-fry the potatoes. Drain on paper towels and keep warm in a turned-off oven.

Vegetables

Meanwhile, sauté the mushrooms in the butter and oil. Mix the garlic, eggs, vinegar, cream, salt and pepper in a bowl.

Place the potatoes in a shallow dish. Add the mushrooms and pour the sauce over them. Toss gently and serve. This dish must be served very warm.

Galette aux Pommes de Terre

A Crisp Potato and Salt Pork Cake Seasoned with Fresh Herbs

Golden and crisp outside, moist inside, this makes a glorious winter meal served by itself or as an accompaniment.

For 8 people:

4 *onions, peeled and minced*
2 *tablespoons lard*
2 *pounds potatoes, peeled and thickly sliced*
 Salt
 Freshly ground white pepper
 Thyme
2 *bay leaves*
2 *pounds lean salt pork (or country ham), cut into small dice*
4 *tablespoons sweet butter (or lard)*
3 *tablespoons chervil (or parsley or chives), finely chopped*

Preheat the oven to 350°.

Sauté the onions in hot lard. Put them in a round ovenproof dish. Dry the potato slices thoroughly with paper towels and add half of them to the onions. Sprinkle with salt, pepper and thyme and place the bay leaves on top.

Sauté the salt pork for a few minutes and put on top of the potatoes. Add the remainder of the potatoes and sprinkle with pepper only. Press down hard with your hands and dot with butter (or lard).

Bake for 1 hour. Run a knife around the inside edge of the dish to loosen and unmold on a warm round serving dish. Sprinkle with herbs and serve very warm.

Les Légumes

Gâteau au Céleri

A Celery, Parsley and Egg Gratin

Light and delicate, this is a lovely first course, and also a splendid accompaniment to pork, chicken or beef. The celery leaves add color and flavor to the dish—don't discard them!

For 8 people:

2 *celery hearts (about 1 pound each) with leaves*
3 *tablespoons minced parsley*
4 *egg yolks*
1½ *cups grated Swiss cheese*
Salt
Freshly ground pepper
Freshly grated nutmeg
4 *egg whites*

Cook the celery hearts in a large saucepan of salted water for 20 minutes. Drain and purée them in a food processer or a Moulinex mill. Add the parsley, egg yolks, cheese, salt, pepper and nutmeg.

Preheat oven to 375°.

Whip the egg whites and fold them gently into the celery-and-egg-yolk mixture. Pour into a buttered ovenproof dish and bake for 20 minutes. The crust should be firm.

Serve with a tomato sauce (p. 65), a Béchamel sauce or by itself.

Gâteau de Carottes

A Carrot Cake with Mushroom, Shallots, Cheese and Herbs

A superb first course for a light meal, or a colorful accompaniment to any meat dish.

Vegetables

For 8 people:

2 *pounds carrots, peeled and quartered*
¼ *pound mushrooms, diced*
2 *shallots, peeled and finely chopped*
4 *tablespoons sweet butter*
1 *tablespoon vegetable oil*
4 *to 5 eggs, beaten*
3 *tablespoons cream*
½ *cup grated Swiss cheese*
2 *tablespoons finely chopped chervil*
  Salt
  Freshly ground black pepper
  Freshly grated nutmeg

Garnish

Cabbage or spinach leaves, blanched
2 *tablespoons minced parsley*

Cook the carrots for about 20 minutes in a saucepan of boiling, salted water. Drain.

Meanwhile, sauté the mushrooms and shallots for 5 minutes in 2 tablespoons of butter and 1 tablespoon of oil in a large skillet.

Purée the carrots, mushrooms and shallots in a blender, a food processor or a Moulinex mill (for a less mushy consistency).

Add the eggs, cream, cheese and chervil to the purée; add salt and pepper to taste and nutmeg. It must be highly seasoned.

Preheat the oven to 350°.

Pour the mixture into a buttered ovenproof dish, dot with the remaining butter and bake for 20 minutes.

Let cool until lukewarm and then unmold onto the center of a serving plate covered with cabbage leaves or spinach leaves for a colorful effect. Sprinkle with parsley and serve.

Note: For a lighter cake, the egg whites can be whipped separately and 3 tablespoons of cream added to the mixture. This should not be unmolded but served in the baking dish.

Les Légumes

Gâteau de Pommes de Terre

A Crisp Potato Cake Seasoned with Herbs and Cheese

Wonderful-looking, this is a splendid accompaniment to any roasted meat or fowl dish.

For 8 people:

- ½ cup vegetable oil
- 5 tablespoons sweet butter
- 10 large boiling potatoes, peeled and cut into ½-inch slices
- ½ pound Swiss cheese, grated
  - Salt
  - Freshly ground pepper
  - Nutmeg
- 3 bay leaves
- 3 tablespoons minced fresh herbs
- 1 garlic clove, peeled and minced

Preheat the oven to 350°.

Melt one-third of the oil and 3 tablespoons of the butter in a large skillet and sauté one-third of the well-dried potatoes for 15 minutes. Scrape the bottom of the pan from time to time with a spatula. Put the potatoes in a well-buttered ovenproof dish and cover with one-third of the cheese, salt, pepper, nutmeg and a bay leaf.

Add one-third of the oil to the skillet and sauté the second third of the potatoes for 15 minutes. Add to the ovenproof dish, covering with another layer of cheese, salt, pepper, nutmeg and 1 bay leaf. Do the same with the last batch of potatoes. Cover the dish with foil and bake for 35 minutes.

Unmold onto a warm serving dish. Dot with the remaining butter, sprinkle with fresh herbs, garlic and pepper and serve at once.

Vegetables

Gratin d'Oignons

Onion Gratin

A luscious dish from Lyon, perfect for serving with a roasted meat or a pork stew.

For 8 people:

4 pounds onions
2 tablespoons sweet butter
2 tablespoons oil
Salt
Freshly ground black pepper
Nutmeg
3 tablespoons heavy cream
4 tablespoons grated Swiss cheese
1 tablespoon sweet butter

Preheat the oven to 350°.

Mince the onions by hand or with a food processer and cook them slowly in the butter and oil on top of the stove for 10 minutes, stirring, until soft.

Add the salt, pepper, nutmeg and cream. Check the seasonings and pour the mixture into a buttered ovenproof dish. Sprinkle with cheese, dot with butter and bake for 30 minutes.

Serve in its baking dish.

Grapiau

A Grated Potato, Onion, Egg and Cheese Pancake

Les Légumes

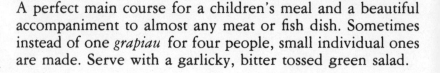

A perfect main course for a children's meal and a beautiful accompaniment to almost any meat or fish dish. Sometimes instead of one *grapiau* for four people, small individual ones are made. Serve with a garlicky, bitter tossed green salad.

For 8 people:

*8 to 10 potatoes, peeled and grated by hand or in a food
    processor*
2 eggs, beaten
*2 onions, peeled and grated, either raw or sautéed in 2
    tablespoons sweet butter*
2 tablespoons flour
Salt
1 tablespoon good brandy
Pinch of freshly grated coriander
1 cup grated Swiss cheese
Freshly ground pepper
4 tablespoons oil (preferably walnut)
3 shallots, peeled and minced
2 tablespoons minced parsley

Rinse the potatoes and dry them thoroughly with a kitchen towel. Put them in a large bowl and add the eggs, onions, flour, salt, brandy, coriander, cheese and pepper.

Heat the oil in one or two large skillets and cook the mixture for 15 minutes, then place about 8 inches below the broiler flame for 10 minutes. The pancake should be very crunchy on both sides yet moist in the center.

Sprinkle with the shallots and parsley and serve warm.

Gratin Dauphinois I

Potato Gratin Enriched with Nutmeg, Egg and Cheese

The only vegetable to grow in the Dauphiné and Savoy, the potato is the main ingredient of two of the most delicious dishes: *gratin savoyard* and *gratin dauphinois.*

Dauphinois and Savoyard were not kissing cousins and neither are the gratins. The first is more delicate, the second more rustic. Both are superb accompaniments to fish and meat preparations and should be served with a dry white wine.

The variations on this dish are endless. Here are two of my favorites.

Vegetables

For 8 people:

> 9 *large potatoes (about 3 pounds)*
> 2 *cups milk*
> *Salt*
> *Freshly ground white pepper*
> *Freshly grated nutmeg*
> 1 *egg, beaten*
> 1 *garlic clove, peeled*
> 1½ *cups grated or shredded Swiss cheese (or half Swiss and half Parmesan)*
> 3 *tablespoons sweet butter*

Peel and cut the potatoes into thin slices (don't rinse them) and dry thoroughly with a kitchen towel.

Preheat the oven to 325°.

Bring the milk to a boil, add the salt, pepper, nutmeg and potatoes. Cook for 10 minutes, stirring frequently to prevent sticking. Stir in the beaten egg.

Rub an ovenproof dish with a garlic clove, then with a little butter. Spread half of the potato-and-milk mixture in the dish, and sprinkle with half of the cheese. Add the rest of the potatoes, sprinkle with the rest of the cheese and dot with butter. Bake for 1 hour. The dish must be creamy, and golden crisp on the top. To prevent it from drying out (if the meal is delayed), place a sheet of foil over the top and turn off the oven. This will keep it warm and soft.

Note: Often two turnips are added to the potatoes for that extra touch.

Gratin de Potiron

A Highly Seasoned Pumpkin Gratin

Pumpkin was used by the Romans with honey. In Burgundy there are many versions of luscious pumpkin soups. The Nouvelle Cuisine chefs sometimes turn it into elegant sherbet.

Les Légumes

This traditional gratin is a true delight served as an accompaniment or by itself. You may substitute the tasty butternut squash for pumpkin.

For 8 people:

> About 4 pounds (9 cups) pumpkin (or butternut
>   squash), peeled and cut into large pieces
> 2 tablespoons vegetable oil
> 4 onions, peeled and minced
> 12 thick slices of bacon (each piece cut in half)
> 4 eggs, beaten
> Salt
> Freshly ground white pepper
> Pinch of freshly grated nutmeg
> 2 tablespoons bread crumbs (preferably homemade)
> 1 cup freshly grated Swiss cheese
> 1 tablespoon sweet butter

Place the prepared pumpkin (or squash) in a large pot of boiling, salted water. Cook for 20 minutes.

Heat the oil and sauté the onions for 5 to 10 minutes. Remove and set aside. Add the bacon to the skillet and fry until crisp on both sides. Set aside. Pass the cooked pumpkin through a sieve or a Moulinex mill. Let it drain to get rid of as much water as possible, pressing down with your hands.

Preheat the oven to 375°.

Place the pumpkin purée in a large bowl. Add the eggs, salt, pepper and nutmeg and stir. Check the seasoning. Add the bacon and pour into a buttered ovenproof dish. Sprinkle with bread crumbs and cheese. Dot with butter. Bake for 30 minutes. Serve in its cooking dish.

Haricots Rouges

Red Beans Cooked with Wine and Spices

This can be served as a vegetable dish or as an accompaniment to broiled meat. A cheek and an ear of pig were traditionally added to the beans for extra flavor as they cooked, but they are not essential. For a smoother dish, you may pass the beans through a Moulinex mill or food processor and add the crisp pork on top just before serving.

Vegetables

For 8 people:

1½ pounds dried red beans
1 carrot, peeled
1 large onion studded with 1 clove
1 garlic clove, peeled
Bouquet garni
½-pound piece lean salt pork or bacon
1 cup red Burgundy-type wine
1 onion
3 tablespoons sweet butter
1 cup red wine
Salt
Freshly ground pepper

Soak the beans in cold water overnight. The next day, put them in a saucepan with the carrot, onion with a clove, garlic clove, bouquet garni, pork, wine and water to cover. Bring to a boil and simmer for about 2 hours. (Check the bean-package directions for cooking time.)

When the beans are tender, remove the carrot, onion, bouquet garni and pork and drain the beans.

Chop a fresh onion and sauté it in 2 tablespoons of the butter. Dice the pork and add it to the onion. Sauté for a few minutes on all sides, then add the wine and let it reduce for 5 minutes. Add the beans and simmer for 3 minutes. Add salt, pepper and 1 tablespoon of butter and serve at once.

Le Paillasson

A Crisp Potato Patty

These crisp little "mats" *(paillassons)* of golden potatoes are served throughout Burgundy and in Lyon. They must be small, and the two secrets of success in making them are to use several skillets (and prepare a *paillasson* only for two or three persons at the most) and to sprinkle on the garlic and parsley at the last moment. Make as many batches as you have guests and keep them warm in a turned-off oven.

Les Légumes

Paillassons are a good accompaniment to beef, poultry, pork and lamb and are a child's idea of the absolute treat.

For 2 people:

4 large potatoes
Salt
Freshly ground black pepper
5 tablespoons sweet butter
2 tablespoons vegetable oil
2 garlic cloves, peeled and minced
2 tablespoons minced parsley

Peel and dry the potatoes and cut them into matchstick-sized pieces. Sprinkle them with salt and pepper. Heat 4 table-spoons of the butter and the oil in two small skillets (each about 5 inches wide). When they are frothy, add the potatoes, one-half in each skillet. The potatoes will spread and be about 2 inches thick. Cook over medium heat for 5 minutes, pressing down with a fork.

After 5 minutes, turn the *paillassons* over. (Add a little butter and lower the heat if necessary to prevent burning.) They should be ready in about 15 minutes.

Mix together the garlic, parsley and 1 tablespoon butter.

Place the *paillassons* on a warm dish and spread with the garlic mixture just before serving.

Pommes de Terre Lyonnaise

A Sautéed Onion and Potato Accompaniment

For 8 people:

10 potatoes (3–3½ pounds), unpeeled
4 onions, peeled and thinly sliced
4 tablespoons vegetable oil
6 tablespoons sweet butter
Salt
Freshly ground black pepper
Freshly grated nutmeg
3 tablespoons minced parsley

Vegetables

Boil the potatoes in a large pot of salted water. Cook for 30 minutes, or until soft.

Meanwhile, prepare the onions and sauté them in the oil and 5 tablespoons of the butter over rather low heat for 10 minutes; season with salt. Remove from the pan and set aside.

Peel the potatoes, holding them with a kitchen towel. Slice them ½ inch thick. Reheat the butter and oil and sauté the sliced potatoes for 3 minutes. Add the onions, salt, pepper and nutmeg and cook for 2 minutes, shaking the pan.

Add the remaining 1 tablespoon of butter and the parsley before serving.

Gratin de Verdure

A Spinach, Egg and Herb Gratin

A delectable dish, easy to prepare ahead of time, that goes well with a baked ham, a leg of lamb or poultry.

For 8 people:

- 4 *pounds fresh spinach (and/or watercress), or 4 10-ounce packages frozen spinach*
- 2 *onions, peeled and chopped*
- 1 *tablespoon vegetable oil*
- 11 *tablespoons sweet butter*
- 2 *cups milk*
- 1 *bay leaf*
- 6 *tablespoons flour*
- 4 *egg yolks*
  Nutmeg
  Salt
  Freshly ground black pepper
- 4 *egg whites, stiffly beaten*
- 8 *tablespoons grated cheese (preferably Parmesan or Romano)*

Cook the spinach rapidly. Drain well, squeezing with your hand.

Sauté the onions in the oil and 3 tablespoons of the butter until soft, then add the spinach. Shake the skillet until no

Les Légumes

192

water is left. Remove from the heat.

Preheat the oven to 375°.

Heat the milk with the bay leaf. Knead 8 tablespoons of the butter and flour and heat this mixture in a heavy-bottomed saucepan. Stir in the milk. When the sauce is quite thick, add the egg yolks, stirring briskly, and pour it on the spinach. Season with nutmeg, salt and pepper. It must be lightly flavored.

Fold in the egg whites and pour the mixture into a buttered ovenproof dish. Sprinkle with cheese and bake for 30 minutes.

Gratin Forestière

A Potato, Mushroom and Onion Gratin

From Savoy comes this lovely fragrant gratin, which can be served as a first course or an accompaniment to broiled meat or fowl. It can be prepared ahead of time.

For 8 people:

> 7 *tablespoons sweet butter*
> 2 *tablespoons vegetable oil*
> 1½ *pounds firm white mushrooms, cleaned, dried and sliced*
> 2 *onions (or 8 shallots), peeled and sliced*
> 1 *garlic clove, peeled and lightly crushed*
> 8 *potatoes (about 3 pounds), peeled and thinly sliced*
> *Salt*
> *Freshly ground white pepper*
> 5 *tablespoons minced parsley*
> 1 *cup light cream*

Heat 4 tablespoons of the butter and the oil in a skillet and sauté the mushrooms for a few minutes. Remove from the pan. Sauté the onions for a few minutes and remove from the heat.

Preheat the oven to 350°.

Rub an ovenproof dish with the garlic clove, then butter it carefully. Place the first layer of one-half of the well-dried potato slices in the bottom of the dish. Sprinkle with salt and pepper and dot with half of the remaining butter. Add the mushrooms and sprinkle with salt, pepper and parsley. Add the onions and then the rest of the potatoes. Sprinkle with salt and pepper and dot with the remaining butter.

Bake for 15 minutes. Pour the cream all over the top, letting it go through evenly. Continue baking for 20 minutes. The gratin should be crisp and golden on top.

Note: One version of this asks for grated cheese (about 3 tablespoons) on top of the gratin.

Gratin Savoyard

A Potato Gratin Seasoned with Onions and Garlic and Baked under a Cheese Crust

This poor cousin of the more elaborate gratins is superb with a leg of lamb, a pork roast or a plain chicken.

For 8 people:

10 potatoes (about 3½ pounds), peeled and thinly sliced
4 onions (or shallots) peeled and either minced or thickly sliced
1 cup milk
1 cup broth
Salt
Freshly ground white pepper
Freshly ground nutmeg
1 garlic clove, peeled
Salt
Sweet butter
1½ cups grated or shredded Swiss cheese

Preheat the oven to 375°.

Prepare the potatoes and onions, drying the potatoes well. Heat together the milk, broth, salt, pepper and nutmeg. Rub an ovenproof dish with garlic, then salt, then butter. Add one layer of sliced potatoes, one layer of onions and half of the milk-broth mixture. Sprinkle with half of the cheese.

Les Légumes

Add the rest of the potatoes, onions, milk-broth mixture, and sprinkle with the rest of the cheese. Bring to a boil on top of the stove, dot with butter and bake for 30 minutes uncovered.

Gratin Rouge

An Onion, Vinegar and Wine Gratin

Another medieval recipe that has been constantly improved; the latest version even includes grenadine.

For 8 persons:

- *3 tablespoons sweet butter*
- *1 tablespoon oil*
- *4½ pounds onions, finely chopped*
- *6 tablespoons sugar*
- *2 tablespoons wine vinegar*
- *Salt*
- *Freshly ground black pepper*
- *Nutmeg*
- *4½ tablespoons red Burgundy wine*
- *1 tablespoon grenadine (optional)*

Heat the butter and oil in a heavy skillet. Sauté the onions for about 10 minutes. Add the sugar, vinegar, salt, pepper and nutmeg; cover and simmer for 30 minutes, stirring from time to time.

Add the wine and cook, uncovered, for 30 minutes more. Check the seasonings and serve. (You may add 1 tablespoon grenadine during the last 5 minutes of cooking.)

Gratin Dauphinois II

Vegetables

A delicious, prettier version, but without cheese. The best accompaniment for roast beef, chicken or even fish.

For 8 people:

1¼ cups milk
10 potatoes (about 3½ pounds), peeled and thinly sliced
1 garlic clove, peeled
2 tablespoons sweet butter
Salt
Freshly ground white pepper
Freshly ground nutmeg
1 garlic clove, peeled and minced
3 shallots, minced
2 eggs, beaten
½ cup light cream
2 tablespoons sweet butter

Preheat the oven to 350°.

Heat the milk to the boiling point and let cool to lukewarm. Prepare the potatoes, drying them carefully with a kitchen towel.

Rub an ovenproof dish with a garlic clove, then sprinkle with salt and rub with butter. Pour the potatoes into the dish. Sprinkle with salt, pepper, nutmeg, garlic and shallots. Stir thoroughly with your hands to coat the potatoes evenly with the seasonings.

Beat the eggs in a bowl, add the lukewarm milk and the cream and pour over the potatoes. Dot with butter and bake for 40 to 50 minutes. Serve warm.

Purée de Choux

A Cabbage Purée

Superb with pork and prepared in a jiffy, this reheats well.

For 8 people:

2 heads of cabbage, cores removed and cut into quarters
2 tablespoons sweet butter
Salt
Freshly ground black pepper

Les Légumes

Blanch the cabbage in a pan of salted boiling water until tender, about 15 minutes. Drain. Pass through a sieve, a blender or a food processor. Add butter, salt and pepper, stir carefully and serve.

Gratin Trois

A Potato Gratin

This classic potato gratin is sheer perfection in its simplicity. You can prepare it ahead of time and reheat for 20 minutes before serving.

For 8 people:

    2 cups cream
 1½ quarts milk
    Salt
    Freshly ground black pepper
    Freshly grated nutmeg
  10 potatoes (about 6 pounds), peeled and thinly sliced
    1 garlic clove, peeled
    4 tablespoons sweet butter

Bring the cream, milk, salt, pepper and nutmeg to a boil in a saucepan. Add the carefully dried potatoes and cook until tender (about 15 minutes).

Preheat the oven to 350°.

Rub a very large ovenproof dish with the garlic clove, then butter it and pour in the potatoes and cream. (There should not be more than one or two layers of potatoes in the dish.) Dot with butter and bake for about 30 minutes.

Haricots Blancs au Vin Rouge

White Beans with a Wine and Shallot Sauce

Vegetables

If you use fresh white beans, serve them as a separate course and eat them with a spoon. If dried beans are used, this is a good accompaniment to pork and lamb.

For 8 people:

3 pounds fresh white beans (or 1½ pounds dried white beans)
1 onion stuck with 1 clove
1 carrot, peeled and chopped
2 onions, peeled and chopped
6 shallots, peeled and minced
2 tablespoons sweet butter
2 tablespoons vegetable oil
5 tablespoons red wine
1 garlic clove, peeled and minced
2 tablespoons sweet butter
2 tablespoons minced parsley
Salt
Freshly ground black pepper

If you use dried beans, let them stand in lukewarm water as directed on the package. If you use fresh ones, shell them only.

Bring the beans, onion with a clove, carrots and onions to a boil in a large pot of salted water and cook until the beans are tender. (See cooking time on package if using dried beans.)

Meanwhile, cook the shallots in the butter and oil until soft. Add the wine and let the liquid reduce, uncovered, for a few minutes.

Drain the beans and pour them into a warm bowl. Add the wine and shallots, the garlic, butter, parsley, salt and pepper. Stir and serve.

Haricots Verts à la Crème

Green Beans with a Light Cream sauce

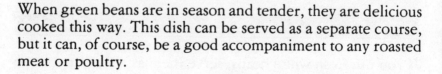

When green beans are in season and tender, they are delicious cooked this way. This dish can be served as a separate course, but it can, of course, be a good accompaniment to any roasted meat or poultry.

Les Légumes

For 8 people:

- *3 pounds green beans, trimmed*
- *2 tablespoons sweet butter*
- *1 tablespoon flour*
- *⅓ cup hot milk*
- *2 yolks*
- *2 tablespoons light cream*
- *Salt*
- *Freshly ground black pepper*
- *1 garlic clove, minced (optional)*
- *2 tablespoons finely chopped parsley*

Blanch the green beans in a large pot of salted water until cooked but slightly crunchy. Drain.

Over medium heat, melt the butter in a thick-bottomed pan. Stir in the flour and then the milk. Add the beans to this light cream sauce.

In a separate bowl, beat the egg yolks and the cream and pour over the beans, stirring gently. Season with salt, pepper, garlic and parsley and serve lukewarm or warm.

Matelote de Pommes de Terre

Potatoes and Onions Cooked with Herbs and Red Wine

Serve this sprinkled with chives, because despite its splendid flavor the color is not appealing.

For 8 people:

- *2 tablespoons sweet butter*
- *2 tablespoons vegetable oil*
- *2 cups red wine, Burgundy type*
- *Salt*
- *Freshly ground black pepper*
- *2 bay leaves*
- *2 teaspoons thyme*
- *2 onions, peeled and thinly sliced*
- *8 potatoes, peeled and thickly sliced*
- *2 tablespoons chopped chives*

Vegetables

Melt the butter and oil in a skillet. Add the red wine, salt, pepper, bay leaves, thyme, onions and potatoes. Bring to a boil, then simmer, uncovered, for 1 hour. Sprinkle with chopped chives and serve at once.

Oignons aux Épinards

Yellow Onions Stuffed with Spinach, Cream, Cheese, Eggs and Spices

This takes rather long to prepare, but it is pretty and very much worth it. It can also be served cold with a little olive oil dribbled over it.

For 8 people:

    8 *large yellow onions, peeled*
    2 *tablespoons and 8 teaspoons sweet butter*
       Salt
 1½ *pounds spinach*
  ½ *cup cream*
  ½ *cup grated Swiss cheese*
      Nutmeg
      Freshly ground black pepper
    3 *eggs, beaten*
 16 *bay leaves*
    4 *carrots, thinly sliced*

Preheat the oven to 375°.

Cut the onions into halves and remove the centers, keeping only three layers on each onion.

Melt 2 tablespoons of the butter in a large skillet over medium heat. Add the shells of the onions in two or three batches. They should become slightly brown after 10 minutes. Gently remove them with a spatula and set aside. Mince the onion centers, sprinkle them with salt and cook them in the skillet over low heat for 10 minutes.

Cook the spinach and dry it thoroughly in a kitchen towel. Place it in a bowl and add the cream, cheese, the minced onion centers, salt, nutmeg, pepper and the eggs. Stir carefully and check the seasoning. Add more cream if the mixture is too dry.

Les Légumes

Fill each onion shell with the mixture. Place 2 bay leaves on each side of the shell and a slice of carrot on top. Tie a piece of string around each shell and across the bay leaves, and dot each shell with 1 teaspoon of butter. Wrap individually in foil and bake in an oiled ovenproof dish for 30 minutes.

Petits Légumes

An Assortment of Turnips, Carrots, Lima Beans, Mushrooms and Cucumbers Cooked with Herbs, Cream and Lemon Juice

This can be served with any meat, but it is also an unusually light and fresh first course.

For 8 people:

16 small pink turnips, peeled and halved lengthwise
16 small carrots (or 8 large ones), peeled and cut into 2- by 1-inch sticks
½ cup lima beans (frozen are acceptable but fresh are better)
2 small cucumbers, peeled and cut in 2- by 1-inch sticks
1 pound white mushrooms, halved
6 tablespoons sweet butter
4 teaspoons thyme
Salt
Freshly ground pepper
6 tablespoons light cream
3 tablespoons finely chopped fresh herbs (chives, parsley, mint)
Juice of 1 lemon

Blanch the turnips in a large pot of boiling salted water for 5 minutes, then add the carrots, lima beans and cucumbers and cook for 10 minutes. Drain.

Sauté the mushrooms in 4 tablespoons of the butter for 5 minutes in a large skillet. Add the remaining 2 tablespoons of butter and the vegetables to the skillet, sprinkle with thyme, salt and pepper and cook, uncovered, for 5 minutes, stirring frequently.

Vegetables

Add the cream and fresh herbs and cook 5 minutes longer. Sprinkle with lemon juice, check and correct the seasoning and serve at once.

Petits Navets en Ragoût

Turnips, Onions, Herbs and Garlic Simmered in Broth

For 8 people:

- 2 *tablespoons vegetable oil*
- 4 *big onions, peeled and thinly sliced*
- ½ *cup bacon, cut in small dice*
- 3½ *pounds small pink turnips, peeled and quartered*
- 2 *bay leaves*
- *Thyme*
- 1 *garlic clove, peeled and crushed*
- *About 1 cup broth*
- *Salt*
- *Freshly ground black pepper*

Heat the oil in a heavy-bottomed pan and sauté the onions and bacon for 3 minutes.

Add the turnips, bay leaves, thyme and garlic and cover with broth. Sprinkle with salt and pepper and bring to a boil. Simmer, covered, for 20 minutes and then, uncovered, for 30 minutes more. Check the seasoning before serving.

Potée aux Lentilles

Cooked Lentils Served with Toast, Spread with Pâté and Bacon and Seasoned with Fresh Cream

Les Légumes

This is a most unusual variation of *potée,* since *potée* in Burgundy is usually a cabbage soup with various additions and this has no cabbage. It comes from Dijon and makes for a wonderfully hearty dinner.

For 8 people:

¾ *pound lentils*
½-*pound piece of bacon (or lean salt pork)*
1 *large onion, stuck with 2 cloves*
1 *carrot, peeled*
3 *teaspoons thyme*
  Salt
5 *peppercorns*
8 *slices stale or toasted wholewheat bread, each cut in*
   4 triangles
2 *tablespoons sweet butter*
½ *pound good pâté, preferably homemade country pâté*
   or liver pâté
6 *tablespoons light cream*

Wash and put the lentils in a pot, add 2 quarts cold water and cook, according to the instructions on the package, with the bacon, onion, carrot, thyme, salt and peppercorns.

Meanwhile, either toast the slices of bread or sauté them in the butter. Set aside.

Spread the pâté on the bottom of a warm tureen or, if it is firm, dice it. Place the toast over it.

Remove the bacon from the pot and dice it. Discard the cloves stuck in the onion. Add the cream and bacon to the pot. Stir well and pour over the bread and pâté. Check the seasoning and serve.

Pommes de Terre aux Herbes

Sautéed Potatoes with Fresh Herbs Coated with a Light Cream and
Yolk Sauce

A splendid accompaniment to any roasted meat or to serve in spring with new potatoes and fragrant herbs as a first course.

Vegetables

For 8 people:

16 *medium potatoes, peeled and diced (do not peel new potatoes)*
6 *tablespoons sweet butter*
2 *tablespoons vegetable oil*
5 *shallots, peeled and minced*
  Salt
  Freshly ground black pepper
7 *tablespoons fresh herbs (chives, tarragon, mint), finely chopped*
1 *cup light cream*
4 *egg yolks*

Prepare the potatoes and dry them thoroughly. Heat the butter and oil and sauté the shallots for a few minutes. Remove and set aside. In the same skillet, sauté the potatoes over high heat. You may do them in two or three batches so that all the potatoes will turn crisp and golden. Remove the potatoes to a warm serving dish. Add salt and pepper, the herbs and the shallots and stir. Cover with a sheet of foil and keep warm.

Mix the cream and egg yolks together well and, with the heat turned off, add the mixture to the skillet, stirring rapidly. Return to the heat for 1 minute, until the mixture thickens a little, then pour it over the potatoes, stir gently, and serve at once.

Pouti

A Potato and Chestnut Purée with Milk or Wine

A traditional winter dish from Savoy that goes splendidly with pork or game.

For 8 people:

9 *potatoes, unpeeled*
2 *pounds chestnuts, unpeeled (or canned)*
  Salt
  Freshly ground black pepper
1½ *cups milk (or white wine)*

Les Légumes

Cook the potatoes and chestnuts in separate pans of salted water.

Peel the potatoes while hot, holding them with a kitchen towel or oven mit as you peel. Purée the potatoes and keep them warm.

Peel the chestnuts, purée them and add them to the potato purée. Whip and season to taste. Continue whipping as you add the milk until you have a light, fluffy mixture.

Petits Oignons à la Bourguignonne

Little Onions Braised with Raisins, Herbs and Wine

An absolutely marvelous accompaniment, whether served warm or cold.

For 8 people:

3 cups tiny white pearl onions
½ cup raisins
1 cup vegetable oil
½ cup wine vinegar
3 tablespoons tomato paste
6 garlic cloves, peeled and crushed
2 bay leaves
1 sprig of thyme (or 1 teaspoon dried thyme)
1 teaspoon savory
1 teaspoon sage
Salt
Freshly ground pepper
Dry white wine (enough to cover everything)

Peel the onions and, with a knife, mark an "x" in the stem end to keep the layers from separating during cooking. Put all the ingredients in a saucepan and cover with wine. Bring to a boil. Cover and simmer for 45 minutes.

Let cool, uncovered. Check the seasoning and serve.

Vegetables

Poireaux à la Savoyarde

Leeks Coated with Bread Crumbs, Cheese and Spices

For 8 people:

10 to 12 leeks (white part only), sliced
7 tablespoons sweet butter
½ cup bread crumbs (preferably homemade), sautéed
    in butter
1 garlic clove, peeled
1 cup grated Swiss cheese
Salt
Freshly ground black pepper
Freshly grated nutmeg

Cook the leeks in a large pan of salted water for 15 minutes. Drain.

Melt 4 tablespoons of the butter in a skillet and add the bread crumbs, stirring over medium heat until golden.

Butter an ovenproof dish and rub it with the garlic clove. Spread a layer of leeks, sprinkle with bread crumbs, cheese, salt, pepper and nutmeg and continue to layer until all ingredients are used.

Pour 3 tablespoons of hot foamy butter on top and broil for about 10 minutes. Serve in its cooking dish.

Purée de Fenouil

Fennel Purée

For 8 people:

5 fennel "bulbs"
2 potatoes, peeled and sliced
Salt
Freshly ground black pepper
2 tablespoons light cream
1 tablespoon chopped fennel leaves

Cut off the base and tops and any tough, fibrous parts of the outer layer of the fennel. Quarter the "bulbs." Place them and the potatoes in a pan of hot salted water and cook for 20 minutes. Drain.

Purée the potatoes and fennel in a Moulinex mill, a food processor or a blender. Stir in the salt, pepper and cream.

This may be reheated over low heat. Sprinkle with the fresh fennel leaves, and serve with pork or fish.

Pommes Sautées

Sautéed Onions and Potatoes Seasoned with Vinegar and Fresh Herbs

For 8 people:

1 cup diced lean salt pork (or bacon)
1 tablespoon sweet butter
12 small white onions, peeled
1 teaspoon flour
1 teaspoon softened sweet butter
2 to 3 cups broth (beef or chicken)
2 tablespoons wine vinegar
Salt
Freshly ground black pepper
Thyme
1 bay leaf
8 potatoes (small boiling type), peeled and quartered
2 tablespoons minced fresh herbs (tarragon, savory, mint)

Sauté the diced pork in the butter for 2 minutes in a heavy-bottomed pan. Add the onions and sauté on all sides for 5 minutes. Mix the flour and softened butter and stir it in. Cook for a few minutes, then add the broth and vinegar. Add salt, pepper, thyme and bay leaf. Add the potatoes, cover tightly and cook over medium heat for 45 minutes to 1 hour. Discard the bay leaf.

Sprinkle with the fresh herbs and serve.

Vegetables

Purée de Haricots Blancs

A White Bean Purée Seasoned with Garlic, Onions and Cream

A superb accompaniment for roasts but mostly for pork. This has a wonderful nutty flavor but must be highly seasoned.

For 8 people:

- 2 *pounds white beans*
- 1 *whole bulb of garlic, unpeeled*
  Bouquet garni
- 3 *potatoes, peeled and cut in half*
- 1 *large onion, peeled and stuck with 1 clove*
- 3 *tablespoons cream*
- 5 *tablespoons sweet butter*
  Freshly ground white pepper

Cook the beans with the garlic and the bouquet garni in a large pot of salted water for about 2 hours—or according to the instructions on the package. Add the potatoes and the onion for the last 20 minutes. Remove the garlic, peel it, then return the flesh to the beans. Remove and discard the bouquet garni and the clove stuck in the onion. Pass everything else through a Moulinex Mill or a food processor. Beat lightly. Add the cream, butter and pepper and serve very warm. Add a few little pieces of butter on top before serving.

Tarte aux Légumes

A Tomato, Onion and Zucchini Pie Seasoned with Herbs

The most fragrant, the freshest, the lightest of summer dishes. It is better warm or lukewarm but can be served cold with a tossed lettuce salad for a buffet.

Les Légumes

For 8 people:

¼ *pound and 3 tablespoons sweet butter*
1 *egg, beaten*
  Salt
½ *pound flour*
1 *tablespoon vegetable oil*
2 *onions, peeled and thinly sliced*
4 *tomatoes, each cut into 3 or 4 thick slices*
4 *zucchini (or 4 cucumbers), unpeeled and thinly sliced*
  Thyme
  Salt
  Freshly ground pepper
5 *tablespoons minced basil (or chives) and parsley*
  Vegetable oil

Make the pastry for the pie crust, adding ¼ pound of the butter, egg and salt to the flour and mixing quickly with your fingertips. Make a ball of the dough, cover it with a kitchen towel, and let it rest for at least 1 hour.

Prepare the filling. Heat 1 tablespoon of the butter and the oil in a skillet and sauté the onions until soft. Remove them into a bowl. Add 1 tablespoon of the butter to the skillet, then add the tomatoes, cut side down. Cook for 5 minutes over low heat. Remove to a bowl, pouring off the liquid. Add the remaining tablespoon of butter to the skillet and cook the zucchini until soft.

Preheat the oven to 375°.

Flatten the dough ball; roll it and fold it three times. Roll it again. It should be smooth and soft. Spread it on a buttered 10-inch pie plate, prick it with a fork and place a few dried beans or pebbles on it to keep it from puffing up. Bake for 20 minutes.

Let the crust cool, then spread the onions on it and sprinkle with thyme, salt and pepper. Spread the zucchini over the onions and sprinkle again with thyme, salt and pepper. Cover with the tomatoes, cut side up and close together. Sprinkle with the basil and parsley (or chives and parsley), salt, pepper and few drops of oil. Bake for 15 minutes and serve warm.

Vegetables

Gratin de Chou

A Cabbage, Apple, Ham, Meat, Shallot, Cream and Cheese Gratin

A vegetable treat that is unusual yet very easy to prepare, since the ingredients are always available. It is a wonderful way to use meat leftovers.

For 8 people:

½ *pound boiled beef, pork or chicken (or any leftover meat)*
¼ *pound boiled ham (or country ham)*
¼ *pound lean salt pork (or bacon)*
1 *large head of Savoy cabbage*
3 *Granny Smith or firm tart apples, sliced*
3 *shallots, peeled and minced*
1 *garlic clove, peeled and minced*
3 *tablespoons minced parsley*
  Freshly ground black pepper
1 *cup light cream*
2 *tablespoons grated Swiss cheese*
1 *tablespoon sweet butter*

Chop the leftover meat, ham and salt pork and mix them well.

Preheat the oven to 350°.

Cook the cabbage in boiling salted water for 20 minutes. Drain and chop finely.

Butter an ovenproof dish. Add a layer of one-third each of the cabbage, apples and meat mixture and sprinkle with one-third each of the shallots, garlic, parsley and pepper. Repeat this procedure twice.

Pour the cream over the whole dish and sprinkle with the grated cheese and butter. Bake for 20 minutes.

Les Légumes

Tomates au Fromage

Baked Tomatoes Stuffed with Cheese and Shallots

This is a good buffet dish that is also a splendid accompaniment to many meat and fish dishes.

For 8 people:

5 tablespoons minced shallots
4 tablespoons minced parsley
Salt
Freshly ground black pepper
3 tablespoons grated Swiss cheese
8 tomatoes
2 tablespoons vegetable oil
3 tablespoons bread crumbs
3 tablespoons sweet butter

Place the shallots, parsley, salt, pepper and cheese in a bowl and mix well.

Cut the tomatoes in half and squeeze gently to remove the seeds.

Heat the oil in a large skillet and cook the tomatoes (cut side down) for 3 to 5 minutes, depending on their ripeness.

With a spatula, remove the tomatoes and place them cut side up in an ovenproof dish. Fill them with the shallot-and-cheese mixture. Sprinkle with bread crumbs, dot with butter and broil for about 5 minutes.

Vegetables

Terrine de Navets

A Turnip, Herb, Ham, Cream and Cheese Gratin

A very tasty dish, easy to prepare ahead of time.

For 8 people:

- 2 *pounds tender pink and purple turnips, peeled and very thinly sliced*
- *Dried savory (or thyme)*
- *Salt*
- *Freshly ground black pepper*
- 1 *cup sliced and shredded ham (country ham or prosciutto)*
- 1 *cup heavy cream*
- 1½ *cups grated cheese (Romano, Swiss or Parmesan)*
- ½ *cup bread crumbs, preferably homemade*
- 2 *tablespoons sweet butter*

Preheat the oven to 375°.

Blanch the turnips in a large pan of boiling salted water for 5 minutes. Drain.

Place one-third of the turnips in a buttered deep ovenproof dish. Sprinkle with savory, salt and pepper, then add a layer of one-third of the ham and one-third of the cream. Continue layering, and seasoning each layer, until all the turnips, ham, and cream are used up. Cover with the cheese and bread crumbs. Dot with butter and bake for 45 minutes to 1 hour. Serve in the baking dish.

Les Légumes

Farineux

Pasta and Grain Dishes

As hunters became shepherds, then farmers, cereals were for a long time the staple of most people's diets. Oats, rye, wheat and corn were prepared in many ways. The Romans enjoyed their *poulte,* which became the Italian *polenta* and, later, *gaudes* in Burgundy.

The Chinese and then the Italians created the raviolis that were to become goat cheese *ravioles* in Savoy.

Matafam (literally hunger-killer), a large pancake of flour and vegetables, was popular; so was *farcement,* a cake of grated potato, raisins, prunes and flour. *Rambollet,* a cake made with potato and egg, was a favorite dish. *Fricot,* a purée of pears and potatoes, was served with game.

For centuries starchy dishes were widely enjoyed in the poor regions of Burgundy and Savoy. Most of them were heavy, dull, true "Christian chokers," as they were later nick-named. So in spite of the memories they may evoke—a grand-mother's specialty, a cheerful meal shared during a village festival—few of those dishes appeal to our taste, which re-quires intensity of flavor and lightness. I have chosen the dishes that traveled well in time and space. And I have added new creations, such as homemade pasta served with tender crayfish or thinly sliced fish and herbs.

Crousets

Crousets were served in Savoy and Dauphiné on Christmas Eve. They are beloved by all children, and delicious with a roast or a turkey.

Pasta and
Grain Dishes

For 8 people:

4 *cups flour*
4 *eggs, beaten*
Salt
2 *cups grated Swiss cheese (about ½ pound)*
4 *tablespoons cream*
4 *tablespoons milk*
2 *tablespoons sweet butter*
6 *walnuts, chopped*

Place the flour in a bowl and form a well in the center. Add the eggs, salt and 3 tablespoons of water and knead lightly until you have a soft, firm dough.

On a table dusted with flour, spread the dough to a ¼-inch thickness. Cut it in strips 1 inch wide. Roll each strip into a cylinder ½ inch in diameter and cut it into sticks 1 inch long.

Preheat oven to 350°.

Put the sticks of dough in a large pot of salted boiling water. Let them simmer for 15 minutes. Drain.

Carefully place the *crousets* in a large buttered ovenproof dish. Sprinkle with the cheese. Add the milk and cream and dot with butter. Bake for 15 to 20 minutes. Sprinkle with the chopped walnuts and serve.

Crozets

Potato and Flour Sticks Seasoned with Cheese

A good accompaniment to almost any dish.

3 *large potatoes, boiled in their skins*
4 *cups flour*
4 *eggs*
1 *tablespoon walnut oil*
Salt
Freshly ground black pepper
1 *cup crumbled blue cheese*
1½ *cups grated Swiss cheese*
1 *tablespoon lard*

Farineux

Peel the potatoes and mash them along with the flour, eggs, walnut oil, salt and pepper and 3 tablespoons of water. (It must be a rather dry mixture.) Stir vigorously. Divide it into small balls and roll them in the shape of short pencils. Cut them into 1-inch pieces and bend them so they look like plump commas. Preheat the oven to 375°.

Bring a large pot of salted water to a boil and poach the *crozets* in three batches (so they have enough room) for 10 minutes each. Drain them.

Place a layer of *crozets* in a buttered ovenproof dish and sprinkle with the blue and Swiss cheeses. Heat the lard to the boiling point and sprinkle it on top of the dish. Heat the *crozets* in the oven until lightly browned.

Pâtes Fraîches

Homemade Noodles

This clearly comes from the South by way of Lyon.

It can be served for dinner with rich classical dishes, such as *Boeuf Bourguignon* (p. 220) or *Travers de Porc aux Herbes* (p. 168), or with sautéed vegetables, fillets of fish or tender crayfish, or as a main luncheon dish.

> For 8 people:
>
> 4 *cups unbleached flour*
> 6 *eggs, slightly beaten*
> 1 *tablespoon salt*
> 2 *tablespoons olive oil*
> 1 *teaspoon peanut oil*
>   *Sweet butter*

Put the flour in a large bowl and make a well in the center. Put into the well the eggs, salt, 2 tablespoons of water and olive oil, and, with your fingers, work it gradually into the flour. Place the dough on a floured counter or table and knead it for 15 to 20 minutes. Flouring your hands and the counter or table often, push the dough away from you with the heel of your hand, then gather it back into a mass and repeat until the dough is smooth and elastic. Let it rest, covered with towel, for 1 to 2 hours.

Pasta and
Grain Dishes

Divide the ball into eight parts (each the size of a fist). Roll each part through the pasta machine into thin layers, starting at No. 1, then 2, then skipping to 4 and finally 5 or—if you like thin noodles—6. Sprinkle a little flour on the machine every time you put in a new layer of dough so it will not stick to the metal. In using No. 6, be sure to reach underneath and pull out the thin strip as it is being rolled. If allowed to pile up under the machine, the strips will stick together. Sprinkle flour on all the trays you have (use counters and tables also) and let the sheets of thin pasta dry on them for 30 minutes. Then cut the sheets in the machine into thin or wide strips, as you prefer. Dust lightly with more flour and let them fall loosely onto the floured surfaces.

Bring a large pot of salted water to a boil. Add the peanut oil and drop the noodles into the pot. Cook, stirring twice, for 5 to 10 minutes over medium heat. Drain in a colander and pour into a shallow dish. Add desired amount of butter at once.

Riz aux Herbes

Rice with Herbs

Quickly prepared and a good fish and stew accompaniment.

For 8 people:

1½ cups raw rice
3 bay leaves
2 teaspoons thyme
2 tablespoons olive oil
2 tablespoons sweet butter
Freshly ground pepper
2 tablespoons chopped herbs (tarragon, chives, fresh thyme)

In a large kettle, bring 7 quarts of salted water to a boil and add the rice while slowly stirring with a fork. Add the bay leaves and thyme and boil, uncovered, for 20 minutes.

Rinse the rice under cold water and drain in a colander.

Farineux

Transfer it to a saucepan, add the olive oil and butter and fluff the rice with two forks.

Reheat, stirring lightly with two forks a few times, for 5 minutes just before serving. Sprinkle with pepper and the fresh herbs.

Ravioles
Cheese-Filled Pasta

This is a delicious Savoy and Dauphiné version of the Chinese and Italian dish. You can use a Greek or American goat cheese, since French goat cheese seems harder to find in America. A pasta machine is a great help.

For 8 people:

2½ cups unbleached flour
2 tablespoons olive oil
2 eggs, beaten
2 teaspoons salt
⅔ cup goat cheese
2 eggs
2 cups grated Swiss cheese (about ½ pound)
Salt
5 tablespoons chopped parsley
4 tablespoons sweet butter
Broth (or water)
3 tablespoons grated Swiss cheese

Sift the flour into a large bowl. Make a well in the center and pour in 1 tablespoon of the olive oil, the beaten eggs, salt, and 6 tablespoons of water. Mix with a fork until all the flour is absorbed, adding another tablespoon of water if necessary. Knead for 10 minutes, either in the bowl or on a floured counter, until the dough becomes smooth and elastic. Form a ball of the dough, place it in an oiled bowl, cover with a clean cloth and let it rest for 1 hour.

Place the pasta machine on the table and flour it. Divide the dough into four balls the size of small oranges. Roll each ball through No. 1, then 3, then 5, then 7. Reach underneath and pull out the thin strip as it is being rolled. If allowed to pile

Pasta and
Grain Dishes

up under the machine, the strips will stick together. Lay the paper-thin sheets of dough on a floured tray or table to dry for 10 minutes.

If you do not have a pasta machine, roll each small ball of dough on a floured board as thinly as you can.

Prepare the stuffing. Crush the goat cheese, eggs, Swiss cheese and salt with a fork or a blender. Sauté the chopped parsley in 2 tablespoons of butter and add to the mixture.

Place a sheet of dough on a floured surface, put a teaspoon of filling every 2 inches along the entire sheet, making 2 long rows. Place another sheet of dough on top of the mounds and carefully press around each little heap with your fingers, sealing the two layers together. With a pastry wheel, cut around each heap so that you have neat little squares that look like plump cushions. If the pasta strips have become too dry to adhere to one another, dip the pastry wheel into warm water and work them together. When all the squares are cut, sprinkle them with a little flour and allow them to rest for 1 hour before cooking.

Bring a large kettle of broth or salted water to boil. Add the remaining tablespoon of olive oil. Lower the heat and gently slide the *ravioles* in. Simmer gently for 10 minutes. When they rise to the surface they are ready. Take them out with a slotted spoon and drain them in a colander.

Arrange the *ravioles* in a warm dish, dot with the remaining 2 tablespoons of butter, sprinkle with grated cheese and serve at once.

Farineux

Les Plats de Festin

Festive Dishes

Boeuf Bourguignon, Fondue Bourguignonne, Fondue Savoyarde, Gratinée Lyonnaise, La Pauchouse, Pot-au-Feu Bourguignon, Potée Bourguignonne and the two versions of *Saupiquet* are the sumptuous party dishes presented here.

A crisp salad or a few light appetizers can precede these splendid dishes and a light fruit dessert or a single good cheese conclude the meal. Nothing more is required for a hearty feast.

They can be prepared ahead of time and you can gather as many guests as you wish—nothing will go wrong or need your attention at the last minute. You will truly be able to share the feast.

And because these dishes are exuberant, highly flavored and generous, they can be the core of all your celebrations.

La Fondue Savoyarde

Fondue of Cheese, Wine and Brandy

This is a mountain dish usually eaten in fall and winter when the sheep are brought down from the mountains and shepherds and villagers celebrate. It is also eaten during the *veillées,* when village people meet to speak and sing and shell walnuts (for making walnut oil) and entertain each other in large groups.

This is a lovely dish to share with friends. Don't serve too much wine. Better to drink water instead, and a little kirsch.

You will need a tabletop brazier (preferably fired by butane) and a long-handled fork as well as a standard fork for each guest.

Festive Dishes

For each person:

- *1 garlic clove*
- *2 tablespoons sweet butter*
- *1½ cups grated or shredded Swiss cheese*
- *7 tablespoons dry white wine*
- *½ teaspoon cornstarch, stirred in 2 tablespoons water*
- *½ cup kirsch*
- *Freshly ground black pepper*
- *Freshly grated nutmeg*
- *1 bowl of diced bread*

Put a heavy-bottomed enamel or copper pan over a lit brazier and rub it with the clove of garlic, then add the butter. Add the cheese and wine and cook over a low flame, stirring with a wooden spoon until you have a smooth mixture. When it reaches the boiling point, add the cornstarch and water and stir in the kirsch. Keep stirring. Add pepper and nutmeg. If you think the fondue is too thick, add a little more wine and check the seasoning again.

Each guest will use a long-stemmed fork to spear a piece of bread, then coat it in the hot fondue cooking in the center of the table. The bread should be transferred to a standard fork to avoid burning the lips.

When most of the fondue has been consumed, break one or two yolks and the rest of the diced bread into the pot and stir until golden.

Note: There are many variations on this recipe. Some marinate diced pieces of cheese in milk, then stir it with egg yolks over a low flame and sprinkle it with truffles, but the recipe above is the classic one.

Boeuf Bourguignon

Beef Stew of Burgundy

Les Plats
de Festin

There are so many variations of this dish that the definitive one cannot be determined. It can be made with beef heart or beef cheek or any good American eye of round or round steak. It is better prepared ahead, degreased and reheated, and is best served with a plain potato or pasta accompaniment and a sharp celery or fennel purée (p. 206) or with boiled chestnuts.

For 8 people:
- *3 pounds round steak, rump roast, eye of round or chuck, cut into 2-inch cubes*
- *3 tablespoons brandy*
- *1 quart good red wine*
- *5 yellow onions*
- *2 bay leaves*
- *5 whole peppercorns*
- *1 sprig of thyme*
- *1 tablespoon vegetable oil*
- *3 tablespoons lard (or 3 tablespoons sweet butter and vegetable oil)*
- *½ pound (about 2 cups) bacon (or lean salt pork) cut into small cubes*
- *2 tablespoons flour*
- *3 carrots, sliced*
- *20 pearl onions (or 10 yellow onions, cut in half)*
- *3 whole garlic cloves, peeled*
- *Grated nutmeg to taste*
- *1½ pounds mushrooms, thickly sliced*
- *1 tablespoon butter*
- *2 tablespoons minced parsley*

Place the beef cubes in a large bowl with the brandy, wine, 1 yellow onion (peeled and quartered), bay leaves, peppercorns, thyme and oil. Cover and store on the lowest shelf of the refrigerator for 48 hours.

Heat the lard in a heavy-bottomed pan and sauté the bacon on all sides. Remove and keep for later use. Add the drained meat cubes to the skillet and sauté on all sides for 10 minutes. Sprinkle flour over them and stir with a wooden spoon. (The flour will form a light crust on each piece.)

Bring the marinade to a boil and pour one-half of it over the meat. Cook the meat, uncovered, for 30 minutes. Chop the remaining yellow onions. Add the rest of the marinade, the onions and the reserved bacon to the meat. Cover and cook gently for 2½ to 3 hours. Add the carrots, pearl onions, garlic and nutmeg. Check the seasoning and cook for 30 minutes. Let cool. Remove the bay leaves, peppercorns, and

Festive Dishes

the sprig of thyme, cover and refrigerate overnight.

The next day, remove as much fat from the top of the pan as possible. Reheat and check the seasoning. Sauté the mushrooms in the butter until they are browned and add to the pan. Cover and cook for 10 minutes. Serve in a warm dish, sprinkled with parsley.

Fondue Bourguignonne

Cubes of Beef Cooked in Oil and Served with a Variety of Sauces

A newcomer to the Burgundy repertory, this is an easy dish to prepare and a festive experience to share with friends.

Serve with a hearty red wine and a large bowl of green tossed salad.

To serve this communal dish, you will need a tabletop brazier (a butane-fired one is best), and a long-handled fork as well as a standard fork for each guest.

For 8 people:

5 pounds very tender fillet or sirloin of beef, diced (2-by 2-inch cubes)
1 quart peanut oil
1 bowl of homemade mayonnaise flavored with lemon
1 bowl of homemade mayonnaise flavored with curry
1 bowl of homemade mayonnaise flavored with Spanish saffron
1 bowl of spicy tomato sauce
1 bowl of tiny onions
1 bowl of cornichons
1 bowl of capers

Place the oil in a heavy-bottomed enamel or copper pan over a lit brazier in the middle of the table. Heat it to just the boiling point and then adjust the heat to maintain the temperature. Pass the various bowls of sauce to each guest.

Each guest will cook his or her meat for a few seconds, changing forks for dipping so as not to burn the lips or to cloud the oil with the sauces, then dip the meat in one of the sauces and nibble capers, gherkins or onions with it.

Les Plats
de Festin

Gratinée Lyonnaise

A Superb Version of Onion Soup Enriched with Eggs, Cheese and
Madeira Wine

Whether it is at dawn after the theater or in the evening for a large family dinner, onion soup is always a treat. It should be followed by a plate of highly seasoned country ham and sausages or, better, by a plate of raw oysters and a good beer. It should be accompanied by an old brandy or Calvados, the fine apple brandy.

For 8 to 10 people:

> 4 pounds (about 12 cups) yellow onions, peeled and
>   thinly sliced
> ¾ cup and 4 tablespoons sweet butter
> 3 tablespoons flour
> 2 quarts chicken broth (or beef broth or water)
>   Salt
>   Freshly ground white pepper
> 10 slices of stale bread, lightly toasted
> 4 tablespoons Madeira
> 4 cups grated Swiss cheese
> 2 whole eggs
> 1 onion, finely grated (optional)

Sauté the sliced onions in ¾ cup of the butter in a large covered skillet until they turn golden. Sprinkle them with flour and stir with a wooden spoon for a few minutes. Meanwhile, heat the broth and blend it little by little with the onions. Add salt and pepper and simmer for 30 minutes, uncovered, skimming the froth off the top from time to time.

Preheat oven to 400°.

Sauté the slices of bread in 4 tablespoons of butter until crisp on both sides (or simply toast and butter them). Pour 3 tablespoons of the Madeira into an ovenproof dish, or, if you prefer, into small individual ovenproof bowls. Add a layer of the bread and sprinkle with half of the grated cheese.

Beat the eggs with the remaining tablespoon of Madeira and pour the mixture into the broth, stirring constantly. Pour the broth over the bread and cheese, sprinkle with the remain-

Festive Dishes

ing cheese and bake for about 20 minutes. Just before serving, a nice touch is to lift the cheese crust slightly and beat 1 tablespoon of grated onion into each bowl.

Variation:
You may wish to add ½ cup of wine to the stock while preparing the soup, then 4 tablespoons of good brandy just before serving.

Le Pot-au-Feu Bourguignon
Burgundy's Version of the Boiled Dinner

Every province boasts its own version of this wonderful boiled dinner, but it is in Burgundy that it becomes a truly superb creation. It is, of course, never boiled, but gently simmered. In this harmonious dish composed of many ingredients, the meat remains moist and tasty, the vegetables crunchy and full of flavor, and the broth heady yet lean. It is, in fact, such a treat that in the old days the broth used to be kept for new mothers, old people and lovesick teenagers. At springtime a branch of the boxwood tree dipped in the broth scared away bad spirits, snakes and ill omens for a whole year.

Pot-au-feu is a glorious meal in itself, and only a crisp tossed green salad and a robust red wine are needed to accompany it. The secret of a great *pot-au-feu* is to prepare it a day ahead and degrease it completely before you add the vegetables. The bones, the vegetables and the meat must be fresh and well trimmed. Remember that the dish has to be highly seasoned to be genuinely *bourguignon,* so taste the broth before serving it and prepare two or three sauces to accompany the meat. Since everything can be prepared ahead of time, you, too, can relax and enjoy the feast.

Les Plats
de Festin

For about 10 people:

1 large onion studded with 2 cloves
1 tablespoon vegetable oil
2 large beef bones (about 1 pound)
3 pounds brisket of beef, tied with a string
3 pounds rump roast (or sirloin tip or boneless chuck),
    tied with a string to keep its shape
2 pounds short ribs
1 oxtail, cut in 4 pieces
5 quarts chicken broth (or cold water)
1 carrot, peeled
1 celery stalk
1 garlic bulb (with about 7 cloves), unpeeled
3 bay leaves
2 sprigs thyme
10 peppercorns
    Salt
1 4-pound stewing hen
½ cup chicken livers
1 tablespoon sweet butter
1 onion, finely chopped
1 cup lean bacon (or lean salt pork)
3 teaspoons thyme
    Freshly ground pepper
1 egg, beaten
1 cup cooked rice
1 garlic clove, chopped
½ cup finely chopped parsley
2 onions, peeled
10 carrots, peeled
4 large Polish sausages (or any similar sausage)
1 celery heart
10 potatoes, peeled
10 turnips, peeled
1 small head of green cabbage
10 slices of bread, each cut into 2 triangles and fried
    in butter
½ cup grated Swiss cheese
    Kosher salt
2 large marrow bones, cut into 10 1-inch pieces by the
    butcher

Festive Dishes

Accompaniments

Tomato sauce (p. 65)
Vinaigrette
1 bowl of kosher salt
1 bowl of pickled gherkins (cornichons)

Brown the clove-studded onion in oil in a heavy skillet for 2 minutes. (You will add it to your broth to give it a pretty caramel color.)

Place the bones in the bottom of a very large pot, add all the meat on top, and cover with chicken broth (or cold water). Bring to a boil and cook for 5 minutes, skimming the froth off the surface. Add the clove-studded onion, the carrot, celery, garlic bulb, bay leaves, thyme, peppercorns and salt. Bring to a boil and skim off once more. Partially cover and simmer for 2 hours.

Meanwhile, prepare the stuffing for the hen. Cut the chicken livers with scissors. Heat the butter in a skillet and sauté the chopped onion, cooking over low heat for 3 minutes. Add the bacon (or lean salt pork) and the chicken livers and cook for 2 more minutes, tossing. Remove from the heat; add the thyme, pepper, egg, rice, chopped garlic and parsley. Check the seasonings and stuff, then sew the chicken closed.

Add the stuffed chicken to the bones and meat and cook for 1½ hours. Remove from the heat, cover and refrigerate overnight.

The next day, carefully remove all the fat on the surface of the broth, the clove-studded onion, the bay leaves, thyme and garlic bulb. Bring the broth with the bones, meat and chicken to a boil. Add the whole onions and carrots and cook for 15 minutes, then add the sausages, celery heart, potatoes and turnips. Simmer for 30 minutes. Check the seasoning.

Boil the cabbage separately in a pan of salted water for 15 to 20 minutes. Meanwhile, prepare the croutons, the grated cheese, the sauces you want to serve, the bowls of kosher salt and pickled gherkins.

Press a teaspoon of kosher salt on both openings of each marrow bone to prevent the marrow from melting away, and add the bones to the cabbage to cook for 10 minutes.

Preheat the oven to 300°.

When you are ready to serve, place the beef on a warm ovenproof serving platter. Remove the strings and slice the

Les Plats
de Festin

meat. Season with salt and pepper and pour a tablespoon of broth over it. Cover with foil and place in the oven. Remove the chicken from the broth. Scoop out the stuffing, slice it and place it in the center of a warm ovenproof platter, surrounded by the pieces of chicken. Pour a little broth over everything, cover with foil and put in the oven.

Arrange the vegetables on a warm ovenproof serving dish and place the thickly sliced sausages and marrow bones in the center. Cover with foil and place in the oven to keep warm.

Serve the broth in soup bowls with croutons, sprinkled with cheese. You may also want to add—as old Burgundy gourmets do—1 tablespoon red wine to each bowl of soup or else 1 tablespoon cream and 1 tablespoon sherry, stirring well.

Then comes the second course, served on three platters: beef, chicken, sausage, marrow bones and vegetables. Be sure to serve small teaspoons or butter knives with the marrow bones so that each guest can scoop out the marrow and spread it on the warm potatoes.

Pass the sauces, kosher salt and gherkins.

Note: You can use the leftover broth two days later by adding to each bowl of hot broth 1 egg yolk mixed with 1 tablespoon of cream and 1 tablespoon of chervil and stirring vigorously.

You can use the leftover meat or chicken in croquettes, shepherd's pie, or in a cold salad with sliced potatoes, shallots soaked in a spicy vinaigrette sauce, or in a *Boeuf à la Mâcon* (p. 111) cooked with sliced onions and vinegar.

La Pauchouse

A Fish Stew Prepared with White Wine, Onions, Garlic and Cream

The name comes from *poche,* the fisherman's bag where he puts his catch, and it can be spelled either "pauchouse" or "pochouse." It is a sort of Burgundy bouillabaisse, a fragrant fish stew, with a rich sauce.

The mixture of four kinds of fish—pike, perch, eel and carp —and dry white wine is the essence of the dish, but each restaurant and each family has its own tricks to personalize its *pauchouse.* It is a cousin of the *meurette,* which is made with red wine.

Festive Dishes

The recipe we have comes from medieval sources. Serve with white wine of the kind used in the preparation of the dish.

For 8 people:

2 *tablespoons vegetable oil*
20 *garlic cloves, peeled and crushed*
4 *shallots, peeled and chopped*
10 *pearl onions (or 4 quartered yellow onions)*
2 *bay leaves*
1 *sprig of thyme*
10 *peppercorns*
6 *cups dry white wine*
2 *pounds pike, chopped in 2-inch pieces*
2 *pounds carp, chopped in 2-inch pieces*
1 *pound eel, skinned and chopped in 2-inch pieces*
1 *pound perch, chopped in 2-inch pieces*
  Salt
  Freshly ground black pepper
4 *tablespoons flour*
4 *tablespoons sweet butter*
6 *tablespoons cream*
8 *slices of bread fried in butter and rubbed with garlic to make croutons*

Put the oil in a heavy-bottomed dish and add the garlic, shallots, onions, bay leaves, thyme and peppercorns. Pour the wine into the dish and cook over medium heat, covered, for 10 minutes, stirring from time to time. Add the pieces of fish, sprinkle with salt and pepper, cover and simmer for 15 minutes.

Knead the flour and butter into a paste. Add to the sauce and simmer for 10 minutes. Remove from the heat and add the cream. Check and correct the seasoning.

Place crisp croutons and pieces of fish on each plate and pour through a sieve some of the broth on top.

Potée Bourguignonne

Burgundy Boiled Dinner with Shoulder of Pork, Spareribs, Sausages, Ham and a Variety of Vegetables

Les Plats
de Festin

228

This hearty and invigorating dinner slowly simmered in the Burgundy way celebrates the perfect harmony between the region's garden and its pork. It is good reheated, so you had better make an abundant *potée*. In some parts of Burgundy, white or green beans are added.

For about 16 people:

  1 *head of green cabbage, trimmed and quartered*
  1 *shoulder (or butt) of pork*
  1 -*pound piece of lean salt pork*
    Half of a precooked ham—about 4
      pounds
  1 *pig's knuckle*
  1 *pound spareribs*
    Kosher salt
  6 *leeks, trimmed*
 10 *whole carrots, peeled*
  8 *whole turnips, peeled*
  4 *garlic cloves, peeled*
  3 *onions, peeled and each studded with 1 clove*
    Bouquet garni
 10 *peppercorns*
  4 *smoked sausages*
  2 *large Polish cooking-type sausages, such as kielbasa*
 10 *large potatoes, peeled*
    Salt
    Freshly ground black pepper
    Dijon-style mustard

Blanch the cabbage in a large pot of salted water for 5 minutes. Drain and set aside.

Place all the meat except the sausages in a large pot of cold water with salt. Bring it to a boil and cook for 1½ hours, removing the foam from time to time.

Add all the vegetables except the cabbage and potatoes; add the bouquet garni and the peppercorns. Cook for 20 minutes. Add the sausages, potatoes and cabbage and cook for 30 minutes. Degrease as much as you can.

Serve the broth with toasted bread. (The broth will be very tasty, but will be better kept for the next day, when you can degrease it more easily.)

Place all the meat and sausages in the center of a large warm shallow dish. Slice the sausages. Pile the vegetables all around. Pour a ladle of broth over the dish, sprinkle with salt

Festive Dishes

and pepper and serve with a bowl of mustard.

Saupiquet I

A Whole Ham Baked with Vegetables, Spices, Wine, Cream and
Fresh Herbs

This is a medieval dish, interpreted through the centuries in
so many ways that I had to be very, very selective in my
choice. The following two versions are piquant yet mellow in
some subtle way and will be wonderful for a festive meal.
Serve with *Champignons de Dijon* (p. 177), *Crépinette aux Marrons* (p. 32) or a tossed salad.

>   1 precooked 6–8-pound smoked ham
>   3 carrots, peeled and sliced
>   3 onions, peeled and sliced
>   8 tablespoons sweet butter
>   2 garlic cloves, peeled
>   3 teaspoons thyme
>   2 bay leaves, crushed
>   5 juniper berries, crushed
>   Freshly ground pepper
>   3 cups white wine
>   1 quart stock (preferably beef)
>   2 pounds mushrooms, cleaned and sliced
>   2 tablespoons vegetable oil
>   Salt
>   Freshly ground pepper
>   Juice of 1 lemon
>   2 cups cream
>   Fresh tarragon (or any other fresh
>   herb), minced

Cover the ham with cold water and simmer it, covered, according to the directions given by the butcher or written on
the package, until very tender.

Remove the ham from the liquid. Peel off the skin and
discard most of the fat.

Sauté the carrots and onions in 4 tablespoons of the butter
for 5 minutes. Scatter them in the bottom of a very deep pan
and put the ham on top. Add the garlic, thyme, bay leaves,

juniper berries and pepper. Pour the wine and stock into the pan, cover and bring to a boil. Simmer for 1 hour.

Meanwhile, sauté the mushrooms in 4 tablespoons of butter and the oil for 10 minutes. Sprinkle with salt, pepper and lemon juice and set aside.

Preheat the oven to 300°.

Pour all the cooking juices from the ham into a saucepan. Degrease carefully and cook, uncovered, over high heat until the liquid is reduced to 2 cups. Slice the ham and cover it with foil, keeping it warm in a turned-off oven.

Pour the reduced liquid over the mushrooms and reheat. Stir in the cream and check the seasoning.

Spoon this sauce over the ham, sprinkle with tarragon and serve the rest of the sauce in a bowl along with the sliced ham.

Saupiquet II

Ham Cooked with Garlic and Herbs and Served with a Vinegar, Shallot, Juniper and Cream Sauce

A more pungent version.

> 1 7-pound uncooked ham
> Coarse salt
> Freshly ground pepper
> 3 garlic cloves, peeled and cut into ¼-inch slivers
> 3 bay leaves
> 2 tablespoons thyme
> 1 teaspoon sage
> 1 teaspoon savory
> Salt
> 1½ cups wine vinegar
> 10 shallots, peeled and finely chopped
> 5 juniper berries, crushed
> 3 cups light cream
> Tarragon, finely chopped
> Watercress

Preheat the oven to 350°.

Remove the skin, the top part of the bone and part of the

fat from the ham and rub with coarse salt. Let the ham sit for 2 hours. Dry it with a clean cloth and rub it with pepper. Insert the garlic slivers with a sharp knife all over the ham.

Crush together the bay leaves, thyme, sage and savory and sprinkle the mixture all over the ham, pressing to make it stick; sprinkle with salt and pepper.

Place the ham in a deep baking dish and bake, uncovered, in the oven for 2 to 3 hours. Then cover with foil and cook for 1½ hours more.

During the last half hour, prepare the sauce. Heat the vinegar and add the shallots and juniper berries. Boil for 20 minutes, or until most of the liquid is gone. Stir in the cream and check the seasoning.

Remove the ham from the oven and slice it. Put the slices of ham on a warm serving dish and spoon the sauce over them. Sprinkle with tarragon and serve surrounded with watercress.

Les Plats
de Festin

Les Fromages

Cheese

Cheese adds to the enjoyment of wine tasting and is a true part of Burgundy's patrimony because it has been prepared by generations of attentive monks and patient farmers' wives.

When milk turns, it is usually put in an earthenware pot pierced with holes. As the cheese becomes firmer it is placed on a wooden tray covered with a layer of straw. Salted water is spread on the surface, and according to the season the crust becomes pale gold or red. The cheese is ready after fifteen to thirty days and may be covered with ashes to help it dry. Three quarts of milk are needed for an average cheese.

In Burgundy, making cheese is an endless activity because it has always been the main food for grape pickers and workers in the fields.

There is a wide variety of cheese made from cow's milk as well as from goat cheese. The rich pastures along the rivers are territory for dairy cattle, while goats graze near the vineyards on the rocky hills.

Cheese made from cow's milk is eaten fresh in desserts or whipped with fresh herbs *(claqueret).* It can be mixed with white wine, brandy, leeks and broth and then fermented, or dried and then marinated in oil or brine. The main soft fresh cheeses are *Sainte Marie des Laumes* and *Sainte Reine d'Alise,* along with many highly flavored cheeses from Beaujolais. Then there are the soft cheeses with washed crusts, such as *Epoisses,* with its orange crust and sumptuous texture and flavor; *Boule des Moines Pierre Qui Vire; Saint Forentine;* and *Soumaintrain.* There are many *tommes;* there is *Emmenthal* (a sort of Swiss cheese), and *Bresse Bleu,* a blue cheese as smooth as gorgonzola.

In Savoy, east of Burgundy, there is a rich kind of *Emmenthal,* a *Reblochon* and different *tommes,* flavored with brandy, fennel and herbs.

Goat cheese can also be served fresh with thick cream. It

Cheese

tastes best from April to October, after the ewes have produced their young. Goat cheeses are shaped like logs, cones or balls; are wrapped in plane, grape or chestnut leaves, and sprinkled with pepper, grape seeds, herbs or ashes. As they dry in straw the crusts turn pale blue. They always have evocative names: *Bouton de Culotte* (pants button), *Claquebiton, Chevreton, Plardon, Picodon.*

Finally, there are home preparations. The *cancoillotte* is a creamy mixture of butter stirred with *meton* (the milk left after making *Emmenthal*). To ferment it, *cancoillotte* used to be kept under the family-bed eiderdown in farmers' houses in the past. It is served with garlic, salt, pepper and white wine.

Then there is the invigorating *fromage fort,* a tasty mixture of fresh cheese, white wine, walnut oil, brandy, salt and pepper that is fermented; it is used as a spread for warm toast.

There is also the *fromage pourri* (rotten cheese), made with goat cheese wrapped in leaves, sprinkled with brandy and kept in earthenware pots for three weeks.

Usually the wines served with the cheeses come from the same regions, and white wines are generally served with goat cheese, hearty red wine with strong cheese made from cow's milk, light red wine with mild cheese.

Baguettes

Deep-Fried Cheese Sticks

These make good appetizers.

For 8 people:

½ pound Swiss cheese cut in sticks ½ inch thick and 2
inches long
1 cup milk
¾ cup flour
2 eggs, beaten
¾ cup bread crumbs
6 tablespoons sweet butter
Parsley

Les Fromages

Place the cheese sticks in the milk for 2 hours. Drain and roll them in the flour, then in the eggs and finally the bread crumbs.

Fry the cheese sticks in the butter for 2 minutes on each side and serve with fried parsley.

Délice de Fromages

A Blend of Various Cheeses, Wine and Broth

A hearty mixture from Beaujolais, perfect for a robust dinner, a picnic or a buffet. Use the different cheeses available where you are.

For 8 people:

- *3 tablespoons goat cheese, grated or diced*
- *3 tablespoons freshly grated cow's-milk cheese of any kind*
- *2 tablespoons freshly grated Swiss cheese*
- *2 tablespoons cottage or farmer cheese*
- *½ cup vegetable broth, made with leeks or celery*
- *2 tablespoons dry white wine*
- *1 tablespoon sweet butter, softened*
- *1 teaspoon freshly ground pepper or nutmeg (optional)*

Mix all the cheeses in a large bowl and crush them with a fork. Stir in the broth, then the wine and the butter to make a thick soft mixture. Check the seasoning. You may want to add a little pepper or grated nutmeg.

Spread on toasted bread and serve with a hearty red wine.

La Cervelle de Canut

A Highly Seasoned Blending of Fresh Cheese, Herbs and Wine

A traditional Lyon dessert, also called *claqueret battu*. It is invigorating, and you can use whatever fresh herbs are availa-

ble. It must be beaten vigorously, "as if it were your wife"
goes the saying. A *canut* is a worker in the silk factories of
Lyon, the French silk capital.

For 8 people:

1 pound white farmer cheese (or cottage cheese mixed
with 3 tablespoons sour cream)
Salt
Freshly ground black pepper
1 cup minced chives, tarragon and dill
1 garlic clove, peeled and minced
3 tablespoons light cream
1 tablespoon sour cream
2 tablespoons dry white wine
1 tablespoon good wine vinegar
2 tablespoons vegetable oil

Whip the farmer cheese (or cottage cheese and sour cream).
Add the salt, pepper, herbs and garlic and continue whipping.
Add the light cream, sour cream, wine, vinegar and oil and
stir well. It will be smooth and creamy. Check the seasoning
and chill. Spread on lightly toasted slices of wholewheat
bread.

Fromage Fort du Beaujolais

A Cheese Blend with White Wine

This and the *Cervelle de Canut* (above), are the two main classic
cheese blends in Lyon.

½ cup grated goat cheese
½ cup grated cow's-milk cheese
½ cup Swiss cheese
½ cup farmer cheese
½ cup grated Parmesan or Romano cheese
¼ cup vegetable broth (preferably made with leek and
celery)
¼ cup dry white wine
2 tablespoons sweet butter

Les Fromages

Mix all the ingredients by hand or in a blender or food processor and add the broth and wine to make a soft paste. Place in a tightly closed pot for 15 days.

Spread on toast or endive leaves or eat as is with a spoon. Drink a Beaujolais wine with it, of course. This can be served as an hors d'oeuvre or at the end of a meal.

Chèvre Chaud

A Tossed Salad Topped with a Melted Goat Cheese

A lovely first course.

Prepare a mixed green salad. Season it with wine vinegar and olive oil or only walnut oil. Place a 1-inch-thick round of creamy goat cheese on a cookie sheet and leave it for 2 minutes in a 325° oven.

Spread a little salad on each individual plate and place a piece of the melted goat cheese on top. Serve at once.

Les Desserts

Desserts

The Greeks and the Romans used honey, spices and pepper in their pastry, and Burgundian cuisine has kept some of these curious pungent blends in some desserts. The famous *pain d'épice* follows the original medieval recipe, but many of the overly elaborate desserts—heavy fruit pancakes, creamy custards, chestnut or corn-flour confections—have been lightened and sharpened in taste in the past few years. Rich, bland desserts have no appeal to our palates, so the addition of fruits, spices, brandy and liqueurs, of tart fruit purées and bitter sauces, has increased. A tray of cheese is also truly appealing when served along with a beautifully arranged basket of pears, grapes, cherries or melon.

I looked for exciting desserts to complement any meal in selecting the following recipes.

Bugnes Lyonnaises

Light Fritters

For 8 people:

½ cup sweet butter, softened
½ cup sugar
1 teaspoon salt
Peel of 1 lemon, grated
3 egg yolks
2 tablespoons rum
2½ cups unbleached flour
1 tablespoon vegetable oil
Oil for deep-frying
Confectioners' sugar

Mix together the soft butter, sugar, salt and grated lemon peel until fluffy. Stir in the egg yolks, one at a time, then the rum. Add the flour and stir. Add the oil, cover with a towel, and let stand for 3 hours.

Shape the dough into walnut-size balls and flatten them until they are very thin. Cut in half and deep-fry in very hot oil for about 3 minutes on each side. Drain on paper towels and sprinkle with confectioners' sugar.

Beignets à la Crème

Cream Fritters

Custard

3 cups light cream
1 cup unbleached flour
6 egg yolks, beaten
1½ cups sugar
Peel of 2 lemons, grated

Batter

2 egg yolks, beaten
2 tablespoons sugar
¾ cup unbleached flour
1 teaspoon salt
1 tablespoon sweet butter, softened
⅔ cup water

Oil for deep-frying
Sugar

Heat the cream in a heavy-bottomed pan. While stirring, slowly add the flour, beaten egg yolks, sugar and lemon peel. Continue stirring. When the mixture coats the spoon, remove from the heat. Let the custard cool until it sets. Cut into 2-inch squares.

Prepare the batter by mixing together all the ingredients. Dip the cubes of custard into the light batter and deep-fry them until they turn golden. Drain on paper towels and sprinkle with sugar.

Desserts

Beignets au Caillé

Delicate Fritters Made with Cheese, Flour and Egg Whites

There are endless varieties of fritters in Lyon and in Burgundy. They can be made of potato flour, grated cheese, and called *talmouzes;* of corn flour, egg whites, bread crumbs; and of all kinds of fruit and blossoms.

These fritters are made with freshly made curds *(caille),* but it can be replaced by a mixture of sour cream and cheese, which are easier to find.

For 8 people:

½ *cup cottage cheese*
½ *cup sour cream*
1 *cup unbleached flour*
3 *eggs, beaten*
1 *teaspoon salt*
6 *tablespoons sugar*
2 *tablespoons orange-blossom water or lemon juice*
  Oil for deep-frying
1 *cup confectioners' sugar*

Mix all the ingredients in a bowl. The mixture should be smooth and thick. Heat the cooking oil and deep-fry 1 tablespoon of the mixture at a time until each fritter turns golden. Drain on paper towels and sprinkle with sugar while still warm.

Biscuit de Savoie

A Light Cake Made with Cornstarch, Flour, Eggs and Lemon

Prepared in Chambéry, Savoy, in the middle of the fourteenth century, and tested by generations of cooks, this is one of the most popular cakes. It is served either with a bowl of stewed fruit, or coated with a fruit coulis (p. 248), with tangerines in Armagnac (p. 262) or with a warm butter-chocolate sauce.

Potato flour, which is traditionally used, is replaced here by

Les Desserts

240

plain cornstarch or arrowroot, which is easier to find and equally light.

For 6 to 8 people:

1½ *cups and 4 tablespoons sugar*
6 *egg yolks*
6 *egg whites*
1 *cup unbleached flour*
1 *cup cornstarch*
2 *teaspoons grated lemon peel*
2 *tablespoons orange-blossom water (or lemon juice)*
2 *teaspoons confectioners' sugar*

Butter a tall mold and dust it with flour. Whip 1½ cups of the sugar and egg yolks until they form a pale yellow ribbon.

Preheat oven to 350°.

Whip the egg whites and 4 tablespoons of sugar until stiff. Combine the flour and cornstarch. Fold the egg whites and flour alternately into the yolk mixture. Add the lemon peel and orange-blossom water. Pour into the prepared mold. It should only be three-quarters filled.

Sprinkle the top with confectioners' sugar and bake for 35 to 45 minutes, until cooked through. If the top begins to brown, place a sheet of wet paper on it.

Remove from the oven and let cool. Wrap in foil to keep fresh.

Biscuits au Citron

Light Crisp Cookies

⅓ *cup confectioners' sugar*
1 *cup unbleached flour*
½ *cup powdered almonds*
⅔ *cup sweet butter, softened*
1 *egg, well beaten*
Pinch of salt
Peel of 2 lemons, grated

Desserts

Mix the sugar, flour and the almonds. In another bowl, combine the butter, egg, salt and lemon peel and mix vigorously.

Stir in the sugar mixture. Cover and refrigerate for a few hours.

Preheat the oven to 350°.

Roll out the dough as thin as you can and cut it in strips or circles. Place the pieces on a well-buttered cookie sheet. Bake for 10 minutes, or until golden.

Beignets de Compote

Applesauce Fritters

This delicate dessert comes from Lyon and remains a favorite among fritter lovers.

For 8 people:

  2 egg yolks, beaten
  ⅔ cup sweet white wine
  2 tablespoons sugar
  ¾ cup unbleached flour
  1 teaspoon salt
  1 tablespoon sweet butter, softened
  2 pounds apples (Granny Smith or any other tart
    apples), peeled, cored and grated
  2 tablespoons sugar
  1 lemon peel, grated
    Oil for deep-frying
  2 egg whites, stiffly beaten but not dry
    Confectioners' sugar

Blend the egg yolks, wine and sugar with a fork. Stir in the flour, salt and butter to form a smooth batter. Cover and leave in a warm place, such as a turned-off oven, until ready to use.

Cook the apples with the sugar and lemon peel, uncovered, until soft.

Heat the oil in a skillet until it is very hot. Delicately fold egg whites into the batter (it should be very smooth). Take a tablespoon of the applesauce at a time, dip it in the batter for a second, then drop it into the hot oil. Fry the fritters until golden on all sides, turning them with a pair of tongs after about 3 minutes. Remove with a slotted spoon and drain on paper towels. Keep warm in a low or turned-off oven.

Les Desserts

Line a large serving plate or a basket with a napkin, place the fritters on it, sprinkle with sugar and serve warm. Some like to sprinkle a little brandy on the warm fritters just before serving.

Caramels

> 2 cups light cream
> 1 ounce unsweetened chocolate, cut in pieces
> 1½ cups sugar
> 2 tablespoons honey
> 5 teaspoons sweet butter

Bring to a boil 1 cup of the cream, the chocolate and the sugar. Add the rest of the cream little by little, stirring all the time with a wooden spoon. Add the honey, then the butter, a teaspoon at a time, until you can clearly see the bottom of the pan. Remove from heat.

Pour into a buttered square mold and let cool for 2 hours. When it is no longer too soft, cut into squares and wrap individually in waxed paper.

Cassolettes Meringuées

Black Cherries in Red Wine, Covered with Meringue and Baked

An elegant dessert you can make with fresh or canned black cherries and serve with a sweet wine.

For 8 people:

> 2 pounds black cherries
> ¾ cup sugar
> 1 teaspoon cinnamon
> 1 cup good red wine
> 6 egg whites
> Pinch of salt
> ⅓ cup confectioners' sugar

Desserts

Wash and pit the cherries. Place them in a heavy-bottomed pan with the sugar, cinnamon and wine. Simmer for 10 minutes, shaking from time to time.

Place the cherries in individual ovenproof dishes.

Preheat the oven to 200°.

Whip the egg whites with the salt and gradually beat in the confectioners' sugar until stiff. Cover each little dish with the egg whites. Sprinkle with confectioners' sugar and bake for about 40 minutes. Serve warm or lukewarm.

La Châtaigne

A Chestnut Pie

This delicate dessert is Burgundy's poor man's treat, since chestnuts have always been the cheapest commodity in the region. Colette, the writer, remembered her favorite dessert as a child: she would place a few boiled chestnuts in a clean handkerchief, sprinkle them with sugar and crush them to make a sweet warm purée.

For 8 people:

2 pounds chestnuts (fresh or canned)
2 teaspoons fennel seeds
1 clove
1½ cups sugar
½ cup sweet butter, softened
3 egg yolks, beaten
3 egg whites, stiffly beaten
½ cup chopped almonds or hazelnuts

Preheat oven to 300°.

Boil the chestnuts in a large pot of salted water with the fennel seeds and the clove. Peel, crush and pass them through a sieve or a Moulinex mill. If you use canned blanched chestnuts, add ½ teaspoon of fennel seeds and a touch of powdered clove to your purée.

Stir in the sugar and butter, then the eggs yolks. Carefully stir in the egg whites and pour into a well-buttered ovenproof

Les Desserts

dish. Sprinkle with the nuts and bake for 40 minutes. It can be served lukewarm or cold with a bowl of cream.

Clafoutis I

A Fruit Dessert

Clafoutis comes in many different guises. It can be prepared with red or black cherries, peaches, pears or apples, and sometimes it is baked in a pastry shell. I have chosen two versions. The first tends to be essentially a custard; the second, more of a cake.

For 8 people:

> *2 pounds black cherries, unpitted*
> *2 cups milk*
> *3 eggs*
> *1 egg yolk*
> *1 cup plus 3 tablespoons sugar*
> *3 tablespoons sweet butter, softened*
> *1½ cups flour*
> *2 tablespoons kirsch*
> *Pinch of salt*

Break a few cherry pits with a nutcracker and put them in the milk to add flavor to the custard. Bring the milk to a boil and cool. Mix the eggs, egg yolk and ½ cup plus 3 tablespoons of sugar vigorously. Add the butter, flour and kirsch. Stir until smooth. Pass the milk through a sieve into the egg mixture, stirring.

Preheat the oven to 350°.

Prepare the caramel: Heat ½ cup of sugar and 1 tablespoon of water until browned and pour into a well-buttered ovenproof mold. Add the egg-and-milk mixture, then add the cherries, letting them sink in slowly.

Place the mold in a large pan containing 1 cup of warm water and cook for 10 minutes on top of the stove. Bake for 40 minutes. Remove from the oven, wait a few minutes, then unmold. Serve warm or cold.

Desserts

245

Clafoutis II

For 8 people:

2 *pounds cherries, unpitted*
2½ *cups flour*
1 *cup sweet butter*
1 *cup sugar*
4 *eggs*
3 *tablespoons milk*

Preheat the oven to 350°.

Mix together all the ingredients. Bake in a well-buttered dish for 30 minutes.

Coeurs à la Crème

Fresh Cheese Coated with Fruit Purée

The old Abbé Burjeud invented the "triple cream dessert" to make anguished souls sleep peacefully. To make it, mix 1 cup of heavy cream, 1 teaspoon of lemon juice and 1 teaspoon of minced lemon peel. Let the mixture rest for 15 minutes. Add ¼ cup of orange-blossom water. Whip lightly and chill for two hours.

The recipe given below is for a simpler cream dessert. It can be prepared all year round, is light and fresh and will do beautifully for a buffet or at the end of a simple meal.

For 8 people:

2 *pounds Philadelphia cream cheese*
Pinch of salt
4 *tablespoons heavy cream*
2 *cups sour cream*
½ *cup sugar*
½ *cup raspberries or black currants*
3 *tablespoons kirsch*

Les Desserts

Beat the cream cheese, salt and heavy cream until light. Add the sour cream, stir well and pour into individual molds. Cover with plastic wrap and chill for a few hours.

Meanwhile, make the fruit purée: blend the sugar, fruit and kirsch in a Mouli mill or a blender. If black currants are used, add more sugar to taste.

Either unmold the chilled cheese mixture onto a large serving dish and pass around a bowl of raspberry or black currant purée, or unmold each individual mold onto separate plates and put a few teaspoons of purée over it. A few mint leaves placed on the serving plate would make the dish look even more refreshing.

Corniottes

Little Dumplings Filled with Cheese and Cream

These crisp little caps are sometimes filled with apple and honey only, but the following recipe is more interesting.

Pastry

2½ cups unbleached flour
½ cup (8 tablespoons) sweet butter, softened
   Pinch of sugar
1 egg yolk, beaten
   Salt

Filling

5 tablespoons cheese or cottage cheese
2 tablespoons sugar
1 egg
2 tablespoons sour cream
2 tablespoons light cream
2 tablespoons vanilla (or orange-blossom or rose water)
1 egg yolk
1 tablespoon milk
1 cup grated Swiss cheese

Mix together all the pastry ingredients and 1 to 2 tablespoons of water and make into a ball.

Desserts

Preheat the oven to 375°.

Filling: Mix the cheese or cottage cheese, sugar, egg, sour cream, light cream and vanilla (or orange-blossom or rose water) into a fluffy mixture.

Roll the dough to ¼-inch thickness and cut into circles about 4 inches in diameter.

Place 2 tablespoons of the cheese mixture in each circle of dough. Lift three sides of the circle and, with your fingers, pinch them to make a triangle. Brush with a well-beaten mixture of egg yolk and milk, sprinkle with Swiss cheese, place on a buttered cookie sheet, and bake for 30 minutes.

Serve hot or cold.

Confiture au Potiron

A Delicious Pumpkin Jam with Lemon, Carrot, Wine and Rum

This jam can also be made with pumpkin, apple juice and orange, but I love this version.

> 2 pounds pumpkin, peeled, cut into large cubes
> 2 lemons or 1 orange, peeled and diced
> 1 carrot, peeled and diced
> 2½ cups sugar
> 1 tablespoon dry white wine
> 1 tablespoon dark rum (optional)

Toss the pumpkin, lemons and carrot in the sugar and leave overnight, stirring twice.

Simmer, uncovered, in a wide saucepan for 30 minutes. Add the wine and continue cooking for 10 minutes more. Cool. Stir in the rum and pour into a pot. Serve after 2 days.

Coulis de Fruits

A Thick Purée of Fruits

Les Desserts

You can use either fresh or canned fruit for this *coulis*. It can be stored for a week in the refrigerator or frozen. Put it in the blender for two minutes after you take it out of the freezer for a smooth consistency. It is delicious with Savoy cake, plain ice cream, poached pears or cookies.

For 1 quart of *coulis:*

> *2 pounds of peaches or apricots or berries (red currants, blueberries, etc.)*
> *3 tablespoons lemon juice*
> *2½ cups sugar (as needed)*

Peel, pit and quarter the fruit if you are using peaches of apricots. Put it in a blender with the lemon juice and half of the sugar. Blend and continue adding sugar in small amounts until desired sweetness is obtained.

Note: Use only the drained fruit (not the syrup) if you use canned fruit.

Coupes aux Fruits

Fruit Delight

An extravagant and luxurious fruit dessert.

For 8 people:

> *Juice of 8 large oranges*
> *3 pink grapefruit (each section peeled of all membrane)*
> *15 large prunes, soaked for 1 hour in warm tea or water*
> *1 pound strawberries (cut in half if large)*
> *½ pound blueberries (or raspberries)*
> *7 egg yolks*
> *6 tablespoons sugar*
> *3 tablespoons orange brandy or cognac*

Put the orange juice in a saucepan and bring it to a boil. Lower the heat and add the grapefruit sections, the drained prunes and the strawberries. Heat for 2 minutes, then remove the fruit, covering it with foil to keep it warm. Return the juice to the low heat.

Desserts

Beat the egg yolks and sugar until frothy. Add to the warm juice, stirring constantly until the custard covers the spoon. Check the taste and add more sugar if needed, then the orange brandy.

Place some of the grapefruit, prunes, strawberries and blueberries in each individual dessert bowl and pour the warm custard over them.

Serve lukewarm or at room temperature with thin wafers.

Crapiau de Pommes

Apple and Rum Pancakes Served with Cream

There are many names for this traditional country dessert: *crapiaux, grapiaux, sauciaux.* It is always made with tart apples and a thick pancake batter, and served with cream. The original recipe, *tartouillat (tartouillat* means "to mix"), was made with pancake batter and quartered apples or cooked cherries spread on cabbage leaves and baked. This is a good treat for children or for Sunday-night supper. Not elegant, not very light either, but tasty and warm, it has been dear to generations of little Bourguignons.

For 8 people:

3 *pounds crisp apples (preferably Granny Smith),*
   peeled, cored and thinly sliced
6 *tablespoons sugar*
½ *cup good brandy or dark rum*
3 *cups unbleached flour*
7 *eggs, lightly beaten*
1 *cup milk*
   Pinch of salt
5 *tablespoons sweet butter*
4 *tablespoons confectioners' sugar*
1 *bowl of light cream*

Sprinkle the apples with 2 tablespoons of the sugar and marinate in the brandy for 1 to 2 hours.

Mix the flour, eggs, 4 tablespoons sugar, milk, and salt in a large bowl, stirring vigorously. Add the brandy from the marinade and stir well. Add the apples.

Heat the butter in a skillet and make small pancakes. Sprinkle them with sugar and serve with a separate bowl of cream.

Crème aux Fruits

Light Custard Prepared with Fruit Juices and served with Sections of Fruits

A variation on the old Burgundy dessert *Pommes Sévigné* (p. 272). It can be made with apples, pears, pineapples and, of course, oranges and grapefruit, which are the key ingredient of this otherwise traditional custard.

For 8 people:

4 *apples* or *pears, peeled, cored and poached in syrup (or 1 pineapple, peeled and sliced)*
12 *large oranges*
4 *grapefruit*
10 *egg yolks*
1½ *cups sugar*
4 *tablespoons dark rum*
1 *cup heavy cream, whipped*

Prepare the apples (or pears or pineapple). Peel 10 of the oranges and 2 of the grapefruit and divide them into sections. Be careful to remove all of the white pulp of the skin. Set aside.

Press the juice of 2 oranges and 2 grapefruit through a sieve into a saucepan. Bring the juices to a boil and remove from the heat.

Mix the egg yolks and sugar and, stirring vigorously, add gradually to the fruit juice. Stir in the rum. Place over low

Desserts

heat and stir until thick enough to coat the spoon. Remove from the stove and pour into a bowl.

Preheat oven to 350°.

Whip the cream and fold it into the lukewarm custard. Place the fruit sections in individual ovenproof dishes or one large single dish and cover with the custard. Heat in the oven for 3 minutes. Serve lukewarm. You may decorate the top with strawberries or raspberries just before serving.

Flamous

A Creamy Pumpkin Pudding

Sometimes called *flamusse,* this is also made with sliced pears or apples sautéed in butter. The pumpkin version is the most delicate of fall desserts. Canned pumpkin can be used.

> 4 *pounds pumpkin, peeled, cooked and well drained*
> 4 *tablespoons sweet butter*
> 4 *tablespoons unbleached flour*
> 2 *cups cream*
> 4 *egg yolks, beaten*
> ½ *cup sugar*
> 2 *tablespoons brandy*
> 1 *lemon peel, grated*
> 4 *egg whites*
> 2 *tablespoons crystallized sugar*

Peel, cut and blanch the pumpkin in very little water for 20 minutes. Drain, and put it through a sieve.

Heat the butter in a thick-bottomed pan. Add the puréed pumpkin and stir with a wooden spoon over low heat. Add the flour, stirring, then the cream. Remove from the heat and quickly stir in the egg yolks, sugar, brandy and lemon peel.

Preheat oven to 325°.

Beat the egg whites until stiff and fold them delicately into the pumpkin mixture. Pour into a buttered ovenproof dish and bake for 25 minutes.

Cool for a few minutes and unmold. Sprinkle with sugar before serving.

Les Desserts

La Flamusse aux Pommes

A Warm Apple Dessert

Of the many different ways this dessert has been made, the most curious was to dip slices of apple in a crepe-like batter, spread them on buttered cabbage leaves and bake them in an oven. The leaves would disappear, leaving a puzzling taste.

This is a rich, lovely dessert, easy to prepare and highly palatable.

For 8 people:

2 tablespoons sweet butter
8 large Granny Smith apples, peeled and cut into thick slices
4 eggs, beaten
1 tablespoon flour
2 cups milk
3 tablespoons sugar
2 tablespoons dark rum (or orange-blossom water)

Heat the butter in a skillet and cook the apple slices slowly.
Preheat the oven to 350°.

Beat the eggs, add the flour, milk, sugar and rum (or orange-blossom water), stir well and add the cooked apples. Pour into a buttered ovenproof dish.

Bake for 30 to 45 minutes and serve warm in its baking dish.

Fruits Cuits au Vin

Stewed Fruit in White Wine with Spices

Poached in wine and spices, fruit can make the lightest and liveliest of desserts. Apricots, pears, quince, peaches can be stewed with white wine separately or together. This must be done a day ahead for greatest flavor.

Desserts

For 8 people:

1 quart sweet white wine (Sauterne type or a dry Chablis type of white wine)
2 cups sugar (or, better: ½ cup sugar, ½ cup honey)
1 whole lemon, sliced
1 whole orange, sliced
2 bay leaves
1 clove (or 3 coriander seeds)
3 pounds fruit, peeled, pitted and sliced (quince should be very thinly sliced)
Mint leaves (optional)

Heat the wine, sugar, lemon, orange, bay leaves and clove (or coriander). Add the fruit when the liquid is hot but not boiling. Lower the heat and simmer for 15 to 20 minutes. Check to see if the fruit is tender. Place it in a large glass or china bowl, cool and let rest overnight in the refrigerator. Remove the bay leaves and clove and sprinkle with whole mint leaves if you have them. Serve cold.

Framboises à la Neige

Floating Island Prepared with Raspberry Purée

A light and lovely dessert to serve after an elaborate meal.

For 8 people:

2 pounds raspberries, fresh or frozen (or strawberries or red currants)
Sugar to taste
16 egg whites
Pinch of salt

Pass the berries through a blender, pour the purée through a sieve and add sugar to taste. Chill.

Beat the egg whites with the salt until stiff.

Heat about 2 quarts of water in a wide skillet. Using a ladle, scoop up the egg whites and dip each ladleful in the simmering water. Cook each ball for 30 seconds on each side, place on a layer of paper towels and set aside.

Just before serving, pile the white balls in a shallow dish and serve the raspberry purée in a separate bowl.

Fruits Caramélisés au Vin Rouge

Carmelized Fruits Cooked in Red Wine

A tart, lovely dessert. Prepare a day ahead for a richer flavor and serve with *Massepains* (p.263).

> For 8 people:
> *1 pound large pitted prunes*
> *1 orange, unpeeled, sliced*
> *1 sliced lemon, unpeeled, sliced*
> *½ pound raisins, preferably the large black Spanish type*
> *5 coriander seeds*
> *5 bay leaves*
> *¾ cup sugar*
> *About 1 quart red wine, enough to cover*
> *2 oranges, peeled and very thinly sliced*
> *2 lemons, peeled and very thinly sliced*

Let the prunes stand in tea or water for 3 hours. Place them in a large saucepan with the unpeeled orange and lemon slices, raisins, coriander, bay leaves, ¾ cup of the sugar and enough red wine to cover. Bring to a boil, uncovered, reduce the heat and cook for 20 minutes. Cool in the juice and let stand for a day.

A few hours before the meal, remove the prunes and raisins and set aside. Bring the wine, herbs and unpeeled orange and lemon slices to a boil and reduce by half until it becomes syrupy. Discard the unpeeled orange and lemon slices. Add the peeled orange and lemon slices and cook for 5 minutes. Let the mixture cool.

Place the prunes and raisins in a large glass bowl. Pour the liquid over them, placing the slices of lemon and orange all around the dish and the bay leaves in the center.

Put 1 cup of sugar and 2 tablespoons of water in a thick-

Desserts

bottomed pan. (Always use the same pan for this purpose and keep it strictly for making caramel.) Place over high heat and boil about 5 minutes, until the syrup turns dark brown and is caramelized.

Trickle the caramel lightly over the fruit. Let the whole dish cool and, just before serving, poke the top of the caramel layer with a fork to crack it so it will be easier to serve.

Galette Grand-mère

An Apple Cake

For 8 people:

Cake

1 *package active dry yeast*
1 *tablespoon sugar*
1 *small egg*
Salt
1 *tablespoon sweet butter, softened*
1½ *cups all-purpose flour*

Topping

2 *tablespoons (approximately) sweet butter, softened*
Sugar
Cinnamon
1 *ripe apple (or pear), peeled, cored and thinly sliced*

Dissolve the yeast in ¼ cup of lukewarm water with 1 tablespoon of sugar for 5 minutes. Beat the egg in a bowl and add the salt, butter and 1 cup of the flour. Mix quickly with your fingertips. Add the yeast mixture and work quickly, adding as much of the remaining flour as needed to make a firm, elastic dough. Knead briefly, form into a ball and put in a greased bowl. Cover with a tea towel and put in a warm place (such as in an oven with a pilot light) for 1 to 1½ hours, or until it has doubled in size.

Preheat the oven to 400°.

Knead the dough briefly and press it into a greased 10-inch quiche or tart pan. Smear with the butter and sprinkle with

Les Desserts

sugar and cinnamon. Put the fruit slices on top of the butter in a circular pattern, then sprinkle again with sugar and cinnamon. Leave at room temperature for 20 minutes, then put on the top shelf of the oven and bake for 15 to 18 minutes.

This can be frozen and reheated. It is delicious when sprinkled with more sugar and caramelized under the broiler.

Gâteau au Caramel

A Rich, Caramel-flavored Cake

For 8 people:

Pastry

½ cup sweet butter
1½ cups sugar
1 egg
4½ cups flour
Salt

Filling

½ pound brown sugar
½ cup powdered almonds
½ cup sweet butter
3 tablespoons cream
2 egg yolks

Mix the butter and sugar. Add the egg and knead until well mixed. Add the flour and salt. Pound and stretch the dough away from you with the heel of your hand to be sure all the ingredients are well blended. Shape the dough into a ball, cut it into four parts, place them one on top of the other, then mix them again vigorously into one ball. Repeat this process three times. Finally shape the dough into a ball, cover with a clean cloth and leave for one hour at room temperature.

Preheat oven to 375°.

Spread the dough ¼ inch thick on a well-buttered 12-inch mold. Cover with a sheet of foil and weight it down with dried beans. Prick the foil and dough with a fork and bake for 30 minutes. Remove the foil and beans.

Meanwhile, mix the brown sugar, almond powder, butter,

Desserts

257

cream and egg yolks. Pour into the cooked pie shell. Reduce the oven heat to 350° and bake for 15 minutes.

Gâteau aux Noix et au Rhum

A Rich Walnut Rum and Apricot Jam Cake

A sumptuous dessert.

For 8 to 10 people:

Pastry

2 tablespoons sweet butter, chilled
2 cups unbleached flour
2 tablespoons vegetable oil
¼ teaspoon salt
2 tablespoons sugar

Filling

9 tablespoons apricot preserves
½ pound walnut meats, chopped (about 1½ cups)
½ pound sugar
8 tablespoons sweet butter, softened
1 tablespoon cream
4 egg yolks
4 egg whites
4 tablespoons confectioners' sugar
2 tablespoons dark rum
24 large walnut halves

Mix the butter rapidly with the flour, oil, salt and sugar. Add 4 tablespoons of cold water. Knead rapidly with the heel of your hand into a thick dough. It should not be sticky. Wrap it in a piece of plastic wrap and refrigerate for at least one hour.

Pass the apricot preserves through a sieve to make a purée.

Spread the chilled dough on a buttered 12-inch-wide tart mold. Cover with 6 tablespoons of the apricot purée.

Preheat the oven to 375°.

Mix the walnuts, sugar, butter, cream and egg yolks thoroughly in a large bowl. Beat the egg whites and gently

Les Desserts

add them to the walnut mixture. Spread this mixture on the apricot purée in the pastry shell. Bake for 50 minutes. Cool on a rack and unmold onto a large platter.

Mix the confectioners' sugar and the rum into a thick paste.

Spread the top and sides of the cooled cake with the remaining 3 tablespoons of apricot purée, top with the sugar-and-rum mixture and decorate with walnut halves.

Galette de Goumeau

A very plain, traditional country dessert.

Pastry

3 cups flour
½ cup plus 2 tablespoons sweet butter
1 tablespoon lard
1 egg
3 tablespoons hot water

Filling

1 egg
3 tablespoons cream
Salt
Freshly ground black pepper
½ cup raisins

Preheat the oven to 375°.

Knead all the pastry ingredients into a soft dough. Spread the dough in a quiche or tart pan.

Mix the ingredients for the filling and pour it into the pan over the dough. Bake for 20 minutes.

Gouerre au Cirage

A Prune Pie

There are all kinds of *gouerre,* fruitcake made with apples or pears. This one, because it is made with prunes, is called "shoe-polish pie."

Pastry

2 cups unbleached flour
7 tablespoons sweet butter
Pinch of salt

Filling

½ pound large prunes, pitted
3 tablespoons apricot preserves
1 tablespoon good plum brandy
3 tablespoons confectioners' sugar

Mix the flour and butter, kneading lightly. Add the salt and ½ cup cold water briskly. Make into a ball. Cover with a towel and leave in the bottom part of the refrigerator for at least 1 hour.

Soak the prunes in cold water for 2 hours.

Preheat the oven to 400°.

Roll the dough ¼ inch thick and spread it in a 10-inch-wide buttered mold. Prick it with a fork.

Crush the pitted prunes with a fork and mix them with the apricot preserves. Fill the pastry shell with this mixture. Bake for 40 minutes.

Remove the pie from the oven and place it on a rack to cool. Sprinkle with plum brandy and confectioners' sugar and serve.

You may also, when it is cooled, sprinkle it with crystallized sugar and place it under the broiler for a few minutes to caramelize the top. Place on a rack to cool and serve luke-warm or cold.

Gaufrettes au Miel

Honey Wafers

A light crisp waffle, fragrant with honey and orange-blossom water.

> 5 *cups flour*
> ½ *pound honey*
> 3 *egg yolks*
> 2 *tablespoons orange-blossom water (or brandy or grated lemon peel)*
> 1 *quart milk*
> ¼ *pound sweet butter, melted*
> 2 *egg whites, stiffly beaten*
> *Confectioners' sugar*

Mix all the ingredients. Cover and set aside for at least 4 hours.

Heat an oiled waffle iron. Cook and serve hot, sprinkled with confectioners' sugar.

Mousse au Chocolat

Chocolate Mousse with Orange Peel

My very favorite of all chocolate mousses. It must be made at least eight hours before serving.

> For 8 to 12 people:
>
> *Peel of 4 oranges, grated*
> 1¼ *cups sweet butter, softened*
> ½ *cup orange juice*
> 1 *pound semisweet chocolate bits or chopped pieces*
> 9 *egg yolks*
> ½ *cup sugar*
> 9 *egg whites, stiffly beaten*
> 2 *tablespoons confectioners' sugar (or grated black bitter chocolate)*

Beat the grated orange peel with the butter until the butter becomes frothy.

Bring the orange juice and chocolate slowly to a boil in a saucepan, then remove from the heat and let cool.

Beating vigorously, slowly add the egg yolks, then the sugar to the chocolate and juice. The mixture has to be smooth. Stir in the orange peel-butter mixture. Gently fold in the egg whites and pour into individual cups or a large

Desserts

bowl. Cover with plastic wrap and refrigerate for at least 8 hours.

Sprinkle with confectioners' sugar or grated black bitter chocolate just before serving. Pass a bowl of *Mandarines à l'Armagnac* (see below) along with the chocolate mousse.

Lait de Poule

A Light Custard

This is the best of medicines against colds or just the melancholy of long winter evenings. Have a good book and a warm blanket handy.

For 1 person:

- *1 cup hot milk*
- *2 tablespoons sugar*
- *1 egg yolk, beaten*
- *Pinch of nutmeg*
- *2 teaspoons cognac (or bourbon)*

Heat the milk, add the sugar, egg yolk and nutmeg and stir over low heat for 5 minutes. Add the cognac and drink. Preferably served in a bowl or mug.

Mandarines à l'Armagnac

Small Tangerines with Brandy

This is a superb accompaniment to chocolate cake, Savoy cake, chocolate mousse, plain vanilla ice cream and *rigodon*. It must be kept about two months. Look for the smallest tangerines you can find—clementines, if possible—and use a good-quality Armagnac brandy.

Les Desserts

4 pounds tangerines, peeled
1 quart brandy
2 cups granulated sugar

Peel the fruit very delicately by hand and make sure that all the white is removed and the skin is not broken.

Place the whole tangerines if they are small (or sliced, if they are larger) in a jar and add the sugar. Shake the jar twice. Then pour in the brandy and close tightly. Store the jar in a dark place for one month, turning it upside down every week. Add a little sugar and wait another month before testing.

If you want to use kumquats instead of tangerines, use 1 cup more sugar.

Massepains

Light Almond and Lemon Wafers

Delicious, crisp, light cookies made in different versions throughout Burgundy.

About 60 cookies:

2½ cups sugar
2 cups ground almonds
1 tablespoon flour
4 egg whites, stiffly beaten
Rind of 2 lemons, grated

Mix the sugar, almonds and flour. Slowly fold in the beaten egg whites and the grated lemon peel.

Preheat the oven to 350°.

Drop by teaspoonfuls on a sheet of buttered foil on a cookie sheet and flatten each mound slightly with the back of a spoon. Bake for 10 minutes.

Let the cookies cool before removing them from the foil. Store in an airtight box.

Desserts

Mousse au Citron

A Lemon and Wine Custard

A tart, invigorating dessert you can serve with *Massepains* (p. 262) or thinly sliced *Pain d'Épices* (p. 267). Don't worry if there is a fluff of egg white on top.

For 8 people:

Rind of 1 lemon, grated
12 tablespoons sugar (or more, according to taste)
Juice of 4 lemons
2½ cups dry white wine
10 egg yolks, beaten
10 egg whites, stiffly beaten

Mix the grated lemon peel and sugar, and add the lemon juice. Pour into a heavy-bottomed pan and stir in the white wine over low heat. (You can use a double boiler instead of a pan.) Add the egg yolks, stirring constantly. When the custard is thick enough to coat the spoon, remove from the heat, add the egg whites and pour into a large glass bowl or individual dishes. Cover with plastic wrap and refrigerate.

Noeuds d'Amour

Love Knots Fritters

These crisp little bows are fritters made at Christmastime and served in large baskets lined with white napkins.

4 cups unbleached flour
3 eggs, beaten
1 teaspoon salt
1 teaspoon good brandy or dark rum
1 tablespoon orange-blossom water
½ cup sweet butter, melted
Oil for frying
Confectioners' sugar

Pour the flour on a table. Make a well in the center and add the eggs, salt, brandy, orange-blossom water, and butter. Stir, then knead well. Make a ball. Cover it and let it stand for about 3 hours.

Roll out the dough ¼ inch thick. Cut it into 1-inch-wide strips and then into 10-inch-long ribbons.

Heat the oil in a large pan until very hot. Fold each ribbon into a bow and fry in the oil, one at a time, for 3 to 5 minutes, turning each with tongs. Remove with a slotted spoon and drain on paper towels. Sprinkle with confectioners' sugar. These can be eaten warm or cold.

Nonnettes

Little Honey and Almond Cakes Made with Rye Flour, Flavored with Rum and Stuffed with Apricots or Marmalade

These delicate little honey-and-spice cakes were prepared as early as the sixteenth century in convents, hence the name *nonnettes* (little nuns). They are sometimes covered with bitter chocolate and become *duchesses* because of their fancy look.

For 1 dozen cakes:

1 cup honey, as fragrant as possible
½ cup sugar
¼ teaspoon salt
½ teaspoon soda
2 cups rye flour
½ cup chopped almonds with their skins
¼ cup dark rum
2 teaspoons anise powder (or anise seeds)
½ teaspoon cinnamon
½ teaspoon powdered cloves
½ cup Malaga raisins or diced glacéed fruits
12 tablespoons apricot purée or orange marmalade

Preheat the oven to 325°.

Heat the honey, ½ cup of water and sugar in a large bowl. Turn off the heat; add the salt and soda and, little by little, vigorously stir in the flour. (You may use a food processor or

Desserts

a blender.) Add the almonds, rum, spices and raisins. Pour into buttered muffin pans, filling to only two-thirds of each mold. Bake for 25 minutes, or until a knife plunged into the center of the cake comes out clean.

Remove the cakes from the oven. Let them cool in their molds for 15 minutes before unmolding onto a cake rack to finish cooling.

Meanwhile, pour the apricot purée (or marmalade) into a saucepan and heat over low heat.

Slice the cold cakes horizontally through the middle, pour some warm jam on the bottom half and replace with the top half. Cover the top with more jam or sprinkle with confectioners' sugar or with a light icing. Wrap in foil individually.

Omelette aux Pommes

A Soufflé Apple Omelet Flavored with Rum

Sweet omelets are always exciting, whether they are filled with fruits, jams or ice cream. This light, tart omelet must be served with a bowl of cream, whipped with Calvados. You must use two skillets.

For 8 people:

5 apples (Granny Smith or any other tart apple), peeled and sliced
1 cup dark rum
9 tablespoons sweet butter
10 egg yolks
2 cups sugar
*10 egg whites, stiffly beaten
Confectioners' sugar*
1 bowl heavy cream
3 tablespoons Calvados

Soak the sliced apples in rum for 1 hour. Remove them and cook them in 6 tablespoons of the butter for 15 minutes over low heat.

Stir the egg yolks, sugar and rum marinade together until frothy. Gently fold in the beaten egg whites.

Over medium heat, heat the remaining 3 tablespoons of butter in two skillets and pour half of the egg mixture into each. Cook for 5 minutes. Holding a plate over each skillet, invert the omelet onto the plate, then slide it back into the skillet for 2 minutes more. Place the two omelets on a warm serving dish. Spread the cooked apples in the center and fold each omelet. Sprinkle the tops with confectioners' sugar and serve at once with a bowl of cream flavored with brandy.

Pâte de Cassis

4 pounds very ripe black currants
2 pounds sugar (approximately)

Wash and put the currants in a large pan. Add ½ cup of water and bring to a boil. When the fruit is soft, crush it and pass it through a Mouli mill or a sieve. Mix the purée with an amount of sugar equaling three-quarters of the purée's volume and boil for 5 minutes.

Pour into a dish 1 inch deep. Leave it for a few days in a cool place. Cut into cubes and sprinkle on all sides with granulated sugar. Keep in a tin box.

Pain d'Épice

The Rich Burgundy Version of Gingerbread

It was the practice of Greek and Roman cooks to spread their pastry with honey. The Arabs mixed flour with the honey and brought the idea to Europe in the Middle Ages, during which spices were added and Dijon became known for its honey-and-spice bread. As early as the fourteenth century, this type of bread was mentioned in chronicles as an aid to digestion, and it was served at all banquets. In the eighteenth century the standard version was finally established: it specified ten spices, egg yolks, rye flour and good honey.

This is the recipe I found to be the tastiest. *Pain d'épice* is best served in very thin slices, lightly buttered, with tea or coffee.

    1 pound honey
    5 cups light rye flour
    1 teaspoon coriander
    ½ teaspoon cinnamon
    1 tablespoon aniseed
    ½ teaspoon powdered cloves
    1 teaspoon grated nutmeg
    5 drops lemon extract
    2 tablespoons lemon peel, cut in tiny dice
    4 tablespoons crystallized or fresh orange peel, cut in tiny dice
    2 teaspoons soda
    2 egg yolks, beaten
    1 teaspoon milk

Combine the honey and ½ cup water and bring to a boil. Mix the flour, spices, lemon extract, peel of lemon and orange and add the honey and water, stirring vigorously. Cover and let stand 20 to 24 hours.

Mix the soda and egg yolks and add the batter, which should be very soft and smooth. (Add a little water to soften it if needed.) Stir well.

Preheat the oven to 300°.

Pour the batter into two well-buttered loaf pans. Bake for 1 hour. Brush the tops with milk and let cool.

Wrap in aluminum foil. The flavor will improve after three days. Always keep tightly wrapped.

Pogne

A Cake Flavored with Lemon and Rum

When everyone in the Burgundy countryside used to make their own bread, they often kept a handful of dough *(une poignée),* added a little sugar and lemon, shaped it like a crown and made a *pogne.*

Les Desserts

There are many variations of this simple cake made of bread dough. Some are cut in the shape of little fat boys and girls; some have fresh fruit in the summer and pumpkin in the autumn added to the dough. The recipe given here is what I have found to be the tastiest of the *pognes.* It must be prepared a day ahead.

> ½ square yeast (fresh)
> 1 tablespoon lukewarm milk
> 3½ cups unbleached flour
> 6 eggs, beaten
>   Salt
> 1 cup sugar
> 9 tablespoons sweet butter, softened
> ½ tablespoon rum
>   Juice of 1 lemon
>   Peel of 1 lemon, grated
> 1 egg yolk, beaten with 1 tablespoon water

Mix the yeast and lukewarm milk and let stand for a few minutes, according to the package directions.

Put the flour in a mound on the table and make a well in the center. Add the beaten eggs, salt, sugar and butter and knead well. Add the yeast-milk mixture and mix well. Knead until the dough is soft and elastic, then add the rum, lemon juice and grated lemon peel. Knead into a ball, cover and let rise overnight at room temperature.

Preheat the oven to 350°.

Butter a cookie sheet. Using your hands and scissors, make two crowns with the ball of dough, paint their surfaces with the egg yolk–water mixture and bake for 40 minutes.

Le Poirat

A Pear Pie

This pear pie is a medieval dessert that remains a favorite for many family meals in Burgundy. The dough must be very thin, and it must be served lukewarm. *Le Poirat* may be the French answer to England's apple pie brought to France during the Hundred Years' War.

Desserts

For 8 people:

Pastry

4½ cups unbleached flour
1 cup sweet butter
2 tablespoons vegetable oil
1 teaspoon salt

Filling

---

8 ripe pears, peeled, cored and sliced (marinated in brandy or not)
4 tablespoons light cream
3 tablespoons sugar

Mix the flour, butter, oil, salt and 2 tablespoons water together. Knead for a few minutes, then make a ball. Cover with a towel and let stand for 2 hours.

Preheat the oven to 350°.

Spread the dough as thinly as you can on a floured table. Place half of it in a well-buttered 10-inch baking dish. Cover the dough with the sliced pears (be sure they are well drained if you have marinated them first), then cover with the rest of the dough, leaving a 2-inch hole in the center.

Prick the dough with a fork and bake the pie for 45 minutes. Remove from the oven and pour the cream through the center hole into the pie.

Bake for 15 minutes more. Sprinkle with sugar and serve with a bowl of cream or custard or ice cream.

Raisiné

Pears and Quinces Cooked in the Juice of Fresh Grapes

A beloved dessert in Burgundy, this is served with crisp lemon cookies (p. 241) or a bowl of cream. But for a medieval or Nouvelle Cuisine taste, it is also a splendid accompaniment to roast duck or pork.

6 pounds very ripe white grapes
2 pounds tasty ripe pears, peeled, cored and quartered
2 large ripe quinces, peeled, cored and sliced
Sugar to taste (omit entirely for a tart raisiné)

Les Desserts

Crush the grapes through a sieve. Bring their juice to a boil and let it reduce, uncovered, for 30 minutes. Remove the froth on the surface with a slotted spoon.

Add the pears and quinces and let them cook over a low flame for 1 hour, uncovered, stirring from time to time. Add sugar to taste, if you wish, and cook for 10 minutes more.

Let cool and pour into glass jars. Cover the jars and keep in a dry place.

Poires en Manteau

Pears Filled with Raisins, Flavored with Rum and Wrapped in a Thin Pastry Shell

A favorite dessert for buffets and family meals.

For 8 people:

Pastry

½ cup unbleached flour
½ cup sweet butter
1 egg, beaten with 1 tablespoon milk
Pinch of salt

Filling

1⅓ cups raisins
5 tablespoons dark rum
8 large ripe pears, peeled and cored
4 tablespoons sweet butter
1 egg yolk mixed with 2 tablespoons milk

Place the flour in a large mixing bowl and mix in the butter and egg beaten with milk. Add 3 tablespoons of water and salt and blend quickly with one hand as you gather the dough into a mass. Press the dough into a ball. It should not be sticky. With the heel of one hand, press the pastry down on the table away from you. Gather the dough into a mass, kneading for a few more minutes. Sprinkle with flour and wrap in waxed paper or a kitchen towel. Let stand for 1 hour.

Desserts

Place the raisins in a bowl, sprinkle with rum and let marinate, stirring once or twice, for 1 hour.

Preheat oven to 375°.

Fill each pear with raisins, then close the hole with ½ tablespoon butter.

Place the dough on a floured board. Knead it briefly into a flat circle. Roll it out with an even stroke, back and forth. It should be ⅓ inch thick. Cut 8 large squares. Place each pear in the center of a square and pinch the corners so the pear is tightly wrapped in its coat. It should look like a hut. Brush the pastry with the egg-yolk-and-milk mixture. Place the 8 pears in a buttered ovenproof dish and bake for 25 minutes. Serve warm or lukewarm with a bowl of fresh cream.

Pommes Sévigné

Cooked Apples Covered with a Light Custard and a Soft Meringue

The beautiful Madame de Sévigné was the most brilliant observer the court of Louis XIV. She was also the most *gourmande* of women.

For 8 people:

8 large apples (preferably Granny Smith), peeled and
cored
1 teaspoon cinnamon
1 clove
6 tablespoons sugar
2 cups milk
4 egg whites, stiffly beaten
4 yolks
1 tablespoon grated black chocolate (or nutmeg)

Cook the peeled and cored apples with the cinnamon and clove, 6 tablespoons of water and the sugar in a covered pan until soft. Let them cool in the syrup, then drain them, setting the syrup aside, and place them in the center of a large, shallow serving dish.

Les Desserts

Meanwhile, heat the milk in a large skillet and poach the stiffly beaten egg whites, 1 tablespoon at a time, in the milk

for about 2 minutes on each side. Drain on paper towels.

Pass the milk through a sieve. Beat the egg yolks into the syrup and pour into the warm milk, stirring constantly over low heat. When the mixture coats the spoon, pour it over the apples. Place the cooked egg whites around and sprinkle the whole dish with grated black chocolate or a little nutmeg.

Rigodon

A Light Pudding Enriched with Nuts and Served with Stewed Fruit

A classic of Burgundy recipes. A sweet dessert served with stewed fruit.

For 8 people:

1 quart milk
¾ cup sugar
Pinch of salt
Pinch of cinnamon
¼ pound stale brioche (or pound cake), diced
7 eggs, beaten
2 tablespoons arrowroot (or cornstarch)
10 hazelnuts, minced
10 walnuts, minced
2 tablespoons sweet butter
1 cup peaches stewed with red wine or stewed apricots, cooked apples, jam or Coulis de Fruits (p. 248)

Bring the milk, sugar, salt and cinnamon to a boil and turn off the heat. Preheat the oven to 350°.

Place the diced cake in a large bowl. Pour a little of the warm milk on it, add the eggs, arrowroot and remaining milk, stirring vigorously. Add the nuts.

Pour into a deep, buttered ovenproof dish, dot with butter and bake for 30 minutes.

Serve cold or lukewarm unmolded, covered with a thick layer of stewed peaches or stewed fruit, warm jam, or a *coulis* of fruit.

Desserts

Note: Some people add sliced apples or pears to the mixture before baking it.

Le Pouding

A Creamy Pudding, Flavored with Lemon and Caramel

A delicate, warm dessert.

For 8 people:

Peel of 2 lemons
3 cups milk
1 cup sugar
4 tablespoons sweet butter
¾ cup flour
4 egg yolks, beaten
4 egg whites, stiffly beaten

Preheat the oven to 350°.

Bring the lemon peel, milk and ½ cup sugar to a boil. Mix together the butter and flour and add the warm milk mixture, stirring vigorously. Remove the lemon peel. Bring the mixture to a boil and remove from the heat. Cool for a few minutes, stir in the egg yolks, then fold in the egg whites.

Put the remaining ½ cup of sugar and 1 tablespoon water in a mold and pour the pudding mixture into it. Place the mold in a large dish with about 2 inches of water around it and bake for 50 minutes.

Let stand about 10 minutes, unmold and serve lukewarm.

Pouding de Pain d'Épice

Gingerbread, Raisin, Lemon and Orange Peel, Egg and Rum Pudding

Les Desserts

The trouble with *pain d'épice* is that the stale slices become very hard. This recipe solves that problem.

For 8 people:

2 cups warm milk
3 eggs, well beaten
1 pound pain d'épice (or gingerbread), sliced
1 cup raisins
Peel of 1 lemon, grated
Peel of 1 orange, grated
½ cup dark rum
2 tablespoons sugar

Pour the milk over the eggs and add the *pain d'épice.* Preheat the oven to 325°.

Butter a round ovenproof dish. Place the raisins on the bottom, pour in half of the *pain d'épice*-milk-egg mixture, add the orange and lemon peel, rum and sugar, and pour in the rest of the mixture.

Place the dish in a large pan with ½ cup water around it and bake for 1½ hours.

Unmold. Sprinkle with sugar and a few drops of rum. Serve warm with perhaps a bowl of plain vanilla ice cream or a compote.

Raisin à l'Eau de Vie

Grapes in Brandy

2 pounds grapes, very ripe and firm, black or white,
washed and dried, with ½ inch of stem left on
½ pound sugar
2 cloves
4 peppercorns
2 2-inch strips of orange peel
2 2-inch strips of lemon peel
Good brandy to cover

Wash and dry the grapes. Place them in a large glass jar with the rest of the ingredients. Leave in a dark place, turning the jar upside down every month. They will be ready around the sixth or seventh month.

Serve on vanilla ice cream, with a *rigodon* (p. 273), or in small glasses after a meal.

Desserts

Sorbet au Marc

A Tangy Brandy Sherbet

It is important to choose a good brandy, since cold increases all flavors, bad or good. This dessert is wonderful after a hearty meal.

For 8 people:

> 6 *cups sugar*
> *Peel of 1 lemon*
> *Juice of 4 lemons*
> 4 *egg whites*
> ½ *cup marc (brandy)*
> *Mint leaves*

Heat 5 cups of the sugar and 4 cups of water for 1 hour, uncovered, to make a thick syrup. Add the lemon peel and juice and cook for 30 minutes. Let cool. Remove the lemon peel.

Pour the liquid into ice-cube trays in the freezer and let it set but not freeze.

Beat the egg whites with 1 cup of sugar until stiff, add the marc and pour over the partially congealed liquid. Return to the freezer until ready. Stir well before serving.

Serve in a bowl with mint leaves stuck in the center or in individual glass dishes.

Soupe à l'Abricot

An Apricot Dessert

The dukes of Burgundy loved this, and it is one of the prettiest desserts. Use very ripe, plump apricots or peaches. If you cannot find any that have enough flavor, use canned fruits.

For 8 people:

24 *ripe whole apricots*
1 *cup red wine*
¼ *cup and 2 tablespoons sugar*
  Peel of half a lemon, grated
10 *croutons, fried in butter*

Place the whole fruit in a thin-bottomed pan. Cover with the wine and 2 tablespoons of water and cook until soft (about 10 minutes). Pass the fruit through a sieve into a saucepan, discarding the pits. Stir in ¼ cup of the sugar and the grated lemon peel. Bring to a boil and cook for 2 minutes.

Serve warm or cold with the croutons and sprinkled with 2 tablespoons of sugar.

Soupe au Vin en Dessert

A Wine, Egg, Raisin and Spice Dessert

This is a most unusual soup, which should be served after a rather light meal. It is a rich medieval dessert and quite heady.

For 8 people:

5 *slices homemade or good bread, crusts removed and diced*
5 *tablespoons sweet butter*
6 *eggs*
1½ *quarts red wine (hearty Burgundy type)*
3 *tablespoons sugar*
1 *tablespoon Spanish saffron*
½ *cup raisins*
1 *teaspoon cinnamon*

Sauté the diced bread in the butter until golden, tossing for about 5 minutes.

Beat the eggs lightly, then slowly add the wine and 1 cup of water. Cook over low heat, stirring. Add the sugar, saffron, raisins and cinnamon and cook for about 10 minutes. This should be served warm with the crisp bread cubes.

Desserts

Tarte aux Pommes

An Apple Dessert Flavored with Orange, Lemon and Raisins

This unusual apple dessert can be served with a bowl of plain cream or with a light orange custard.

For 8 people:

> 3 eggs
> 1 cup and 2 teaspoons sugar
> 1 cup flour
> 1⅓ cups heavy cream
> 9 tablespoons sweet butter, softened
> 2 pounds (about 4) tart apples (such as Granny Smith), peeled and sliced
> 2 tablespoons orange peel, grated
> 2 tablespoons lemon peel, grated
> ½ cup raisins (preferably Malaga type)

Preheat the oven to 400°.

Beat the eggs and 1 cup of sugar until light and foamy. Add the flour and cream, stirring vigorously. Add the butter and stir. Add the apples, orange and lemon peel and raisins. Pour into a buttered mold and bake for 15 minutes. Then raise the temperature to 425° and cook for about 15 minutes. Cool for a few minutes and serve lukewarm, sprinkled with 2 teaspoons sugar, along with a bowl of cream or custard.

Gâteau aux Prunes

A Plum and Cinnamon-Almond Custard Cake

Les Desserts

This is a very tasty dessert made with either little yellow mirabelle plums or tart green plums, or with pale yellow ones. You can use canned fruit if it is tasty and firm. The *gâteau* may be served warm or cold.

For 8 people:

Pastry

1⅓ cups flour
¾ cup sweet butter, softened
1 egg, beaten
1 teaspoon salt
1½ teaspoons sugar
2 teaspoons milk

Filling

---

3 eggs
9 teaspoons sugar
¼ cup ground almonds
Pinch of cinnamon
⅔ cup flour
2 cups hot milk
3 tablespoons sweet butter
4 tablespoons sugar
1½ pounds plums (or about 3 cups canned fruit), pitted

Place the flour on a table. Make a well in the center and place the butter and egg in the center. Mix well with your hands. Sprinkle with salt and sugar and mix a few minutes longer, working with the tips of your fingers. Then push away from you with the palms of your hands and add the milk to the dough. Gather the dough into a ball, cover with a piece of wet cloth and let it rest for an hour or overnight in a cool place.

Prepare the filling. In a saucepan, beat together the eggs, sugar, almonds and cinnamon. Beat in the flour and stir with a whisk.

Bring the milk to a boil and stir it quickly into the egg mixture. Place over low heat and stir continuously for 4 to 5 minutes to make a custard. Remove from the heat and cool.

Preheat the oven to 400°.

In a large skillet heat the butter and add the sugar and the plums. Cook over low heat for about 5 minutes and cool.

Roll out the dough on a floured table to ¼-inch thickness and place it in a buttered mold. Pour in the cooled custard, arrange the plums, skin side down if possible, and bake for 35 minutes. Cool before serving.

You can sprinkle the cake with a little sugar and plum brandy a few minutes before it is ready to serve.

Desserts

Tarte Lyonnaise aux Miettes

A Crisp Pastry Shell Filled with Bread Crumbs, Almonds, Eggs and
Orange and Lemon Peel and Covered with Meringue

A classic dessert in Lyon, this pretty and light tart is always a
children's favorite.

For 8 people:

Pastry

3 *cups unbleached flour*
2 *eggs, beaten*
1 *cup sweet butter, softened*
½ *cup sugar*
1 *teaspoon salt*

Filling

1 *tablespoon milk*
½ *cup bread or cookie crumbs*
8 *teaspoons powdered or minced almonds*
2 *eggs*
2 *egg yolks*
Peel of 1 orange, grated
Peel of 1 lemon, grated
½ *cup and 3 tablespoons granulated sugar*
3 *teaspoons sweet butter, softened*
2 *tablespoons kirsch (optional)*
2 *egg whites*
2 *tablespoons confectioners' sugar*

Prepare the pastry. Working quickly with the tips of your
fingers, mix all the ingredients together on a well-floured
board. Pound and stretch the dough away from you with the
heel of your hand to be sure all ingredients are well blended.
Shape the dough into a ball, cover with a clean cloth and leave
for 2 hours at room temperature.

To make the filling, mix the milk and bread crumbs in a
saucepan and heat for a few minutes. Pour into a blender and
add the almonds, whole eggs, egg yolks, orange and lemon

Les Desserts

peel, ½ cup granulated sugar, butter and kirsch. Blend until the mixture is smooth. Beat the egg whites with 3 tablespoons granulated sugar until stiff.

Preheat the oven to 375°.

Spread the pastry as thinly as possible in a buttered mold. Prick it all over with a fork. Spread the filling over the pastry and cover with the beaten egg whites. Sprinkle with the confectioners' sugar and bake for about 30 minutes.

Les Boissons de Ménage

Homemade Beverages

In the Middle Ages only young wines, beer and *hypocras* were drunk, and it was only in the sixteenth century that brandy became popular, along with liquors made with sugar, cinnamon and various flavors.

In France, black currant bushes grow wild in places where there is chalky dry soil. Until the eighteenth century the fruit was used in Burgundy mostly for medical purposes. Leaves were crushed and used in herb teas; berries were cooked with sugar, crushed into juice and used by doctors, priests and housewives to treat a variety of diseases—fever, plague or simply digestive problems. In the nineteenth century the famous liquor made from black currants was first concocted and was to become one of France's most popular drinks.

Black currants grow in Burgundy wherever there is good wine. They are the complementary crop of wine growers, and in July the black-currant picking is as important as the grape picking a few months later. The fruit is a staple in Burgundy and the berries are used in compotes, desserts of all sorts, jellies, preserves, candies, syrups, sherbets and a variety of drinks, including the famous kir.

I have included here only the Burgundy recipes agreeable to the modern palate. They can be served as aperitifs before meals, with dessert or between meals.

Crème de Cassis

3 pounds very ripe black currants
2 quarts red wine
4 pounds sugar (approximately)
1 cup brandy

Wash the berries and crush them coarsely. Add the wine and marinate for 48 hours in a covered bowl.

Pass through a sieve and add 2 pounds of sugar for each quart of juice. Bring to a boil, stirring, and boil for 5 minutes. Let cool. Pass through a sieve and add the brandy while stirring. Keep in tightly closed bottles. It will keep indefinitely.

Liqueur de Cassis

3 *pounds black currants*
1 *cup raspberries (optional)*
  Pinch of cinnamon
1 *clove*
2 *or 3 black currant leaves*
1 *quart brandy*
1 *pound sugar*

Wash the currants (and if desired, the raspberries) and place them in a large bowl. Add the cinnamon, clove, currant leaves and brandy. Cover and keep in a cool place for 45 days.

Drain the fruit. Combine the sugar with 1 cup of water and add to the juice. Keep in tightly closed bottles and drink after two months.

Ratafia de Cassis

10 *pounds black currants*
 9 *quarts brandy*
   Pinch of cinnamon
10 *cloves*
 3 *pounds sugar*

Crush the currants coarsely and place them in a large container. Add the brandy, cinnamon and cloves. Leave the mixture in the sun for 50 days.

Pass the mixture through a sieve. Dissolve the sugar in 1

Homemade
Beverages

cup of water and add to the juice. Keep in tightly closed bottles. It can be used after two months.

Eau de Coing

Quince Water

Grate a few unpeeled quinces when they are yellow, ripe and fragrant. Leave them in a bowl for 3 days, then add the same quantity of brandy and ½ pound of sugar for each quart of liquid.

Keep in a dark place for a year before drinking it.

Hypocras

Some medieval treats like *vespétro* were made with angelica seeds, coriander, cinnamon and sometimes with bitter orange and spices. This was one of the favorites until the sixteenth century.

> Pinch of cinnamon
> Pinch of crushed vanilla bean
> *1 clove*
> *⅓ cup sugar*
> *3 quarts dry white wine*

Mix everything and keep for 3 weeks in a closed jar. Pass through a sieve and keep in well-closed bottles in a cool place.

Kir

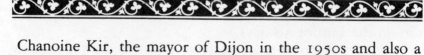

Chanoine Kir, the mayor of Dijon in the 1950s and also a

left-wing canon who was a highly controversial figure, may be best remembered for inventing what has become almost a national drink—*le Kir*.

For each person:

1 teaspoon black currant liquor or black currant crème
1 glass of dry white wine (preferably Bourgogne Blanc Aligoté or Pouilly Fuissé)

Serve chilled. *Kir* can be made with champagne instead of wine and is then called a *royal*.

Liqueur Rouge

Red Liquor

2 quarts brandy
1 pound wild cherries
1 pound red currants
1 pound raspberries
1 cup black currants
    Pinch of cinnamon
1 clove
1 pound sugar

Mix everything except the sugar and keep for 6 weeks in a closed jar. Pass through a sieve. Add the sugar and 1 cup water and keep in bottles.

Ratafia de Framboise

Raspberry Ratafia

This is delicious made with wild strawberries, too.

2 pounds raspberries, cleaned and trimmed
4 cups brandy
2 cups sugar

Homemade
Beverages

Marinate the raspberries in the brandy in a closed jar for 2 months, stirring with a wooden spoon from time to time. Pass the fruit through a sieve, crushing it with a spoon. Add the sugar and ½ cup of water and bring to a boil. Remove from the heat at once. Cool. Add the brandy in which the berries have marinated. It is now ready to drink.

Ratafia de Genièvre

Juniper Ratafia

This can also be made with sloes, cranberries, dog rose berries, wild cherries and blueberries.

> *1 cup juniper berries, crushed*
> *4 cups brandy*
> *1½ cups sugar*

Crush the berries in a mortar or blender. Bring them to a boil with 3 tablespoons of water. Let boil for 3 minutes. Cool. Add the brandy. Put in a closed jar and leave for one week in a dark place. Pass through a sieve, pushing with a wooden spoon. Heat the sugar and 4 tablespoons of water until the mixture becomes syrupy. Add it to the berry juice. Pour into bottles and keep for 1 month before tasting it.

Ratafia de Raisins

Grape Ratafia

There are many *ratafias*. Some are made with cherry juice, brandy, clove and wild cherry; some with bitter lemon, coriander, cinnamon and brandy.

This *ratafia* is served before a meal or as a sweet afternoon wine with cookies and is easy to prepare.

> *About 3 pounds black or white grapes*
> *1 quart marc*

Crush and pass the grapes through a sieve. Mix 2 quarts of the juice with the marc. Keep for a few weeks in a wooden cask before bottling.

Ratafia de Noix

Walnut Ratafia

A hearty drink to prepare in the early summer, when both the beige walnut shells and the green kernels are still so soft that the entire fruit can be pierced by a knitting needle.

    50 green walnuts
    4 cloves
    1 teaspoon freshly grated nutmeg
    4 stamens of Spanish saffron
    2 quarts good brandy
    2 pounds sugar

Put all the ingredients in a closed glass jar and leave in a dark place for 2 months. Pass the liquid through a sieve. Add the sugar and keep in the closed jar in a dark place for 3 months more. Pour into bottles.

Vin Chaud

Red Wine Simmered with Spices

    1½ quarts hearty red wine
    ½ pound sugar
    1 lemon, unpeeled, cut into thin slices
    1 clove
    5 sprigs of thyme
    1 bay leaf

Heat the wine and sugar to the boiling point. Add the lemon, clove, thyme and bay leaf. Remove from the heat after 5 minutes and serve at once.

Homemade
Beverages

Vin de Genièvre

Juniper Wine

1 cup juniper berries, crushed
4 cups dry white wine
½ cup sugar

Place the crushed berries in a jar with the wine and sugar. Close tightly and leave for 3 weeks in a dark place. Pass through a sieve. It is now ready to enjoy.

Vin de Noix

Green Walnut Wine

This comes from Dauphiné, a region to the east of Burgundy, famous for its large walnuts, which are picked in June, when the shell is still tender and can be pierced with a pin.

3 quarts hearty red wine
2 cups good brandy
2 pounds sugar
14 green walnuts, quartered
1 unpeeled orange

Mix everything and leave in a jar for forty days, shaking it from time to time, then pass it through a sieve into bottles.

Close tightly and keep in a dark place for a few months so the flavor will mellow.

Le Vin

Wine

Wine from its beginning has always been accepted as a present from the gods. It is as old as civilization, and wine grapes have been growing in the rocky soil of Burgundy for over two thousand years. Here it is a part of daily life. It has been the core of rituals, pagan as well as Christian, since around the second century of our era, when mine workers grew fond of Greek wines. Later a grape was developed that could bear cold winters, and soon vineyards spread along the Rhone Valley and found their favorite place in Burgundy.

Wooden barrels replaced earthenware amphorae, and honey and spices were added to the wines to cover their acidity. Wine was not yet wine as we know it, since it was drunk very young. But it was widely enjoyed and soon became a highly profitable commodity. In the sixth century the king of Burgundy gave vineyards to the monks, and by the early Middle Ages the Church was the principal producer of wine. It was whispered that the monks expended as much effort on tending to their wine as they did to spread the gospel.

Philip the Bold, "First Great Duke of the West, Lord of the Best Wine of the Christian Kingdom," regulated the methods of selecting, growing and tending the vines and the wine. Later the kings of France, all very fond of Burgundy wine, kept a vigilant eye on the quality of the region's crops.

After the Revolution the vineyards were taken away from the Church by the state and sold to the people, hence a pattern in Burgundy of small ownership that still prevails. In the nineteenth century the vineyards were decimated by phylloxera. But American plants became immune to it, and soon, by growing on American rootstock to replace the old vines, the vineyards were replenished.

The production of wine in Burgundy is small compared with that of Bordeaux—only twenty-eight million gallons a

Wine

year—but it is rich in quality and diversity.

The land and the vine are important, but the devotion of the winegrowers (more than thirty-three thousand in Burgundy now) is essential. Fine wines come from pruning and growing the vines, then tending and aging the wine. This work starts in the fall after the harvest when the soil has to be plowed and cleaned. In winter, pruning has to be done, and in spring, plowing and removing of excess buds. In summer, there are two more plowings, training and spraying, and in the fall there is finally the harvest.

Good wine comes mostly from good management and technique. Made by the fermentation of grape sugar, it needs elaborate care. The yeast grows in fresh juice and produces enzymes, which convert the sugar to alcohol and carbon dioxide. The grape skins give tannin, color and even flavor to the wine. The difference between red and white wine does not stop at the color but comes from the tannin that passes from the skin to the juice during vatting.

Red wine is made with black grapes fermented with their skins, crushed and vatted for six to seven days. The skins and pulp of the grape floating on top of the juice are called the *chapeau* (hat) and may be as much as three feet thick. The *chapeau* must be punched down a few times a day during fermentation, or the wine may be pumped through a hose over the *chapeau.*

Then the wine is drained and poured into oak barrels to age. The oxygen, which enters through the wood and cork, helps to "mature" the wine. The color deepens, and the taste becomes less harsh as it ages. Particles settle to the bottom. Twice a week more wine is added to the barrel to make up for the evaporation, so there is no space for bacteria to develop.

During the first year the wine is cleaned ("racked") about four times, and during the second year, about twice more. It is during this second year that the wine mellows and develops its bouquet. The third year the wine is cleared of any suspended particles left and undergoes a *collage* (a fining) with white of egg, blood or gelatin. After that the wine is bottled in the typical squat, slope-shouldered Burgundy bottle and aged for two to ten years.

White wines are made without grape skins, pressed as soon as possible and poured into barrels to ferment. The fermentation must be cool and slow, and here oxygenation plays a

Le Vin

much smaller role than it does with red wines. The barrels are only partially filled, since the must (the not yet fermented juice) expands and the grape particles rise to the top. The temperature is kept at 60° to 70°F., and one racking is done after the first fermentation.

After twelve to eighteen months in the barrel, dry white wine is bottled. It is the fresh early taste of grapes that gives white wine its flavor, so it should be drunk quite young; it does not improve with age.

When the sun is not warm enough to provide the requisite sugar, *chaptalisation*—the addition of sugar to the must—is needed. This gives the wine a higher alcoholic content and sometimes even improves its flavor. Its use is widespread in Burgundy but always under strict government control.

The greatest wines of Burgundy come from the slopes of the Côte d'Or, a low range of hills along the western edge, beginning in Dijon and ending south of Santeny. The region is divided into two main parts. In the north, the Côte de Nuits, a narrow strip of hills, provides great red wines, such as Nuits-Saint-Georges, Vougeot, Gevrey-Chambertin, Vosne-Romanée, Musigny, which must be aged between five to ten years. South of this, Côte de Beaune offers splendid white wines, such as Meursault, Montrachet, Volnay, and a delicate red wine, Pommard.

Then there are the Hautes-Côtes with Bourgogne Aligoté and Passe-Tout-Grains, fruity pleasant wines.

Farther south, Côte Chalonnaise gives good red and white wines, such as Givry, Mercurey, Montagny, and the Côte Mâconnaise has its delicious Pouilly-Fumé and Mâcon.

Beaujolais, a light and pleasant wine, and Morgon and Brouilly come from the area near Lyon.

The main vine in Burgundy is the Pinot Noir, which produces red wines. The Gamay makes a light Beaujolais and plain red wines. The main vine for white wines is Chardonnay, which is the source of all the great white wines. Pinot Blanc and Aligoté provide pleasant light white wines.

The identity of a Burgundy wine comes from its vine and what is described on the bottle as a *climat*, which means a place whose soil and climate give the wine its quality. There are 419 *climats* in Côte de Nuits and about 900 in Côte de Beaune. A *climat* may belong to different owners. The finest are the fifty *Premiers Crus* and the eighteen *Grand Crus*. As Talleyrand observed, "When one is served such a wine one takes the

Wine

glass respectfully, looks at it, inhales it, then having put it down, one discusses it."

To the east of Burgundy, in Savoy, Dauphiné and Jura, there are many pleasant and fresh wines—dry light wines, sparkling wines and a delicious yellow wine prepared with grapes that have dried on straw for three months before being pressed, fermented and aged for four years. It is a sweet natural wine served with dessert and is called *vin jaune.*

Wines should please the palate, match the food they are served with and also balance one another. Usually, therefore, one starts the meal with a dry white wine, which is followed by a red one, then a great red wine, and, finally, sweet wines with desserts and champagne with fruit.

Light white wine tastes best with fish, ham, chicken, snails, crayfish, sausages; light red wine, with light soups and mild cheese; hearty red wine with peasant soups, vegetables, meat, game, highly flavored cheese and some fowl dishes.

But all these rules may be broken according to what tastes best to the host.

Le Vin

Menus

Menus

To entertain is a serious matter. In the eighteenth century, women of quality were given three funeral orations—one by a philosopher and two by regular guests at her table.

Choosing a menu requires taste and imagination. Clichés—pigeon with peas, veal with noodles, duck with turnips—should be avoided. It is better to serve such combinations as lamb with a purée of lima beans, veal with onion *confits* or chicken with melted leeks. One should remove the commonplace from the menu; otherwise the conversation can also become trite and ruin the feast.

As in all good marriages, the different dishes must keep their own personalities. The different flavors should offset or enhance one another, answer to one another, associate but never be absorbed. There must be contrasts—warm and cold, creamy and dry, sweet and salty—to bring balance and liveliness to a meal.

A meal is eaten first with the eyes, so, of course, a veal cream dish should never be followed by a pale custard dessert, nor should a *rouget* fish be served before rare beef or a beet salad and a strawberry cake.

I have chosen here a few menus to convey the Burgundy spirit.

Le Déjeuner entre Amis
Lunch

Salade de Céleri
Filets au Safran
Le Paillasson
Pommes Sévigné

———————

Potage de Porée à la Ribelette de Lard
Le Saladier Lyonnais
Coeurs à la Crème

Le Déjeuner Élégant

Oeufs en Meurette
Poulet au Fromage
Gâteau de Pommes de Terre
Salade de Nevers
Fruits Cuits au Vin

———————

Délices d'Endives
Côte de Boeuf Bourguignonne
Gratin d'Oignons
Champignons de Dijon
Salade de Pissenlits
Raisiné et Massepains

Le Dîner entre Amis
Dinner

Soupe Nevers
Saupiquet 1
Gratin Rouge
Crépinette aux Marrons
Laitue Bourguignonne
Gouerre au Cirage

Le Régal Aillé
Boeuf Bourguignon
Pâtes Fraîches
Purée de Fenouil
Salade à la Menthe
La Cervelle de Canut

Le Dîner Élégant

Saumon aux Herbes
Jambon à la Saulieu
Gâteau au Céleri
Gratin Trois
Sorbet au Marc

Chèvre Chaud
Canard à la Menthe
Petits Navets en Ragoût
Raisiné
Salade aux Griaudes
Framboises à la Neige

Menus

Le Pique-nique
Picnic

Salé (salty dishes)

Fricandeau
Tarte Bourguignonne
Terrine de Canard
L'Enchaud
Délice de Fromages

Sucré (sweet dishes)

Nonnettes
Massepains
Noeuds d'Amour
Pogne

Le Buffet
Buffet

Froid (cold dishes)

Terrine de Canard
Saumon aux Herbes
Filets de Harengs
Fromage Fort du Beaujolais
Bersaudes
La Cervelle de Canut
Jambon Persillé
Corniottes
All the Salads
All the Desserts

Chaud (hot dishes)

Saupiquet I et II
Ravioles
Boulettes Dorées de Montagne
Croquettes aux Herbes
Tarte Bourguignonne
La Gougère
Les Petits Paniers
Saucisson Chaud Lyonnais
Petits Poissons à la Bourguignotte

Le Goûter
Snack

Sucré (sweet dishes)

Biscuit de Savoie
Nonnettes
Lait de Poule
Pain d'Épice
Pogne
Caramels

Le Machon
Snack

Salé (salty dishes)

Filets de Harengs
La Gougère
Fricandeau
Délice de Fromages
La Cervelle de Canut
Fromage Fort du Beaujolais

Menus

Moutarde

Mustard

In 400 B.C., Aristophanes mentioned the taste of a stew seasoned with mustard. The Romans used a mixture of seeds and vinegar called *sinapis,* and they introduced the Gauls to this condiment, which they believed to be also a medicine.

Burgundy became the center of the preparation of mustard; in the fourteenth and fifteenth centuries it was eaten not only with meat and fish but also with soups. When the cardinal of Euze became pope, he named one of his cousins "first *moutardier,*" whose official attire was a green suit worn with a necklace; with an allowance of a thousand ducats, he enjoyed a cozy life in exchange for keeping a vigilant eye on the mustard situation in the papal palace. "I tickle the mouth and I sting the nose" was the motto of this *moutardier.*

Philip the Bold, duke of Burgundy, whose motto was *Moult me tarde* (I am impatient), is said to have ordered a hundred and eighty pounds of mustard for one of his festive meals.

Mustard is an annual. It has yellow flowers, and the seed, round and purple-brown with a yellow center when its shell is removed, holds all the active ingredients of mustard. The crushing of the seeds (of the species *Brassica nigra* or *Brassica juncea,* or a mixture of both) is done in a mill, and the crushed seeds are mixed with the juice of unripe grapes or with grape must or with vinegar or wine. Salt, sugar, spices and herbs may be added in small quantities.

The thick mixture is put through a sieve and pulverized. The soft, smooth paste that results is kept in large containers, where its flavor is developed for about ten days before it is ready for sale.

Mustard enhances the taste of food and is said to be good for the digestion. One can understand why Louis XI used to go out to dinner carrying his own pot of mustard for fear of having to do without.

Until the sixteenth century, mustard makers sold their

La Moutarde

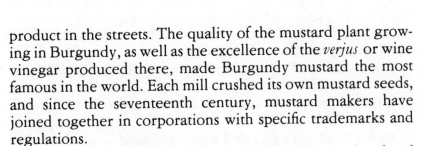

product in the streets. The quality of the mustard plant growing in Burgundy, as well as the excellence of the *verjus* or wine
vinegar produced there, made Burgundy mustard the most
famous in the world. Each mill crushed its own mustard seeds,
and since the seventeenth century, mustard makers have
joined together in corporations with specific trademarks and
regulations.

Today the preparation of mustard is severely regulated and
follows certain fundamental rules: for example, the taste of
the seeds must never be overpowered by herbs that are too
strong or by vinegar that is too heavy.

Mustard

Spécialités

Special Treats

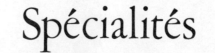

A truffle is a truffle is a truffle wherever it is eaten. A carefully prepared *boeuf bourguignon* can taste as good in New York City as it would in Dijon. But there are a few dishes that will not cross the Atlantic, and to taste them we either have to cross it ourselves or read and dream about them.

Why are such special treats untransportable? The reason is that some depend on local products—a special cardoon, a musky mushroom, a plump snail that cannot be found outside of Burgundy and is too fragile to be shipped. And some dishes are prepared or eaten in ways that would be hard to enjoy in the United States. So I will mention them here only to show the diversity and inventiveness of Burgundy cooking:

Stuffed veal ears seasoned with butter, brandy and bread crumbs, deep-fried in batter.

A leg of wild boar wrapped in its fur, placed in a deep hole in the ground, covered with embers and cooked for a day, then served with red currant jelly.

The *ferchusse,* a mixture of pork lungs, heart and liver sautéed with onions and garlic, cooked with red wine and traditionally eaten on the day the pig is killed.

Sanquette, coagulated chicken blood sautéed in chicken fat with onions, seasoned with vinegar, tarragon and parsley.

Beef or veal brain cooked in red wine and served with onions, mushrooms and croutons.

Tripe filled with spices, garlic and onions and cooked with wine and carrots.

Gratins of pig's feet and pork rind cooked with white wine and herbs.

Salads of sheep's feet and sheep's testicles.

A wild boar's head cooked in water and vinegar, sautéed with onions, garlic, juniper and red wine and thickened with fresh blood.

The *gruotte* made of the lungs, liver and head of baby boar, sautéed with onions, herbs and wine—a favorite of hunters.

Roasted suckling pig stuffed with chopped heart, liver, kidney, garlic and sage and simmered in white wine.

Beef heart marinated in wine and herbs, then cooked for twelve hours.

There are all kinds of sausages prepared in different ways in Burgundy and, mostly, in Lyon: blood sausages made with onions, spinach, cinnamon, sage and rice and either cooked with chestnuts or fried apples and cream, or seasoned with mustard and tarragon; Lyon pistachio sausage, Morteau smoked sausage flavored with aniseed; Seaulieu raw cured sausage eaten with plain potatoes or cooked in a stew; *andouille,* made with pork stomach marinated in spices, mustard and vinegar, then eaten broiled with lemon and mustard or sautéed with shallots and white wine and accompanied by beans and pig's ears.

There are smoked, cured and boiled hams, prepared in endless ways.

Quenelles of pike are served with crayfish butter.

Cheese preparations are often startling. Blue cheese is left in an earthen pot to mature. Sprinkled with dry white wine, it is stirred every day. Then goat cheese is added to it, and the mixture is kept in a warm place and eaten between summer and fall. There is also fresh goat cheese mixed with ewe cheese and butter cooked slowly together and seasoned with sugar; Swiss cheese, goat cheese, butter, brandy and wine melted together and spread on toast; cheese, wine, walnut oil and brandy, left to ferment and eaten on warm toast; fresh cheese wrapped in vine or chestnut leaves, sprinkled with brandy and kept in a cellar for three weeks; cheese mixed with flour, milk and egg and eaten in a pie.

Matefaims, thick pancakes, true "hunger killers," are spread with jam. *Galette à la sermouille,* a pie made of semolina, is served with heavy cream. Chestnut, clove, fennel and egg custard is sprinkled with pistachios, and there are endless desserts based on pumpkin. Cooked black currants are used with crepes, sponge cakes and sweet omelets. Black currant and barberry jam, watermelon jam and verjuice jam are spread on *rigodon* and other pastries. Endless amounts of fritters in the shapes of bows, butterflies, ribbons and balls are made with semolina or wheat flour or potato flour and flavored with fruits and liquors. A Lyon delicacy is fritters of carp roe, seasoned with lemon juice. Fritters of marinated

Special Treats

frog's legs, sprinkled with garlic and parsley, are served with a cream-and-chives sauce.

And, finally, *trempe au vin,* a curious mixture of bread moistened with a hearty red wine and sugar, is given to sea and river mariners and newlyweds for energy.

Index

Index

Index

Index

Index

Index

307

Index

Index

309

Index

310

Index

Index

Index

About the Author

MIREILLE JOHNSTON was born in Nice, educated in France and America, and now divides her time between the two countries. She is the author of *The Cuisine of the Sun: Classical Recipes from Nice and Provence,* and *Central Park Country: A Tune Within Us,* and the translator of the film script for *The Sorrow and the Pity,* by Marcel Ophuls, and *Criticism of Everyday Life,* by Henri Lefèvre. She is married and has two daughters, Margaret-Brooke and Elizabeth.